Living In The Shadow Of Hitler

Thomas Davey

WRITERSWORLD

Living in the Shadow Of Hitler
Thomas Davey

Copyright © 2004 Thomas Davey

www.shadowofhitler.co.uk

The moral right of the author has been asserted

Cover Design by Steve Foote of Tin Racer Design
www.tinracer.com

Edited by Jo Apicella and Wendy Lake

ISBN 1-904181-29-5

WRITERSWORLD
9 Manor Close
Enstone
Oxfordshire
OX7 4LU
England

www.writersworld.co.uk

Dedicated to Phil and Simon

Foreword

Yesterday, when I decided to write this story, I thought I'm not going to be able to sit down and write this all down, I'm not the sort of person who can. I'm not a very good writer and not the best of readers, in fact I had to go to see a specialist in London when I was young, to see whether I suffered from dyslexia. I had a very good education, I went to Woodlands a private school in Warley, but it didn't help me in that way.

I remember when my Dad came back from America in 1981 he brought back all these different gadgets, including a Sony Walkman. At the time no one had ever heard of them, he also bought a dicta-phone for me, but my Mum destroyed it, due to me constantly trying to record her private conversations. All that stuck in my mind, so I went out yesterday and bought one, I will tell the story into the machine and then transfer it onto my computer.

I also thought, how do I start writing this? I need some advice but who do I ask? Tom Davey the car valeter wants to write a book. What's that all about? So while in Tesco's I looked at the book section, I thought if I buy an autobiography it might give me some kind of idea on how to go about it and I had a choice between the autobiography of Daniel O'Donnell and Paul Burrell. Well the Paul Burrell book came first, I wasn't too sure at the time when it came out, but it has his whole story and it's interesting to see his story within the Royal Family and his connection with Princess Diana. I think it is important, which I will go on to explain in regards to my own connection with Princess Diana.

So I bought it. I have my dicta-phone and I will sit down at my computer and type it all out.

The dicta-phone also reminds me of Sarah Connor in The Terminator, when she is in her jeep with her dog and telling her unborn son the story of her life and his unlived life, the future and she drives off into the sunset. That story is amazing especially if it was true but it isn't, The Terminator is finished now, John in the 3rd one managed to reach his destiny, he got to where he was meant to be. The story of The Terminator is amazing and has touched a few people in my family, in fact my Dad had had the film recorded and the sleeve printed, and later on I would find out that Rob (my cousin) had done the same thing. But basically The Terminator is a great story and if it were real, would be unbelievable; my story just happens to be true and *is* unbelievable.

My name is Thomas Davey, and I'm going to attempt to write my story.

I'm coming up to twenty-nine and people will probably think I'm not old enough to write an autobiography. But then, I have a story, which is quite unbelievable, and it happened to me at a young age. I have been through a lot and after reading a small part of this story you may agree it needs to be put down on paper, maybe for the wider audience or maybe just so it's on record.

So today 7/11/03 I will attempt to do this and go through with it. What has made me do this? Well there has been a lot floating around in my mind over the past years and it might help me to put it all in writing.

I have a friend from about 18 years ago, from Brentwood Cricket Club called Daniel Cocklin and he has witnessed part of this story and suggested along with others that I write this book. Dan has asked me to do this in the past but I thought it was pointless, because I could not see the ending, I still can't, maybe there isn't one or maybe it will happen while I'm constructing this, because as I was reminded the other day, I haven't been through what I have to end up washing cars.

Daniel has attempted in the past to find a film company and a publisher to take this story on, but due to the damaging and unbelievable facts, people have been too frightened to do so, so what has changed now? Well every other week we have stories about our Royal Family in the media which are becoming more and more damaging and accepted by the public e.g. Princess Diana being killed in a car accident. So the public are beginning to open their minds a little and don't always accept the story that is first thrown at them.

My Family

I was born on the 19th December 1974 at Harold Wood Hospital near Romford, and the first house I lived in was at 7 Shorter Ave, a three-bedroom semi detached house in a nice part of Shenfield, Essex. So I was very fortunate to have such a nice beginning to my life.

Shorter Ave is quite ironic, my Mum's Mum spent her last days in a warden controlled flat in Shorter Ave and I used to spend a lot of time there, I even had a paper round there when I was a bit older, I used to stay there now and again. I have very fond memories of my Nan; she was very close to me and helped me out a lot. It was in that flat that one evening, I would make a phone call to somebody in Vienna that not knowing at the time would contribute to my major breakdown.

My Mum, Hazel Anne Davey, who now lives in Hutton, was brought up in Gidea Park, her Dad, George Dickman came from Newcastle and her Mum, Violet Dickman was from Wales. The whole family tree needs looking into especially if this story is to go further, but I will tell you what I know.

My granddad died at that house in Gidea Park, I was thirteen, I was very close to him and it affected me quite badly, I remember spending hours in the dining room at the Priest Lane house, crying and not understanding where he had gone. It was the first time I had experienced a death. I was very close to him, it was him who actually taught me to ride my bike without the stabilisers, and it was him who taught me to do my shoelaces up. It's funny the things you remember about your grandparents, he has a strong place in my mind.

When he died my Nan moved to Shenfield, my Mum used to have a brother called Neville, unfortunately he died on the squash court of a heart attack he was about 40, I was about nine, that obviously affected my Mum and the family.

About ten years ago, all of a sudden a man turned up on the scene called Robert Dickman, the son of Neville, whom I had no idea about. My Nan certainly did, but I'm not sure about Mum, they had all completely lost contact. So Robert turned up on the scene, he was 28 and I was 18, it was all quite bizarre, the relationship has taken its time to develop. Now we are a lot closer, I have children and they are trying for children. At the time when we first met, I was in the middle of my turmoil and was a little confused about who this person was and where he had come from. It seems to take me a long time in general to

1

get to know and trust someone. I guess the way he had found us and whom he worked for at the time, made me a bit suspicious. He was working for the government in the Department of Health and he also had a contact through his wife's sister, whose husband was the right hand man to Piers Morgan of the Daily Mirror. So Robert tracked us down through that organisation, I'm sure if the paper had investigated us a little more, he would have stayed away.

To this day, I have not spoken to him about my affair and he has not pushed the subject, making me wonder if he knows anyway through his contacts in the government. We went for a drink once where he lives in Sutton and he spoke a little about his job and told me he was writing speeches for Tony Blair and was dealing with Downing Street at the time. This was an interesting development for me, because it was just recently that I had met someone else who also had contact with Tony Blair and the Royal Family. I sat there with Rob, tempted to go through everything with him, but knowing my Mum would disagree. I didn't, but I did sit there feeling quite secure because if anything big time broke in the news or anywhere else, I had immediate access through to Tony and the Royal Family. I also remember at the time wondering what Rob was all about, he had turned up into our family at a strange time and would come and go over the years. I wondered if his intentions were good and wondered in my suspicious and slightly paranoid way, if he was an MI5 agent trying to get closer to my family. Was there something they didn't know? Or something they wanted? This man coming into the family as a missing member would want to ask a lot of questions and would be ideal for them.

Rob had also met Al Fayed, who plays a small part in this story and a man who my father tried his hardest to reach and speak to. He felt his son had been murdered in Paris and thought he knew the reasons why. Al Fayed also thought this but probably didn't have the same views as my Dad.

My Dad, John Michael Davey, grew up in Dagenham, Essex the biggest council estate in England, purposely built for Fords. He been brought up there, went to school there, the same school in fact that the former Arch Bishop of Canterbury went to. He met my Mum in one of the local pubs, The Volunteer, not sure why my Mum was drinking in there, but I'm glad she did. My Dad left school and joined the Navy, but was unhappy and left and travelled for a while in South Africa, eventually he came back and became a biscuit salesman, which would help him eventually set up his own business selling perfume. His business was named Coombe Promotions, he had a big warehouse in Rainham and he had a major account with Faberge. That was how he made his money, he was very successful and ended up living in Shenfield, he bought the house we lived in Coombe Rise with cash, the lady who owned the house did not take my Dad seriously when viewing the house and so in my Dad's way, paid cash for it there and then. It is the typical story of a Dagenham boy doing well.

His mother Grace Davey, came from Dagenham, his Dad as he calls him, Bill brought Dad up knowing he wasn't his son; he died when my Dad was about thirty and my Dad found out when Bill died. A man from New Zealand appeared on the scene, Joe McCarthy, I think the whole period in my Dad's life affected him in a way that would come out later, and I think it set off certain things in his mind but at the time, didn't affect him or his relationship with his mother. My Dad did manage to spend some time with his real Dad.

Joe was a carpenter and spent a lot of time in the shed that he had built in my Nan's garden, I also remember spending time in that shed, making swords and other strange things. Joe died when I was fourteen, just after this whole affair begun, and so my Dad had to cope with the death of his second father.

So really my name should be McCarthy, not Davey and I have family in New Zealand that one day I would like to track down.

So that is a brief history of both sets of family, I guess it would be nice to look into it a bit more, for instance, my Nan (Dad's Mum) who I owe a hell of a lot to and if it wasn't for her I might not actually be here. She had taken me in a few times throughout my teenage years, and given me somewhere to live, looked after me and fed me but unfortunately she did not have much to do with this story that will unfold, she kept quiet about the whole thing which I thought was a bit strange, my Dad used to remind me, she was in Germany when the war broke out, and I have always wondered about her role in all that. I don't give a fuck anyway, she was great to me, like my other Nan was, they both died at a time when I was standing on my own two feet, I had been through mental illness and I was married and it seemed to be the right time for them to die, I know that sounds bizarre but that's the way I look at it.

Violet Dickman died on the first anniversary of Princess Diana's death 31/8/98

Grace Davey died in 2001 at Hornchurch hospital, her bed was next to a window and her view was of the QE2 Bridge.

Part One

The first ten years of my life were faultless, I had the best upbringing you could possibly have. I don't have too many memories of Shorter Ave but then you don't when you are a baby, so if you need to know the first things I did or the first words I said, I suggest you contact my parents.

The first memories I have, come from Coombe Rise, I lived there until I was about ten, and I can't remember having one bad memory about the place, everything seemed to be so perfect and happy. The one slightly bad memory I had was of my father, while me and all my friends were playing in the garden, one summers day, he surprised us by leaning out of his bedroom window and telling us all to clear off in a very aggressive, unlike him manner. And that was towards the end of living in that house, it must have been in the period of when he was losing his business and on the down side of life, but apart from that I can't remember having any bad memories of the place.

One of my first memories was being at nursery, I remember that vaguely, it was the nursery down by the Pied Piper toy shop in Shenfield, and that's where I met my first friend, he was called Paul Barnes, he had a brother Stuart and his Mum and Dad were Barry and Shirley. They lived at the top of our road Middleton Rd and his Dad had a quite similar story to mine, whereby he had come from the East End, he owned a building company and had done quite well for himself, they were true East Enders. Paul was my best friend for those first ten years until I had to move to Billericay but we met later on in life when we first started going out and clubbing etc.

Most of the memories around that period were when we were all kids and on our bikes, we had massive gardens and our garden would join our friends gardens and we had the woods, so we were always out on our bikes, doing something. And we would have a little gang called The A team, I was Hannibal, Paul was BA, Stuart was Face and Michael was Murdoch and we used to do the things kids do.

We used to play in the woods a lot, we would pretend we were patrolling the whole area, we used to try and chase adults on their bikes and tell them to slow down. I always remember trying to get chased by the Blood Transfusion hospital warden, we used to ride

5

through the grounds and try and get him to chase us. So we spent a lot of time with Paul and Stuart and they were our closest friends. Another good friend was Anthony Woodard and he lived in a house at the back of our garden and his family had come from the West Indies and he was my closest friend while we went to Woodlands Primary School and we would sit next to each other and it appeared we liked the same things such as salami sandwiches. We both loved cricket, Paul and Stuart were more into football. So I had a good friend in Anthony and I always got on really well with his grandmother who was a typical West Indian lady.

Another friend I had was Patrick Moore and I always had to ask him to spell the most simplest of words for me, because I was not very good at writing or reading and he remembers that still today, I think I annoyed him a little.

At Infant school I can't remember too much apart from being in the playground and sports day.

From Primrose Hill, I went onto St Mary's Junior School, I spent one year there and then went back to Woodlands, as my Mum didn't think I was getting a good enough education there. Woodlands had then just opened its junior school in Warley.

At St Mary's I met up with my old mate Paul, who was in the same class as me. It was strange being surrounded by people I didn't know, apart from a few familiar faces, I think everyone else knew each other, they had all come from the same infant school. That was good for me though because when I eventually went onto secondary school, I seemed to know a lot of people from different schools. I remember crying at the gates of St Mary's when my Mum told me on my last day that I wouldn't be going back. I had made some good friends there and remember liking my first girl there, Fiona, we didn't talk much but we both knew we liked each other. She used to live in Parkway and I used to ride my bike down to her house, where I wasn't actually allowed, passing her house and standing by her wall trying to see her.

Around that period, my granddad had always told my Mum, if they're not going to go to church they should go to cubs to install values in them and so I was introduced to religion. My Mum took us to this church on Hutton Mount and that was our first experience of church, I just remember this old man with his black cloak on telling us all these stories of this man called Jesus and singing a load of strange songs with some elderly people. I must have told my Mum there and then, that's not for me I don't want to go back there again, so I didn't. I went to cubs, which was great it was more adventurous and I remember going on cub trips with all my friends on coaches and staying over in these cub/scout adventure sites. In fact I nearly got run over on a cub trip, where I was walking up a steep hill with the rest of the cubs and a car appeared from nowhere and one of the cub leaders dragged me back off the road.

It was at St Mary's, where I remembered my first class and my first teacher, Mrs Hendrix and the main friends I had in that class were Michael Davey (no relation), Mark Judd, Paul Barnes, these were people I went through life with. Richard Lawrence was the first person to ever hit me, he also used to see my closest girl friend Amanda Hartman, but tragically he died quite early in his life, he must have been 22, at a party he fell down some stairs and died, he actually died at a time when a few of our other friends had either committed suicide or died, it was a bizarre period for all of us.

It was also at St Mary's that I began to realise I was quite good at sport; I first started playing football and played for the school team and the cricket team.

I did like the experience of that one-year being at that school.

It has worked out that Paul Barnes who was my best friend as a youngster was related to Amanda.

During the ten years we had formed this group, myself, my brother, Paul and Stuart and we were The A Team, we had our BMX bikes and our sirens for our bikes and we had our pretend guns and rifles, I also had a 007 watch, which I had saved up vouchers from Monster Munch crisps. It was great I thought I was the kiddie, I was Hannibal and we used to ride around the Blood Transfusion hospital where we used to get chased off. And later on in my life, I would be brought back to that same spot and would end up, in my manic state going back to that Blood Transfusion hospital to try and destroy all their vehicles and I was arrested, police turned up everywhere and took me off to the police station and tried to interview me, put me in the cells and then shipped me off to Warley Mental Hospital. I think when you are ill though, you seem to go back to the places where you once enjoyed, I remember riding my bike back from Dagenham and stopping off at my old school Woodlands and going through old pictures with the head mistress' husband, who eventually called my Mum to pick me up, he probably realised I wasn't too well.

Another memory of Coombe Rise, was with my brother in the garden, we had a massive garden with loads of land and we spent a lot of time playing cricket in it and one day I was bowling and for

7

some reason bowled the ball very wide and my brother couldn't hit it and the ball went straight through our lounge window. In the lounge we had glass doors and it was the bottom right panel that got smashed. So I quickly hurried on into the lounge and cleared all the glass up and covered the window with one of my Mum's plants and that was the end of that I thought, until my Dad found out, he must have been sitting in the lounge one night and noticed a draught and so asked me all about it, I didn't lie to him and told him straight what had happened. In a strange way I think he was slightly proud of me for trying to cover up this window, proud of me for not lying, but he did have a go at me for not bowling straight.

Another incident was when I was playing with our friends and we seemed to have so many friends round that period. But while all my friends were in our garden we decided to have a stone fight with the group of kids who came from the garden that joined our one at the bottom. And we began a battle of stone throwing across the gardens through the trees and my protection was the shed at the bottom of the garden, it was like a battle ground, I would come out of the shed and throw these stones and then duck back in, but the next time I attempted to throw a stone one would strike me in the head and I would fall to the ground, my head was bleeding, it had hit me above the eye and I was carried up to the house by my friends. And when my Dad found out he was furious, every time he wanted to warn me about something he would bring cricket into it. He would say if I had lost my eye that would be the end of my cricket career, I was only bloody nine at the time. And later on when I had a motorbike, he would say if you broke a leg, it would be the end of your cricket.

Another thing I remember about Coombe Rise was when I was playing with Stuart, we were throwing stones at cars, I don't know why I was doing that because it wasn't the sort of thing I was normally into. I threw one stone and it hit this lady's car and she got out, so I dashed through a neighbour's garden and through into my garden. I thought I had escaped successfully until I looked round and to my horror, a group of kids were chasing me, they were another group of friends who we didn't like and they knew what I had just done and were trying to catch me and get me into trouble. I reached my back door and it was locked so I banged and banged and my Dad appeared, after I saw him I felt relieved, my Dad, my hero to the rescue. But for some reason he wouldn't open the door and found it amusing, amusing that all these kids were chasing me and he thought I should stick up for myself. I turned round and escaped through the garden's side door leading to the front garden, but by the time I had done that, the lady who's car I had stoned was in the driveway, I was cornered and no way of escape. I told my Dad I had done nothing wrong and he knew I was lying to him, which made the whole thing ten times worse. So for the first time and I think the last, he punished me and bent me over and whacked me a few times.

And deservedly so, throwing stones at cars and then lying about it is not a good idea, but it was the chase I loved whether it be, being chased through the gardens, being chased by the man over at the Blood Transfusion hospital, being chased by the older kids at school, being chased in my car, being chased through Europe by Interpol or being chased out of Austria by the police. There was something I loved about it.

Another one of my close friends, around that period was Richard Donnelly. He was in my class at Woodlands Infant school, and both sets of parents got on well, his Mum was Poppy, his Dad, Tony. Richard used to come round to mine a lot and I used to go round to his house, he had a house in Navestock, in the middle of nowhere with chickens and other animals, he had a derelict swimming pool that we all used to play around, and I remember trying to find flint to try and start fires.

Fields surrounded his house and every time I went there, we would both set off looking for deer, for hours on end. But after Woodlands we would go our separate way, I went to St Martin's and he went to Forest School. And in 1989, when the reason happened to me, for writing this book, Richard had been transferred from Forest to St Martin's, his Mum and Dad apparently not happy with the standard of education he was getting. He was put into my class and it was my responsibility to show him around and introduce him to everyone and it ended up that our old friendship would continue. His Mum would always pick me up and take me to school and now and again Tony would pick me up in his red MR2, with Richard having to sit on my lap due to there being no back seats.

But looking back on all that, I was involved with my Dad and he was involved in something highly politically damaging. I read a few years later, Tony was working for MI5, when I was reading it at the time he was an ex MI5 officer, and had gone onto fight a church organisation in Brentwood and helped Martin Bell run for the Brentwood seat in the election, but that's a story for later.

Richard had joined my school just before I had moved to my father's and before I had knocked the shed down, (when I talk about MI5, through this story, sometimes it is my over imaginative mind getting carried away, it is also thoughts I was having while going through my mental illness later on in life, but other times it is real).

So was it MI5 intention to place Richard in my class, someone who I would trust? I had grown up with him from infant school, was their intention for him to get close to me without him even knowing and getting, not information, but getting a day to day update on my mood, my feelings, attitude and was I coping with the situation? And had he innocently passed that information onto his Dad? If that was the case had MI5 infiltrated me at such an early age? Or was this whole thing a bizarre training course for me being prepared for a mission later on in my life. Why me? Why was I so important? How had they chosen me? And who were really they?

My first Royal experience was with my father and brother; we were in his white BMW and had gone to London for the day, probably to buy a cricket bat or something from Lilywhite's or Harrods. This was not the best first experience of the Royal Family, but Dad wanted to show us where the Queen lived, we drove past Buckingham Palace. As we did, I opened my window and picked up my rifle and aimed at one of the red soldiers, ones with the funny hats, and started pretending to shoot at them. I then closed the window and felt quite pleased with myself. We drove off, I don't think my Dad had any idea what I had just done, until a few blocks up the road when we got pulled over by the police and asked to get out of the car, it was searched and no doubt my Dad had to answer some awkward questions. After, he said nothing about the episode but I always remember asking my Dad, how the police had caught up with us, when we had driven quite away from the palace, I couldn't understand it. And that was all probably put on record somewhere, a little black mark against my Dad's name and mine.

Talking of the white BMW, I remember my Dad always having nice cars, he had a 911, he had two at one point and got rid of them because we used to complain that we couldn't see out of the back windows. So he bought a 5 series and then the 7 series which we all loved, he used to take us to school in it, and we would spin out on to the main road and fly to school, no one would get in our way; we would be at school within minutes. It's things like that you look up to your Dad for, the reasons you love him; you just don't think there is another person better than your Dad. We were treated very well as youngsters, we used to have the most amazing Christmases, with vast amounts of presents waiting for us on Christmas mornings, and I guess we were slightly spoilt. I remember my Dad buying me an Atari games console and I had a go at him for not buying me the Space Invaders game, I've always felt bad about that.

We had a Wendy house in the garden and I used to get on top of the house and my brother would spin it round and round. I used to get in my bedroom and open the windows and climb on the outside, from one window to the other, to prove to myself I could do things, I always liked jumping off of high things as well, like most kids I guess, we used to make ramps in the garden and see who could jump the highest.

I used to play a lot of cricket in the garden, swing ball as well, I used to be very good at that, I had a great eye for the ball and that would help me later on, when I would play a lot of squash. My granddad had his seventieth birthday party round at the house and there were vast amounts of people there it seemed and everyone tried to beat me but no one could.

Some of the holidays we went on, the main three I remember were Barbados, Greece and the Canary Islands. In Barbados we had spent four weeks there, I have three memories of that holiday, one of them is when we went to Barbados Cricket Club, my Dad took us there, we watched some cricket through the gates. My Dad and I used to watch the sun go down every night over the ocean, while sitting on the beach eating cherries. Another memory was when he tried to give me away to three West Indian chaps on the beach and I remember freaking out, crying my eyes out and then the relief of Dad taking me back. I spent a lot of time with my Dad, I loved my Dad, he was funny, entertaining and made everyone laugh.

Tenerife in the Canary Islands I remember quite well, that was disastrous, there were floods everywhere, my brother nearly died in the swimming pool if it hadn't been for my Dad diving in and rescuing him, and my Mum lost a baby there. So I don't recommend that place.

Greece, again I spent most of my time with my Dad, while the rest of the family were at one hotel we would venture off and use another hotel's pool, at the time I didn't care, I thought it was great, I was with

11

my Dad. But now looking back at it, he obviously wanted to be on his own and round that period my Mum and Dad must have started having problems.

This is an interesting part of the story because as you can see my relationship with my Dad was very strong, I spent so much time with him, he used to take us religiously to cricket every weekend in the summer. Wherever he went it seemed I would go with him, I used to love going to his warehouse, playing on the fork lift truck, I used to count his money for him in the office and bag it up ready for him to take to the bank. Towards the end when my Mum and Dad were getting divorced and the house went up for sale, I couldn't understand what was happening, why was something so perfect being taken away? I remember when my Dad went off to America, I had witnessed my Dad go outside and throw the for sale sign up the road, I had seen him smash up the bar at the Cricket Club and I think his temper was running away with him. I think he had been ill and people didn't understand him and he had gone from this happy go lucky rich boy who had everything, to a man who was beginning to lose everything and I remember running after him while he was driving up the road, he was heading to the airport, for a trip to America.

I couldn't understand when I reached the end of the road and stood there staring at him and crying, that he would drive off. I know now he was also crying and hurting, I guess it was at that moment I began to lose my Dad.

It was Mum who spent a lot of time with me at Coombe Rise trying to get me to read, my Dad just didn't have the patience for that, as long as I could hit a cricket ball that was alright for him. So I remember sitting in the lounge, for what seemed hours with my Mum trying to read and I remember the first word I actually read, it was rabbit, Mum used to try and get it into my head about breaking the words down. At school like most kids all I was interested in was playing football in the playground and having a bit of a giggle in class.

The first year of Woodlands came along in 1983, it was also the first year for Woodlands as a junior school, and I was in the second year and had just come from St Mary's. Woodlands was a private school and my Dad had no worries about paying the bill but when my parents split up, it was my Mum who struggled for my last year there. I guess you can say now, that private school done me no good what so ever, I'm not an academic person, I'm not an accountant or solicitor but the memories of the school and things we had experienced was worth all that money. The people I remember in the 2nd year was Jamie Tingle, Jonathan Owen, Brye Rowlands, Lucy Turner, Alan Jarvis, Caroline Acker and Amanda Hartman. Woodlands was a great school all the parents knew each other and all the teachers were close to the parents, it was a very close school like that. It was in fact at Woodlands I first leant how to play squash, we would go to Brenfield Squash Club and the coach Paul Wright would take our class. I would go on to become a good squash player becoming a county player for my age group.

I spent three years at Woodlands, before I went onto St Martin's, I do have very fond memories of the place we had some very close friends there that we still know today. I remember the Christmas plays we use to do, I was Toe-toe in the yellow brick road. My first overseas school trip was with Woodlands and we went on a PGL holiday to Holland and it seemed the whole of the school had decided to go on this trip and it was the first adventure I had away from my parents. I remember doing the entire normal thing you do in Holland, well all the things you do when you're ten. The tulips, the clog factory, the windmills and of course a visit to Anne Frank's home but all the memories are so vivid.

In 1984, I was in the forth year at Woodlands, I was ten. My father's business was crumpling away, the reason, I'm not too sure. I think he had bought too much stock one year, I remember there being a problem with the accountant, which points towards a tax problem. And it was around that period he became ill, he spent some time in Warley Mental hospital and eventually would be diagnosed with Manic Depression. And so my parents marriage began to fall apart, I don't know what my Dad was like at the time, but it is always easy to blame one person. They were both to blame for their divorce, my Mum had an affair with a Jewish man from Chingford and my Dad afterwards would have an affair with someone in Leicester, on a business trip. Even though my Mum had had an affair while my Dad was ill, he had forgiven her and they both tried over again. My Dad could not cope with the guilt of what he had just done in Leicester, and so he tried to cover up his late arrival by smashing his car up and then telling my Mum he had been in a car accident. But he admitted it in the end and he never recovered from the guilt of what he had done. And so, the house went up for sale, sold by Meacock and Jones, but it had to be done my Mum and Dad were getting divorced and they had to split the house half and half.

And so my Mum, myself and my brother moved to Billericay (which was five to six miles away from our friends and school) on the Queens Park estate, 52 Connaught Way and the house was ridiculously small, it was a two bedroom, mid terrace house, it was a nice house though on a recently built estate, there was a car park at the back of the house and a wood at the back of the car park.

My father, well, he went off round the world doing crazy things that manics do, especially if they've got money as well. He ended up having a flat in Thorndon Hall where he was deeply unhappy; he also had a flat in Knightsbridge for a time, while working for Richard King. And he basically ended up blowing all his money and would finally end up living in a flat in Kavanaghs Rd in Brentwood with his best friend from his younger days, Albert Smith.

And so I had moved on to a new chapter in my life, my Mum still managed to take me and my brother to Woodlands and paid for that, she bought herself a new Mini, and I guess round the period of living in that house, we were there for about a year or so, but I remember getting very close to my Mum, we would spend a lot more time together, she still did the things she used to do, she would still take us swimming, she managed to keep things together with the help from her friends and her parents. We visited our grandparents a lot more in Romford and I began to get a lot closer to them.

My Dad, I still remember him helping us move into the house it must have been extremely hard for him, not being with my Mum but still helping her, knowing he couldn't afford the things he once did. I remember sitting outside the house that day when we were moving in, it was a lovely hot day and they were still building the houses round there, we were only renting the house, and we sat there and he got this mirror and reflected this beam off of the sun onto one of the builder's backs who was working in the distance. And we sat there laughing our heads off. I was so close to my Dad and what has happened has just torn everything apart, fucked it all up. And even now I get emotional, just writing about it.

The good things about Billericay, well we had our bikes, we had the woods at the back of the house, where there was a BMX track. I remember when we first moved there, I had come across an ally-way which I was convinced if I rode down would take me back to Shenfield and I would be back with my friends. I remember the disappointment when I eventually rode down that ally and it came out onto the next estate. But that was my imagination at the time, quite wild really.

My brother and I became a lot closer round that period; we didn't know anyone in the area, so naturally we spent more time with each other. His name is Michael Edward John Davey. We went everywhere together, and we would play in the woods, go to Lake Meadows playing fields and go swimming a lot. The only other friend we had was James Rugg and he lived in Billericay and also went to Woodlands. We had a car park at the back of the house and my brother and I would spend hours and hours playing cricket and so the bond between my brother and I would become very strong. We would have the same bedroom together and spend ages talking when bedtime came round. But that relationship would become very distant within three years, when this whole affair would kick in. So I think we were very lucky to have that time back then. It's not until now being the present day that our relationship is starting to develop again.

I had been introduced to squash through my school. So I spent a lot of time at Brenfield Squash Club learning how to play, I liked the game, my Mum also used to play squash while living at Coombe Rise, she also did classes there and I would be put in the crèche. I started playing a lot of squash and my Mum had to drop me off and pick me up all the time. So she got used to coming up the squash club a lot too and it was in the bar area that she met Gary, I think she was with her friend Penny Bowler at the time.

So Gary came on the scene, he used to drive a top of the range Capri 2 litre injection, which was the car to have at the time, the first impression I had of him, was that he was a tall chap about 29. He turned up at our Billericay home and it was the first time I had met him, I remember him walking in with a leather jacket on and I thought he was quite cool. He was Managing Director of Royal Printing in London, which was quite impressive for someone of his age. He had a house in Buckhurst Hill and we used to stay there a few times and it was there I remember him teaching me how to use a leather properly. It would be small things like that, also like when Shirley Barnes told me never to use the sponge after you had dropped on the floor, that I would pick up along the way and would help me in my valeting business in the future.

Gary treated my brother and I well; he took us to places we were familiar with when my Mum and Dad were together. Like in London we would go to the Hard Rock Café. But his main thing with me was squash. He was a very good player so that was our thing; we used to go off to squash all the time, and I would also go to the team matches with him.

Eventually we moved from Billericay and with the money my Mum got from the house in Shenfield she put it along with Gary's money and bought this Victorian house in Priest Lane, Shenfield.

Don't get me wrong we would still see my father, obviously not as much, he was doing his thing round the world. But to move back to Shenfield was brilliant, amazing for my brother and me. We had moved back into the area where all our friends were, and the school I was going to go to was just up the road, St Martin's. We both had our own rooms again and it was great. I think my Dad by then had moved into a flat in Kavanaghs Rd and so we would see him every weekend and on a Wednesday night.

I'm not sure what he thought of Gary at the time, he did actually know him from a friend of his called Chris Vander, who played squash at the club.

Memories of Priest Lane.

Well I began secondary school at St Martin's, I was still playing a lot of cricket I had never ever lost that and still went every weekend with my Dad. So he did see a lot of us, even though it must have been hard for him knowing we were living with another man.

Gary was O.K. though; he looked after my Mum and us, which was a massive responsibly for someone of his age. I used to have a paper round at Priest lane, half a paper round actually which I shared with Matt Everard, I wasn't old enough to have a paper round, I was only 12. But my Dad put a stop to that, he didn't like me doing it so early in the morning; I hated him for stopping me doing my paper round. Looking back on it now I understand it because I would not let either one of my children do a paper round at such an early age.

So everything was hunky-dory so it seemed. We would still go on our holidays; the first holiday Gary took us on was to Portugal. The thing I remember about it was when I tried to get to the top of this very steep hill that looked to me like a mountain at the time, and I fell over and cut my leg wide open, it was Gary who was there to help me, he took me back to the apartment, bathed my wounds and made me feel a lot better. I also met a girl called Brie on that holiday she was from Alaska and we seemed to get on well with each other.

A year or so later we would visit America, we had gone to San Francisco done the Alcatraz bit, went up to the Red Forest then we travelled down to Los Angeles and San Diego and then back to San Francisco, we had spent about three weeks touring California, which was obviously an amazing experience. But I even remembered back then, the affair had not started yet and there was a lot of controversy in the news about a book by Peter Wright called *Spy Catcher* and you couldn't buy it in this country but you could in America, so I always remember flying to America and that was one of the main things I looked forward to, trying to find that book, it wasn't going to Disneyland or anything, that was my main mission, I had to get that book. And we went to San Francisco for the day and we walked past a book shop and I said to Mum and Gary "I've got to go in there to see if they have the book." I remembered the man behind the counter asking me "Can I help you?" in a very pleasant American way. He had the book and so Gary went in and bought it, obviously I never read it at the time, it was a bit heavy for me, it would probably be another ten years before I sat down and read *Spy Catcher*.

That was an amazing holiday.

My Dad started getting us into skiing, we went to the South of France after we had come back from America. My Dad wanted to do his bit but years after I would learn it was money from one of my Mum's friends that paid for both of those holidays. My Dad had borrowed money from Penny Bowler to start up in business again; my Dad had just flown back from America and was dealing with the Indians out in Arizona, trying to get into dealing with Indian jewellery. He brought a few suitcases of samples back, and it looked very nice but wasn't quite the thing at the time; it started to be more fashionable a few years later.

We started to go over to Warley ski slopes where we would be taught how to ski, and then my Dad took us to Austria. We went by train, I guess he thought it was more adventurous than going on a plane. We stayed in one hotel where we would have to get a big lift up to the mountain and my brother and I didn't like that, it seemed to take ages to get there. So we got in a taxi and drove up the mountain and stayed in a hotel in a place called Gerlos, which was fabulous, you just had to get a little lift up and you could ski all the way back down to your hotel. That was an absolutely brilliant holiday and is the only time I have been skiing.

Dad also took us to the South of France; we met up with some cricketing friends, the Webb's and it seemed like a good holiday, I can't remember too much but it was O.K.

So at that point in my life everything seemed to be great, I was playing a lot of squash, getting quite good at it, I was working my way up the leagues, I started playing in championships and I would then go on to play for my county. The best ever squash game I played was against Dean Finegold, he was a year younger than me and for his age group he was number one in the country. It was an Eastern National Open competition and I had reached the quarterfinals and had to play Dean, I knew I couldn't beat him and he knew he could beat me. The whole viewing area was packed with spectators, I think he won the first two games easily, I wasn't playing properly, I knew he was going to win so it didn't seem worth putting in the effort. I remember looking up and Mum and Gary were watching and my Dad also was watching, which was quite a strange thing for me to see. Gary would come down in between the games to give me advice and my Dad from the viewing point would aggressively encourage me. And then something triggered in me and I started to fight my way through this game with a different kind of belief that I could win, I could beat this boy who was ranked one in the country. So the game got to 2-2 and I was playing the best squash I had ever played, with what seemed like hundreds of people watching. It was a brilliant game, full of rallies and good shots, each of the families encouraging. I managed to win that game, I think Dean had relaxed his game and couldn't regain his concentration. Dean shook my hand, I had won and what a feeling it was, I would go on to lose in the Semis.

But I always remember that day, I remember thinking after that if you're in the right frame of mind and have the right attitude I think you can do anything, which I would find out later with regards to my cricket. So I was getting recognised in the squash world, my coach Paul Ansdell told me if I carried on like that I could become a professional player.

My cricket at the time was still developing I was playing in the colts and always up there at weekends during the summer, we would all play on the outskirts of the field while Dad was playing on the main field.

Before the flat in Brentwood, Dad lived in a flat in Dove Mews, Knightsbridge where we used to stay now and again. He was working for someone called Richard King, basically dealing with business deals, I was ten, we had just lost the house in Coombe Rise and my Mum had taken my brother up to her cousin in Wiltshire, we were all spending Christmas there. My Dad had bought my brother and me brand new BMX bikes, but he had to get them all the way to Wiltshire without me seeing them and I was blindfolded the whole way. And I guess this is where the trust thing came in, with regards to me later on trusting him so much. He blindfolded me in the railway station in London and in the taxi to and from the station. I remember him leaving me on the platform blind folded next to the bikes, while he went off and got the tickets but I didn't panic or run off or take the blind fold off and I guess you could say I trusted him that he was still watching me wherever and whatever he was doing at the time. I still remember standing there in my loneliness wondering who was looking at me and wondering what they were thinking, but also knowing Dad would come back. He did and we spent that particular Christmas in Wiltshire, where my brother and I would ride round the whole day on our new BMX bikes, unaware of the bad feeling between our parents.

It was in this period my Dad had become heavily associated with religion, he got into God. He had just come back from New York and everything he was trying in life was not working. While in New York he was wandering the streets on the brink of suicide and stumbled across a church called St Thomas, which is in 5th Ave. He went in and sat down and began to read the bible and it was because of what he was reading that he became so hooked, he just opened it to any page and started reading about a man called Job. Job had lost all his family and house but after a time he would regain it but twice as much. And so that story inspired my Dad; he thought it was a miracle. So he came back to England and started getting heavily involved in Religion. He began to get involved with a religious group in Brentwood and spent hours at people's homes discussing God and Jesus. He would tell all his friends and everyone that he had become a Born Again Christian. I think it was at that point as well he became unwell and you see the connection between religion and mental illness. It is a dangerous subject to get into I think while you are not well, you start feeling bad about yourself about things you have done in the past or what you are doing at the present time, I think you try and live your life in a Godly perfect way, which at the end of the day is impossible, it puts massive pressure on your life and if you are unwell I think you do not need it.

Now it was at this point in the whole story that my attitude towards Gary and Mum had changed. Due to an incident. My Dad by this time had lost his flat in Kavanaghs Rd, Brentwood, and had moved back to his mother's house in Dagenham. And we started seeing my Dad at my Nan's house every weekend, he didn't have a lot of money so we didn't do much. We used to hire out videos and go swimming. Still enjoying ourselves, if I was with my Dad, I was alright.

But there was one day when he had picked me and my brother up from Priest Lane, he wasn't right, my Mum couldn't have known because she would never have let us go off with him. He got us in the car and started driving; we were heading towards Dagenham, and were in Seven Kings. He started ranting and raving, talking about the old days and God. Then he started driving the car without his hands on the wheel, saying God was steering the car and he had complete faith in him, in a manic state, he wasn't calm, his eyes were bulging out of his head. He started going faster and faster along the High St and we began to drift off towards the right. I remember as we were heading towards this bus stop, I whacked the hand brake up which must have stopped us going straight through into the shops. But we did go crashing into the bus stop and there was broken glass everywhere, fortunately no one was sitting in the bus stop. My Dad got out and he told me to guide him to a church, leaving my brother at the bus stop where he was picked up by the police and taken home. But me, I had to find a church for my Dad to go into, I was walking in front of him and he was shouting at me, threatening me not to turn round or run off and to find this church. So after a while I found a church and we went in, everyone turned round and they must of known my Dad wasn't feeling too well. Someone had pulled me into the sitting area, while Dad was crawling along the floor towards the cross and then he just lay there praying. The vicar must have wondered what on earth was going on that Sunday morning but he did manage to carry on his service and my Dad seemed to calm down a little, he got to where he wanted to be I guess. But he was manic and very ill and then we came out of the church, got in a taxi and drove back to Shenfield and back to the house at Coombe Rise, where we all once lived. He knocked on the door and a woman answered, a women who my Dad knew and she invited us in and I remember standing in the hall and having a flood of memories go past me. Then Dad took me home, saw me to the door and walked off.

My Mum was very concerned about my Dad and we got in her Mini and drove round Brentwood looking for him, it was on the corner of his old flat where we found him, he was just staring out toward the sky and to be honest looked like something out of a horror movie. My Mum stopped the car got him in and took him home to Dagenham.

Then I think he spent a day or so in Warley Mental Hospital. He was diagnosed as a Manic Depressive and started taking Lithium, which he accepted at the time, where a lot of people don't accept it but fortunately he did. And he spent a long time at my Nan's resting and recovering. I didn't know what on earth was going on, but I still loved my Dad, I still went over to see him and spent a lot of time with him, but I didn't know what was going on in his life.

My life was O.K. I was still at Priest Lane and at St Martin's. So I was getting on alright at school, when I first went to St Martin's I had a lot of friends there because I knew a lot of people from different junior schools and was also into a lot of different out of school activities e.g. football at Warley Star's, and cricket at Brentwood Cricket Club. So I had a lot of friends, I never actually had a girlfriend though, there were girls that liked me and girls that I liked but I never had a long-term girlfriend at school.

The first two years at school were great, I played in all the school teams and I was also in the middle class for the whole year which considering my learning difficulties when I was young I thought that was a good achievement.

We had come back from that skiing holiday and Gary had bought us a dog, Max he was a Rottweiler. It was my responsibility, as I didn't have my paper round to walk him every morning, whether it was raining or snowing. Gary would give me £3 pocket money a week for doing it. I loved taking him out, it was a good start to my day and then I would ride off to school on my racer that Gary had bought me one Christmas.

So my little life was fine, Mum and Gary's life was fine but my Dads life was in turmoil, he was in a different state all together.

When Gary's brother and wife came over from San Francisco to stay at our house. I was 13 at the time and my brother and me were fighting and messing around in the kitchen. My Mum was upstairs very upset over the death of her father. Gary got hold of us and bashed our heads together twice and just left us on the floor. It was a few weeks before that I had seen Gary pin my Mum down on the floor, not hitting her but shouting at her very aggressively and it was at that point that my views and attitude changed drastically towards that man and my mothers relationship with him. Obviously my Dad was very unhappy about that situation, my Mum had to go and tell him at the Cricket Club, he flipped out and ended up going round to the house confronting Gary over it and a few blows were exchanged.

And so I became this kid who fiercely turned against him and I would take him to the limits and try both my Mum and Gary's patience.

And so in the early part of 1989 I was 14, my Dad had dropped me off, after having us for the weekend and it was that day, I don't know what I had done or said but my Mum couldn't take any more of me and packed my bags and asked Gary to take me to my Dad, which Gary did quite happily, he drove me over to Dagenham, I got out of the car and he put my bags on the door step, got back in his car and drove off.

And there I was in Dagenham, 13 miles away from my friends, 13 miles away from my school and 13 miles away from my life.

My Dad opened the door and I remember me saying "Is it O.K. to come and stay for a while? Mum has thrown me out." I went in, sat down and explained to him what had happened and in a way I thought it was great because I didn't have to go to school anymore, it was too far and Dad didn't have a car.

My Dad wasn't actually doing anything with his life at that point; my Nan had to move into my Dad's room and my Dad and me slept in my Nan's room because it had twin beds. I think I had one day off from school but my Dad insisted I was going to go to school one way or the other.

And my journey to school consisted of a taxi to Chadwell Heath station, then the train to Shenfield, and then I would walk, get the bus or my friend Richard Donnelly would pick me up from the station and take me to school. The journey back was slightly longer because instead of getting a taxi from Chadwell Heath station I would get a bus to save money.

In a way me moving to my Nan's, got my Dad up and running again, the first thing he would do was sign on and he gave all that money to me for my journey back and forth to school.

My Mum was quite surprised by now that I had stayed there so long, I think she was just trying to shock me at first and I would come running home but I was determined to stay with my Dad for as long as I could, I was going to prove to my Mum I didn't need her and I wanted her to apologise to me and ask me to come home.

It would be in the years 1989 and 1997 that the most dramatic things would happen to me.

In 1989 my Dad started getting back on his feet and began looking for a job and ended up working for BAC Windows as a regional sales manager, he was still into religion, he thought it was great because in his mind BAC would stand for Born Again Christian, so he started working for them, he got a company car and basically life started to pick up a little for him.

Due to me living there with my Nan, he had to take some kind of responsibility if he was going to keep me there.

I had stopped playing squash though; I picked up an injury on the squash court just before I moved to my Dads, which stopped me playing anyway. So that little episode put an end to my squash career, the injury, the moving to my Dads, because I couldn't go off and play squash in the evenings in Brentwood and get back to Dagenham of a night.

I wasn't playing cricket because it was wintertime and my Dad made me a promise that we would both be living in a flat by 1st May 1989 in time for the cricket season and he promised me that.

I was still enjoying school, I was in the 3rd year and another chap had come on the scene who had moved from Widford Lodge, Alister Hall, who was a quiet chap at the time but his sense of humour appealed to me and so we became very good friends but he wasn't into anything that I was, he wasn't into any form of sport and he was completely opposite to me but I did like him, I liked his sense of humour and we started to hang about together along with Richard Donnelly who had also just turned up. But step by step my school life went down hill, I wasn't bothered about lessons or anything, I was only interested in having a laugh with my friends, step by step my sport went out the window and I ended up not playing for any of the teams at school. In a way this was because I was starting to rebel against the situation I found myself in, my friendship with Al didn't help either, I'm not blaming him, but in a way it was his influence on me, we were as bad as each other really. I will say now though Al became one of my best friends and has helped me through some of the worst parts of my life.

So those few months I stayed in that house in Dagenham, I must have been a Godsend to my Dad; it had got him up and working again.

While working for BAC, in his company car he started visiting churches in Essex, he went to visit a lot of them. He was unhappy with the fact that the church doors were locked and in God's eyes that was wrong, it didn't matter about things being stolen or vandalised, the church doors should be open no matter what. His thoughts at the time were, if someone like himself had gone to that church in New York and it had of been locked, he would of thrown himself off the bridge. And how many times has it happened in this country, when someone goes to the church for help and the bloody thing is locked. So he spent every spare moment possible at his job to visit these churches and talk to the vicars. And he took on the responsibility to get the Church of England to open their doors. He didn't talk to me too much about it and being a fourteen-year-old kid I was not bothered at all what he was doing, as long as I was getting to school alright and we would still be living in Brentwood by May 1ˢᵗ ready for the cricket season.

There were three strange things that happened to me while I was living there, one of them was when I sat there reading my stars in the newspaper, which my Dad being a religious man was dead against, he didn't like the stars and thought they were evil. And I remember having a pair of roller skates, that I had bought off one of my mates and it was that day I was going to spray paint them and it said in my stars I was going to be using paint and I told my Dad and I said to him "Look they are true, what are you going on about." But in the evening after I had used the spray paints I was very, very ill, being sick, sweating and had a high temperature. In the evening my Dad reminded me about me reading my stars earlier and to look at the state I was in now. And that did shock me a little, it was a bit too coincidental and it did frighten me a little and so I would not read my stars for a long, long time.

Another time, I fainted in the lounge, I got up off my chair went dizzy and fell onto the floor, my Dad said to me it was the holy spirit who had done that. I remember thinking why would the Holy Spirit do such a thing and what did it want with me? I was slightly confused by this but not frightened.

A day later in the evening time, it was time for us to go to bed. We had gone up into our room, shutting the door behind us. The bedroom faced out on to the road and Dad got into his bed and started reading his book and I got into mine. My Nan had some nets up at the window, I was laying there and all of a sudden the nets blew right out towards me, it didn't frighten me, I wasn't dazed but I did turn to my Dad and told him what had just happened. He got up and checked the window to make sure it was shut and it was. Again he said it is the Holy Spirit and you are being touched by it, nothing to worry about, just relax and see what happens. So I thought O.K. again I wasn't rattled by it and felt calm. I went to sleep and carried on, dismissing what my father had just told me.

Then one day in April 1989, I would do something that looking back on, you would wonder if it was the work of God or the work of the Devil. What possible plan did God have by putting a single family through so much? What possible plan did God have by allowing millions of people to be killed? What possible plan did God have by destroying the head of the Church of England? And what possible plan did he have for this 14-year-old boy?

It would be soon after the event in our bedroom, that one Saturday in April 1989 I woke up, got up and walked down the stairs and halfway down I stopped and looked out of the window, that gave me a view of the back garden and at the end of the it there was a shed, it had been built by Joe McCarthy, the man who had come over from New Zealand, and I just looked at it for a while, I had nothing planned for the day.

I walked the rest of the way down the stairs and into the kitchen, opened the back door and again began to look at the shed. It was quite an old fashioned shed, I had spent a lot of time in there messing around with Joe's tools and making weapons and toys. My Nan came into the kitchen and asked me what I was doing, I turned round and asked her if I could knock the shed down. At this stage my Dad had entered the kitchen and over heard what I had just asked, he said, "Don't be stupid Tom, why do you want to do that? It's a ridiculous thing to do," and he was quite adamant that I wasn't going to do it. My Nan, in her way and wanting to please me, turned round and said to my Dad "Oh let him do it if he wants to" My Dad finally agreed and he went off to Southend to see his cousin Michael.

So I went upstairs got dressed and got ready for my long day ahead.

That whole Saturday in April was spent knocking down the shed. Beyond the fence at the back of the garden, the London to Southend train line ran, along with London's District line.

I was in the garden and I had started my project, I opened the shed door and started emptying the contents on to the grass. My Dad said to me before he went that he was going to wave at me as he went past on the train, so every train that went past I would look up to check if I could see him. Then as he promised one train went past and he must of pushed the window down, as you could with the old trains, and waved and I waved back.

I began to empty the inside of the shed I would then carry the bags and tools up towards the back door. I then started to dismantle the shed and it took me the whole day from the roof, door, walls and window.

My Nan spent the whole day with me, bringing out cups of tea and sandwiches.

By the time my Dad got home there was no shed, I had placed everything in separate piles in the garden, tools, bags and boxes in one pile and the panels of wood in another.

I remember the next-door neighbour coming out and he suggested we got a skip and that he knew someone who worked for Ahern and could get it on the cheap. My Dad declined his offer because he thought it was a form of stealing and being a godly person, wasn't into that.

So I started to dig a hole in my Nan's garden for all the rubbish and we lit a fire for all the wood and the rest of the stuff we didn't need.

I passed one of the boxes to my Dad and he noticed a green Mark's and Spencer bag inside. If it had been up to me I would of just throw it on the fire. And looking back sometimes I wish I had.

My Dad opened the bag and took out this antique book. I stopped what I was doing for a while and we both sat down and studied it. It was a very old photograph album.

He put The Album inside and finished what we were doing. After a few more hours, we went in; before I closed the back door I looked at the view without the shed I also noticed the fire smouldering away. I had achieved my goal for that day. But not knowing I had started an affair that would last for the next 15 years.

The Album had a clasp that was broken. The Album contained postcards of mainly religious buildings throughout Europe in Bruges, Gent, Antwerp, Brussels, Trier, Paris, Worms and Frankfurt. On the back of the cards and on the opposite side to them were descriptions of the church's and cathedrals, written in English and German. There was also an address in Speyer, Germany written on one of the cards and writings mentioning a Flemish girl.

My Dad thought that this album was important due to the clasp being broken it meant you could never permanently close it, he connected that to his work with the church. My Nan had no idea where it came from, he asked a few more members of the family but to no avail. So The Album was put on the bookshelf by the telephone and there it stayed.

My father was still pursuing his church project; he had taken it upon himself to get the church doors unlocked and to stay that way. A very important date was coming up for me it was May 1st; my Dad had promised me I would be living in Brentwood by then, just in time for the cricket season.

Towards the end of April, Dad had finished work and walked in, he told me that he had found a flat in Brentwood, his friend Donna who owned Donna Antiques, had a flat in Rose Valley and needed somebody to rent it. We would be moving in on May 1st.

That news was the best news I could have heard, he had kept his promise and I was moving back to Brentwood.

It was a two-bedroom ground floor flat in Rose Valley, which was very close to the railway station; it was a nice flat in a nice block.

It was quite a sad day leaving Dagenham though, we had packed our bags, not forgetting The Album and I remember kissing and giving my Nan a big hug and feeling quite sad for her, she had enjoyed us being there and I knew she would be turning round and walking into a lonely house.

At the same time as us moving into our flat, my Mum, Gary and brother were also moving home, they had bought a four bedroom detached house opposite King George's playing fields in Brentwood, the house was a ten minute walk from my flat.

And so my relationship with them began to develop again. It was my father who had encouraged me in the past to contact my Mum, but because of what she had done to me earlier on in the year I begrudged her for that and I was determined not to contact her I thought she owed me an apology.

So we began seeing each other again I would go there after school and at weekends, I would also start to take my dog out again.

It was in that period that Essex County Cricket Club had written to me and invited me to have trials for the U14 side. My good friend Richard Donnelly, who played for Brook Weald, was also invited. Poppy picked me up from the flat and I remember being very nervous. I knew I had ability and I knew from colts cricket that this ability was a good one. But I was still very nervous heading to Chelmsford and being surrounded by other good cricketers. The trials were held in the indoor coaching school and must have been a good forty fifty kids there. We all took our turn to bat and we would then bowl. It was my turn to bat and I had already noticed the batting before me was not too clever, so I was very confident that I was going to do well. During my net, my confidence grew; I was hitting and timing the ball well. I also bowled quite well. So I came away from that trial extremely confident. I would be notified by post.

I was in the 3rd year at St Martin's. I was in Mr Harris's class, I was still trying at school, I was still involved with the sport teams but school seemed different, I was with my Dad, there had been that split in the family, where I had gone off to Dagenham, so I guess all that had affected my concentration. The situation at school would become a lot worse.

I had a good friend at the Cricket Club called Jamie Wilton; we would spend most of our spare time over the Cricket Club, practising in the nets. He lived right next door to the club.

There was also a Day Nursery at the club and they used the cricket hall for their premises. It was around this time that my brother had made me aware of a girl in the nursery who had expressed a liking towards me. It would take me another eight years to say hello to this girl. It was this girl who I would eventually go on to marry.

Jamie was into motorbikes and so we put our money together and bought a second hand scrambler from my old matron at Woodlands. The bike was a little too big for us and it was extremely fast. And we kept it in the car park at the flat and of a weekend we would push it up to the Cricket Club and ride it around the field, the field next to the Cricket Club. This began to slightly annoy my father because while he was playing cricket on the main pitch, he could hear Jamie and me on our motorbike flying around the field. And he used to say to me if I had fallen off and broken a leg or arm, I wouldn't be able to play cricket anymore, he also thought I should have been practising cricket instead of riding the bike. He threatened to take the bike away, so before he got the chance we moved it from the flat to a hiding place in the woods near Jamie.

It was in this period when I had the motor bike that I began a car cleaning round on Hutton Mount, a wealthy housing estate in Brentwood. I needed the money to run my bike, it was in the summer holidays, and me and a friend James Cooper began knocking on doors to see whether people needed their cars cleaned. It started out as a project for short-term money but over the next two years I would go out every weekend to regular customers.

After a while the bike was stolen from its hiding place in the woods. There are three possible explanations in my mind on how this happened:

Someone had seen us put it there and stole it.

My Dad who was unhappy at the fact I had a motorbike took it.

It was stolen by MI5 because it was jeopardising the mission that was planned for me later on in life and they could not risk me falling off the bike and either breaking a leg or actually being killed.

The bike had served its purpose in a way because it had got me out earning money and started my car-cleaning round. I used the car cleaning materials from Gary's garage, which brought me again closer to Mum and Gary.

This whole story runs in three parallels, one being the story of a normal person going through normal life, the second being the normal person having a second life with the bizarre happenings with his Dad and the third being the story that is seen from someone who at times becomes paranoid and mentally ill and his thoughts at the time while reflecting back on certain events.

One day in the flat, my Dad had gone off to work and I had received the letter I was waiting for from Essex County Cricket Club, I wanted so badly to play for Essex, it meant so much to me, I just wanted to pull that Essex jumper on, the one with the three red swords that represented Essex. And here I had the letter in front of me so I opened it; they had decided to give me three trial games for Essex U14's. Well I jumped for joy; I was elated I rang my Mum, my two Nan's and obviously told my Dad when he came in. My first game was to be at Brentwood School playing against Hertfordshire, My cricket career had begun. My Mum and Dad must of got together and decided between them that my Mum and Gary would be responsible for taking me to Essex games and my Dad would be responsible for my games at Brentwood Cricket Club, which in a way was a good idea. It also meant my father would never ever see me play for Essex but I did respect him for not treading on my Mums ground.

My Dad now had begun to get even more heavily into this church project. He had by now visited seventy vicars and churches in and around Essex; apparently a lot of them had agreed that God in his own way, in a form of signs was talking to my Dad. So he arranged a meeting for all these vicars at a church in Bradwell-on-Sea called St Peters, he had sent seventy telegrams to each of the vicars notifying them of the event. I remember the day well, my Dad had set off for his day fairly early, my brother was at the flat with me and we spent our time watching TV and messing about. He was thirteen.

At this point Dad had put that antique album in Donna's antique shop in Brentwood High St, it was displayed in the window and was put up for sale for £95.

We waited in the flat all day for our father to return, we received no word nor a phone call and to be honest I wondered what was going on, I knew this could be the start of a big campaign for me. It got quite late and we decided to go to bed, we slept in the same room that night, we felt uncomfortable being in the flat on our own.

He returned early the next morning with a look of dejection and looked deeply unhappy and confused. I learnt later, only one of the vicars had turned up and that was the vicar whose church it was. My Dad decided to stay there the whole day and the whole evening as a gesture. My Dad felt understandably dejected by the whole thing, he had spent a lot of time and effort putting this meeting together regarding the church doors. I knew at the time it was going to take a lot more than one meeting to force such a large issue but it could have been the start. Only one vicar turned up. Why? Surely having the church doors opened constantly was a good thing and a

Christian thing. Why would the vicars say God was talking to Dad and then later ignore his meeting?

He came home and must of thought it was the end of that project and era in his life, he had tried and probably due to seventy vicars, being run by a higher force in this country, rubbished his efforts. There was no word from any of them.

That was the end of his door-opening project. So he thought.

My cricket match for Essex was now coming up and I got more and more nervous as the days went by. I remember the day well, it was a beautiful day over at Brentwood School and I was fortunate enough to have already played on the pitch and was aware of my surroundings. Gary and Mum had brought a picnic over along with most of the other families. I felt quite strange my Dad wasn't there, he was the one who had taught me how to play and was the one who began my career, he was over at Brentwood Cricket Club which was literally over the road, so it was slightly strange him not watching me. He had promised me though, if I scored my first hundred that season, he would buy me a new cricket bat.

A few of the other colts and members came over from the club to watch me play but I did fail miserable that day, I scored 0 on my first ever outing for Essex and the walk off that pitch when I had been caught out, was the worst walk off I had experienced, I was holding back the tears, I was so disappointed to have failed in my first game for Essex.

The next couple of games for the county were an improvement; I had also started playing well for the adult teams at Brentwood Cricket Club.

It would be in my 4th game for Essex that I would secure my maiden century. It was at Felstead School playing against one of the minor counties.

Again it was a beautiful day, Mum and Gary were there, and he would sit there reading his paper and Mum, her magazines. They would both stop though while I was batting. That particular day they didn't get to read much.

I batted four and began a long partnership with Imran Mahmood, Imran played for Ilford and had been in the Essex set-up for a few years.

We were both hitting fours around the ground and seemed to communicate well with each other.

I remember Imran coming up to me, in between the over, we were both in our 80's he asked me whether I had ever scored a century before, I said no, he hadn't either.

I think the knowledge of us both knowing that had made us nervous and our communication broke down. Imran was out for 85. I had run him out. Imran walked passed me and said, "Keep going mate."

My century came with a boundary, I hit a spinner back over his head for four, with that I waved my bat to acknowledge the clapping from the crowd. I also remember seeing how proud my Mum was of me.

The side declared soon after that and as we walked off the field, again I would receive loud congratulations from everyone, it was the best feeling I had ever had. During lunch I remember the umpire coming up to me and congratulating me. He told me if I was focused and dedicated in my cricket, I could go a long way.

It was a great day for me not only had I scored my first century, I was told I would be in the team for the rest of the season. I received further congratulations when I got back to the Cricket Club, my Dad was most proud and went round telling everyone. I even received a mention in the school assembly. My Mum bought me a new pair of cricket gloves and my Dad bought me a new cricket bat as he had promised.

My Dad had spent most of his money buying that cricket bat for me. He wanted to do it though he said he had promised me and so we went to Ted Fenton's sport shop and bought me a Gray-Nicolls Dyna Drive, it cost £100.

My Dad had lost his job with BAC windows by now, I think they had finally caught up with the fact he had a lot more miles on his car than he should of and that he was doing things not associated with double glazing.

It was around this time that Donna had turned up with The Album, she said she had little interest from anyone in The Album and gave it back to us.

By now I was a little concerned that my Dad didn't have a job and I was a bit worried about the rent. I knew deep down if my Dad was going to move back to Dagenham, I wouldn't follow him, I would go back to my Mum's house, we had all made up and that relationship had started to develop again. Also by this time my cricket was developing quite well, I had played a lot more games for Essex and gone on to score more runs for them and two further centuries for

Brentwood. I had also just played a quarterfinal Mobil Matchplay competition game and was preparing for the semi final. I also had my car-cleaning round that I had built up over the summer; I was also entering into an important stage in my school life, my GCSE years would begin in September.

So for me to move back to Dagenham I would have been losing too much.

My Dad must of sat down one day and studied The Album more closely. It was quite bizarre that this album had appeared in the first place and had kept coming back into our lives. My Dad wasn't working and his church project had finished.

So one night he sat down and began to look at the writing more closely, finding it a bit strange, regarding the German in it.

I had come home one day and Dad told me he was flying to Germany, he was going to find out more about The Album. He flew to Koln.

He didn't tell me at the time why he was going there or what he was doing.

He wanted to find out who had written this album. To be honest I was becoming a little concerned about what my Dad was doing, you know, you just don't do things like that, I'm sure he could have easily gone to London to find out his answers. But no, he flew into Germany and left me at home for one night.

In Koln by the famous cathedral there is a bookshop just before the main shopping area. He walked into the shop and went straight over to the section he was looking for, he pulled out a book and started to compare this person's handwriting to the handwriting in The Album and noticed an extreme similarity. He walked out of the bookshop and headed back to the Eden Hotel where he was staying. He had obtained the information he had come for. It would be another five years until I would walk into that same bookshop looking for another particular book. Dad flew back the next day.

In the past two weeks leading up to this point I had a strange feeling about the future and could sense something was just about to happen. Now and again through my life I would have these feelings, the strongest being the night just before Princess Diana died.

My Dad walked in and told me whom he thought The Album belonged to. I didn't laugh and I didn't take the mick out of him, I didn't accept what he was saying but I wasn't going to belittle him either.

He made a phone call the following day to a lady called Josephine Day; she was a handwriting expert who lived in Worlds End, Chelsea. My Dad photocopied the handwriting out of The Album (marked blue) and the handwriting out of this particular textbook (marked yellow) and presented them to Josephine Day. We went to London, got out of the underground at Sloane St and walked up the King's Rd towards her flat.

I remember that day very well because I had seen Josephine Day a few months ago on the TV, she was sitting on a panel with other experts, and she was studying people's writing and signatures and describing their personality. So I found that quite interesting and I would chat to her about it. We didn't stay long, Dad gave her the two sets of writings and asked her to compare the two and let him know whether the same person penned them. He said it was for a family matter.

We left her flat and got back on the train and went home.

She said she would ring us when she had finished her examination, eleven days later she rang, she had finished her report and invited us back to her flat to pick up her one page report and to pay for her services.

The day she invited us to her home would be the same day as my most important semi final cricket game for Brentwood. But my Dad insisted I came with him, which made me very angry at the time because my semi final cricket was more important than doing anything else.

We arrived back at Josephine Day's flat in Chelsea and when she opened the door she invited us into her lounge and there was another man there wearing a suit, very smartly dressed man, she introduced him as a doctor, he didn't say a word and had no input in the conversations, he just stood in the background.

Josephine Day had changed since last time I had seen her, she had become this nervous person who wasn't talking as freely, openly and friendly as our last visit, this was quite odd and bizarre to me, she passed my Dad the one page report and told him that both sets of writings were penned by the same person and started to go through all the technical aspects of the handwriting, she could pick out the same characteristics in each of the writings, she even pick out illnesses she could detect in the person who's writing it was and basically explained why they were both penned by the same person. I will quote a few paragraphs from her one page report.

" I have spent two and a half days analysing samples provided by you. My conclusions as a Graphologist of many years practical experience is that the writing of both blue and yellow show similarities, which could possibly be the same person.

The person or persons who wrote both blue and yellow samples show similar characteristics. Very high energy levels. A quick constructive method of thought processes. Creativity to genius level which in the yellow samples, shows a personality tortured by fluctuating moods of deep severe almost suicidal depressions, alternative to highly energetic creative episodes.

I see in the writing (both sets) a gentle somewhat shy character. A well-bred or well-educated man who strove to express his feelings through music, painting and drawing.

In the yellow samples I see signs of the writer harassed by someone or some condition in his environment. As if he often felt pushed or manipulated by others. Perhaps (purely supposition) someone around him who was an extremely domineering character who tried to control the writers environment as well as their own.

Both sets of writing show a sharp mind, an ambitious person who despite his depressions, never ever lost touch with reality. He was not psychotic at any stage of his life, according to what I can assess from these samples.

Having been able to pick up all these characteristics in both sets of samples, the blue and yellow, I would say it is probable, and not impossible, that both sets of writing could have been written by the same individual."

At this point I became a lot more interested in what she was explaining but I couldn't believe it, I knew whom the writing belonged to, I started to become quite excitable. My father showed no emotion. He thanked her for the report and gave her £55.

Before we walked out of the door to leave Josephine Day asked him "Whose handwriting is it?" My Dad turned round to her and said, "It is the handwriting of Adolf Hitler."

She looked at my father, she didn't seem surprised and to be honest I think she already knew.

The book Dad had bought at the shop in Koln was Hitler by Joachim Fest.

We came out of her flat and began to walk back down King's Rd towards the station, I remember feeling a sense of intrigue and excitement. My pace had quickened at the anticipation. My father told me that we were now going to Sotheby's in Bond Street. We had The Album and the one page report that proved The Album was Hitler's. The thought of all this and the knowledge of knowing we were just about to become rich made me even more excitable and I started looking in all the shop windows as I walked down the King's Rd, looking at all the clothes I was just about to buy.

We got back on the underground changed at Westminster, one stop at Green Pk and then got out at Bond St. Looking back at that little trip, didn't mean anything at the time but while on the train, we were carrying an item that contained, (unknowing to us at the time) information that if ever was made public would destroy the institutions that were passing by above: the Government and our Monarchy.

We got out at Bond St and walked down New Bond St towards Sotheby's, I had more nice shops to look at, my Dad was totally focused on Sotheby's.

He knew back then, this album was not all about money, he knew it was valuable but he had just been involved in his church project and I think he thought the money raised from The Album would kick start a big campaign for him.

We walked into Sotheby's; wearing no more than jeans and our t-shirts we had no appointment and walked straight in.

A book expert saw us, a well-dressed man, who looked very experienced, and he sat down with us in a private room and studied The Album, and also briefly looked at Josephine Day's one page report. He looked up and dismissed The Album, he made us aware that Adolf Hitler had never written in English and so was unlikely to be his. He told us the one page report meant nothing and we would have to have a lot more evidence to proof that The Album was Hitler's before Sotheby's would even start to entertain the idea of auctioning it.

With that my Dad erupted into a rage at this man, sent me out and told me to phone the newspapers and to get them down here immediately. "Go," he said and I hurried on out into the street. I was a little shocked at what I had just experienced, Sotheby's were not really interested and I had seen my Dad for the first time erupt into this rage, as I stood on the curb of Bond Street I looked round in confusion for a phone box, who was I going to phone? And what on earth was I going to say? Before I began to set off in search, my Dad came out and stopped me.

That meeting was obviously not planned and this man looking at us in our rags and looking at the one page report and the way it was presented was probably not the best way to start a relationship with a company that had been dealing with auctions for the past 260 years.

However within three years of that day, we would be back at Sotheby's holding a much bigger meeting with a lot more people and with the evidence the man had suggested we obtained.

Would this meeting be as disastrous as the last? Or would it be a success? And would the auction ever take place?

We arrived back in the flat that evening, it had been the most bizarre day; my mind had gone from wondering how my cricket had been getting on, to being totally focused on this album and the riches, which hopefully it was going to generate.

Before I went to bed that night, I received a phone call from Paul Lattimore, the cricket colts organiser, he informed me that Brentwood had won the semi-final and would be playing against Ilford in the final at Essex County Ground in Chelmsford.

What great news and what a great day, a day I will never forget and a day that may go down in history.

I went to sleep that night, my thoughts had once again been refocused, I was now thinking of my cricket match, I knew it would be a big day for me, there would be many people there including Essex cricket coaches and selectors. I had to perform.

So I went to sleep once again thinking about cricket.

From that point my Dad's behaviour became a little odd to say the least. He became strongly aware that The Album we owned was extremely valuable and important. He knew it once belonged to Hitler and knew because it was also written in English; it would cause some awkward questions. He realised then that certain organisations would not like the fact there was new evidence to suggest Hitler could not only understand English but he could also write it. The British Government could not allow such revelations to come to light; it would be too damaging and would open up a serious debate within the media.

Dad started to become paranoid.

I walked into the flat, after a day practising in the nets with Jamie. I was full of joy and as happy as any 14-year-old boy would be, knowing he was soon to be rich.

37

I walked in calling after my Dad, he was standing in the lounge holding a piece of paper up and with his index finger covering his mouth, suggesting to me not to talk, the piece of paper read: "Don't talk the flat is being bugged," he had also set up a number of traps in the flat, so he knew whether someone had been in or not. He knew exactly how far each drawer was open and would make sight indentations in the wood and he would also put a match by the letterbox shutter and if the match had been moved, pushed by the shutter, he would know someone was peeping into the flat.

It reminds me now of an episode of Spooks when Danny sets up a number of different traps in their flat for his work partner Zoë.

My Dad took me outside and told me British Intelligence were bugging the flat and the telephone, he told me to go back in and pack a bag. We got on the train and headed for Central London.

We were going to London to visit Richard King, Dad's former boss. Dad wanted to raise enough money to secure our safety and to obtain the evidence he needed for Sotheby's. Richard is Jewish and so Dad would learn quickly that Hitler was not a good subject to talk about.

Adolf Hitler had been responsible for the death of six million Jews during the Second World War and so obviously not one Jewish person would invest in such a project.

He approached another former business contact in London and he basically laughed at us. No one in their right mind was going to invest money in a man who not only thought he owned a book by Hitler but also needed money to secure his families safety because he thought British Intelligence was after them.

He must of thought my Dad was completely mad.

We left and headed for a hotel, we stayed in a hotel near Baker St called the Portland Hotel, Dad had calmed down a little and began to realise he was being a little too paranoid about the whole situation. He also realised that if he was going to get anyone to invest in him, he was going to have to change his sales pitch.

My Dad had always given me a lot of freedom in my life and while staying at the hotel he suggested I go out and explore. I had got a little bored with sitting in the hotel room, eating sandwiches and watching MTV. So I jumped up and left the hotel, there was only one place I was heading, England was playing Australia in the final test match at the Oval. I headed for Baker St tube station and made my way to the Kennington Oval. How ironic it would be for my tube

38

journey on that day would literally pass the MI5 building, home to British Intelligence. Only hours beforehand had my Dad warned me of their possible activities and here I was passing Milbank, I think my Dad would have had a nervous breakdown if he had known where I was.

It must have been the last day of the test match because I didn't have a ticket and just paid at the turnstiles. It was a fantastic day for me, my hero Robin Smith was batting and he was my favourite batsman, I remember watching him hit the ball all round the ground. I thought to myself I have to get his autograph and then I would leave for the day and head back to the hotel. I made my way to the pavilion area; I slipped through security and managed to get to the area where the England players watched the cricket. Robin Smith was still batting so I just waited and then I had a stroke of luck, it started raining. All the players ran off the field and Robin Smith walked in, he walked out onto the balcony and sat down and started to take his pads off. I was standing on the other side of the balcony; the area was reserved for members only. I couldn't believe that my hero was sitting in front of me just after an innings for England in an Ashes match.

I built up my courage and said, "It's a shame about the weather, you were doing really well."

A lot of professional cricketers I have tried to speak to in the past haven't given me the time of day. Graham Gooch the previous year had refused to give me his autograph and he was rude and walked off, I would see Graham quite a lot at Essex after that, I made no attempt to talk to him.

Robin Smith however was very pleasant and charming, considering he may have had to go back on the field, he spent time talking to me, I didn't get his autograph; a conversation with him meant a lot more.

I left the Oval and headed back across the river to the hotel.

As I walked towards the hotel I could see my Dad standing on the corner, I was so pleased to see him and was looking forward to telling him about my day.

"Hi Dad," I said in my joyful way, he picked me up and pinned me against the wall, and started shouting at me " Where the fuck have you been?" He had been going crazy with worry he thought I had been kidnapped.

We spent the night at the hotel and went back to the flat the following day.

We got home and no, no one had been in our flat.

MI5 or MI6 weren't bugging the flat that day and probably had no idea at that time about The Album. However they would soon be involved and it would be someone very close to me that made me aware of that. There was also the time I visited a lady in Ramsden Heath, she made me conscious of the fact MI5 were monitoring my Dad very closely and were monitoring me only when I was directly involved with my Dad.

Many years later one of our security agencies based in Westminster, London would contact me; they feared the security of two individuals, who feature heavily in this story. They asked me to inform them of certain activities that my Dad was engaging in.

What possible security fears could they of had?

And surely asking a person who was so loyal to his Dad was a risk in itself?

It would have to be the biggest reason of all for me to betray my Dad.

I love my Dad and I knew he was right about so many things but I love my country and this was a matter that concerned national security at its highest level.

It was a difficult choice.

Looking back I can understand why my Dad was behaving in such a way but at the time it was a bit strange, my Dad had become different and more aggressive. He had this album and had begun to come up against doubt and scepticism within the family and throughout his friends. He realised he needed more than just that one page report, he needed something more substantial and not just from one expert, he needed several. Then people would listen.

The day was soon approaching when I would leave my Dad and go back to my Mum's house, there was only so much madness a 14-year-old boy could take.

The last happy memory of that flat in Rose Valley was on a Saturday night. It was a rare moment of happiness in all this between my Dad, brother and me.

We were all in the flat watching a film and when it finished we would all for some reason go outside and start playing water fights with washing up liquid bottles. We spent ages running around the car park trying to squirt each other. We would eventually all come together in the middle of the car park. My Dad looked up towards the stars and noticed a satellite going over, we all looked up and what looked like a small star was making its way across the sky. As we were all watching the satellite the biggest brightest thing you could ever see shot across the sky. My brother stood there in shock and asked my Dad "What was that?" I looked up at my Dad; he looked at me and said, "When will you start to understand?"

My Dad considered that moment as a sign from God, while the satellite was going over he had asked a question, in his mind he said "Your up there with everything you've got? You bastard" (referring to Hitler) and then the comet or asteroid or whatever it was, went over.

I remember walking off, not understanding what had just happened but also remembering that feeling of having religion forced on me. I would make my own mind up about religion.

It would be another 11 years, until I would see another shooting star, it would be two days after September 11th 2001, I was heading for Ireland and I would look up and have a question of my own.

Sometime after that event Dad learnt his friend from cricket, Martin Joselyn just by coincidence had also seen that same comet from his flat in Brentwood.

After another outburst from my father, I decided it was time to move out. My Dad had gone out for the day, so I phoned my Mum and she drove down to the flat with Christine Everard to help me move my stuff out. It was a sad day really, I remember putting all my stuff in bags and passing them out my bedroom window. I stood there alone in the flat for a while, just remembering the past few months and all the good times I had spent with my Dad. And also remembering the change in our lives that had taken place in the flat. I wrote my Dad a brief note and walked out the door.

My Dad lost his flat a few weeks later, due to not being able to pay the rent, he had spent all his money and didn't have a job, and he was spending all his time and efforts on The Album. So he sacrificed not only his son but also his flat as well. What a huge sacrifice that was for the pursuit of such a difficult subject for anyone to understand.

Dad moved back to his Mum's in Dagenham and I moved back to my Mum and Gary's house in Hartswood Rd. Brentwood.

I began to live a normal life again, I started to take Max my dog out every morning to the woods that were directly opposite the house. I would also concentrate on my car cleaning round that James and I had built up; we spent every weekend doing it. The 4th year at school was just about to begin and I would begin my GCSE's. I was in 4A and my form teacher was Mrs Stone.

In the 4th year you had more of a choice of what subjects you wanted to study and so I remember sitting down with Mum and Gary one evening in the lounge, we went through all the subjects on offer. My Mum knew it was important to make the right choices, she used to remind me a lot that I would need a good education, she used to say that even if I was going to play cricket for a living, I would need to do something afterwards. Cricketers have short careers and she tried to drum that into me.

I chose my subjects not really thinking of what I wanted to do when I was older but chose them with the thought that I wasn't going to need a profession or a job when I was older. We had just found this album, which was obviously worth a lot of money, and so what would I need with a profession or even work itself.

So choosing the subjects for my GCSE's had become unimportant and so to be honest I just didn't care what subjects I put down.

And this way of thinking run through my life until I was 21.

I remember back in those early days living with my Mum, just before school started, I become so convinced that I was imminently about to become wealthy. I remember going round on my bike when I was doing my car cleaning round looking at all the different houses on Hutton Mount and remember looking at all the insides of my customer houses and I was basically weighing up which house I wanted to buy. I started to have a much bigger interest in cars all of a sudden, I was just about to have the money to buy whatever I wished and so I started looking in detail at all the different cars I was cleaning, to establish which one I was going to buy. There was only one choice the 911 Porsche.

One of my customers had a blue 911 and he said he would take me out in it one day and weeks went by and I guess he must of forgot. I really needed to know how this car performed and I needed to get the feel of it.

I pulled up on his drive one Saturday and I had let the air out of my back tyre, I knocked on the door and I started to clean his car. At the end he paid me and I asked him if I could borrow his pump, he told me he didn't have one, I said " Is it O.K. to leave my bike here

42

while I walk home to get mine?" And with that he said "No, jump in the car and I'll take you home." Yes, I thought, my plan had worked. It was the first time since my Dad had had a 911 that I had been in one and it was a great thrill.

I remember going to the car exhibition at Earl's Court with James, with a real belief that I could soon afford any car that was there.

This way of thinking became quite a problem for me, I remember one night going to bed with the Yellow Pages and just ticking off companies I was going to ring to come and re-decorate the house I was just about to buy. I was ticking off swimming pool companies, security companies, entertainment shops, and so it was getting a little out of hand, I would phone up the Porsche dealership and they would send me brochures. I would also phone BMW dealership because I thought I should have a second car for carrying my friends around in.

So as I've said, it did get a little bit out of control, I don't know what you call that but there must be a word for it, delusional maybe.

I first arrived back at Hartswood Rd, I'm sure my brother was happy to have me back, that was the first time we had been apart and must have been hard for him as well. So our relationship began again, we would ride to school together, take Max out together and we used to play a lot of cricket in the garden. There was one time when we were playing, I smashed the cricket ball straight through the hall landing window, there was no covering that one up, my mother wasn't there and so I phoned the glazier in Warley Hill and got it fixed before she returned, I paid for the window out of my earnings. My Mum returned later unaware of anything. I told her what had happened over dinner that night, she just nodded her head in disbelief.

In the initial few days of me living at Hartswood Rd, I was quite frightened and concerned of my Dad's reaction against the actions and short note I had written him, maybe it wasn't the best way of telling me, maybe I should of told him straight, but I was frightened of him at that point and, I was confused at what was happening.

Mum was due to go to Bermuda with Gary, he was going on some kind of business trip and she decided to stay with me because she was concerned about my fears and me. When my Dad got angry and was aggressive he was a frightening figure. So she stayed with me and at the time it was very comforting. But we learnt a lot later that Gary had actually planned to ask Mum to marry him. I think that would be just one of many reasons why they would eventually split up and why my Mum deep down blames me, and probably is the reason we haven't got on so well over the years. I never asked for them to split up, but sometimes in life things happen that we just don't understand at the time.

So Dad had moved back to Dagenham and he had a massive task ahead of him, he had to convince someone to invest some money in him, to back him to get this album totally authenticated. It was not going to be easy, he was going to have to use all his tact and diplomacy that he a learnt over the years through his business, he was going to have to use his brilliant sales technique to convince people to put up the money. This whole process would be made a lot harder with many of Dad's friends and colleagues knowing he had just lost his family and business, been through mental illness and had just become a self confessed Born Again Christian. So knowing all that and then telling people he just found a book belonging to Hitler, written in English in his garden shed and then to top it all off, there had just recently in 1983 been the Hitler Diaries hoax where Rupert Murdock had bought and published them in The Sunday Times and had been hugely embarrassed by the whole affair; so you can appreciate the task ahead of my Dad.

But if any man was going to pull this off it was going to be my Dad, my Dad had an amazing personality, he had a brilliant sense of humour, he could also be very serious when needed and was very good at conducting meetings and basically he could turn nothing into something and make it work, he could virtually create miracles.

I remember back in 1988 my brother and I were staying with Dad in Dagenham, he took us up to see England v West Indies at the Oval but we didn't have any tickets, we thought you could buy them on the gate, so we arrived and I was really looking forward to the day, all my cricketing heroes were playing, GA Gooch, RA Smith, CG Greenidge, DL Haynes, IVA Richards, MD Marshall, CA Walsh and CEL Ambrose. But unfortunately we got there and it was an all ticket event, the amount of disappointment that came over me was extraordinary, so we walked round the whole ground twice looking for tickets, seeing if we could get in and as we carried on walking I felt more and more disheartened and I wanted to go home and watch it on the TV.

But as we made our way round to the side of the ground where the massive gas cylinders are, there are some houses there with balconies looking over the ground and there was this one lady sitting there on her chair, there were crowds of people walking past and my Dad shouted up at this lady, "It's alright for some, what's the view like?" jokingly, Dad used to do things like that, it made me cringe and I would shy away in embarrassment. They exchanged conversation for a while and then he joked to her "We haven't got any tickets, is it O.K. to come and sit on your baloney?" I could not believe what happened next she said, "Yes, O.K. no problem." She opened her door and we entered into her house and onto the balcony, she had the most beautiful view of the ground you could wish for and I couldn't believe it, I was standing here on this lady's balcony watching cricket. Extraordinary! We then learnt she was actually the wife of Harry Brind. Harry Brind was the head grounds men of the Oval and she got on the phone to him and asked him whether or not there were any spare seats in the reserved area. I could not understand what was going on at this point, this was extraordinary. Not only had Dad got us in to the ground but also into a sitting area reserved for members only, which had the best view of the cricket. Eventually Harry Brind introduced himself to us and spent a while talking to us. I was in my element, it was a beautiful day and I was watching the best cricketers in the world, England V West Indies. West Indies at the time were the best team in the world and England also had a few of their own good players. The only disappointment of the day came when Viv Richards was out for 0. I remember him walking out towards the middle, in that proud lion like way of his, there was a massive sense of anticipation within the crowd, and this was the moment people had looked forward to.

Lunch came and Harry Brind came over and asked whether my brother and me wanted to walk out to the middle of the square. What a moment that was, in front of thousands and thousands of people my brother and I got up and walked out with the head groundsmen towards the middle. Obviously I wasn't playing but it was a nerve-racking experience with so many people there. I got to the middle and looked round at the crowd, I found it hard to believe that anyone could concentrate while so many people were watching them. I began to soak up the atmosphere, I knew the TV cameras were there and we may have been on television. I thought then, I would be back here one day to play for my country. We walked off the field and I tried to explain to my Dad how it had felt being out in the middle. I would never again set foot on that cricket square.

The game finished and we were taken into the main pavilion and my brother and I went on the autograph hunt and what a moment it was when the great Viv Richards came down the stairs. He began to have a conversation with my Dad about the game and they joked together referring to Viv's duck.

I will never forget that moment nor that day, I will never forget the way my Dad managed to create from nothing, a day that will live in my memory forever, he created a miracle in my eyes and he was the only person I knew who had it in him to take on this project

The day was approaching in September that the whole of Brentwood Cricket club were looking forward to. The day of the Mobil Matchplay Final was upon us. We were playing Ilford at the County ground in Chelmsford. We had hired a coach for the day because of the amount of members who wanted to come and support us. Brentwood U16's had already enjoyed success that year when we had won the Ron Yardley six a side competition in Stanford le Hope. We had some very good players in our team including Paul Collier, Danny Hazel, Dave Elmore, Ben Cocklin, Ricky Hazel and of course myself. We were all looking forward to that game and again Ilford had some very good players as well who were playing for Essex at the time: Gul Khan, Danny Plowright and Sanjay Sanyal. And so we were the under dogs.

We got on the coach, my brother was with me and many of the adult members had come. We were all in good sprits, singing songs, psyching ourselves up and generally being happy. But I also remember sitting there noticing, someone was missing on that coach: my Dad.

He had begun to set about finding somebody to back his project. He was at the point where he was asking friends and former colleagues to put the money up so he could fully authenticate The Album. He knew this was going to take quite a lot of money, which he didn't have.

He was due to meet Yocasta Ferra that day. He had set up a meeting with her and was unfortunately unable to join me at the final.

When he lived in Knightsbridge he met a number of very wealthy and affluent people, he asked a lot of those friends he had met along the way without any success. This was going to be a hard project trying to convince anyone to put the money up.

Susan Gibbs, he had met her in a hairdresser in Sloane St called Neville Daniels when he was living in Knightsbridge. Susan Gibbs was actually the granddaughter of Sir Alfred McAlpine, and so she was vastly wealthy, she lived next door to Harrods. They became very good friends while Dad lived in Knightsbridge, he would see her quite a lot and I remember actually while living in the flat in Kavanaghs Rd Brentwood, it was my Dad's birthday and Susan was taking him out for dinner and I remember Dad saying to me and Albert that he had a feeling that she was going to buy him a 911 Porsche and I remember the feeling of disappointment when he returned without the Porsche but with a tie from Marks and Spencer. And still to this day we take the mick out of him over all that.

He had met up with her a few weeks before the Final and went through with her what had happened to him over the past few years, he had gone through the findings of The Album and what Josephine Day had said. But unfortunately Susan Gibbs was totally uninterested and while in the back of her chauffer driven car, Susan had told the driver to stop at the nearest tube station to drop my Dad off. That was the last time Dad saw her.

That kind of attitude towards The Album became a regular thing.

There was this other women called Yocasta Ferra she lived in Sloane St and she was the ex-wife of the ambassador of the Dominique Republic to New York and Dad had met her while living in Knightsbridge. My father had answered a personal advert she had put in the Tatler magazine and they had become good friends. So Dad contacted her and she suggested a meeting with herself and her present boyfriend William. William was a Swiss banker who also studied Graphology. And so it was on that day they had their meeting.

We arrived at the Essex County Cricket Club and both captains Gul Khan and Danny Hazel first of all tossed a coin to see which changing rooms we were going to be in. Danny lost the toss and so we were in the away changing rooms.

Danny won the main toss out in the middle though and he decided to put Ilford into bat. We had won all our previous games by batting second and chasing.

So Ilford batted first and quickly got in trouble losing a few quick wickets including one of their main batsmen Danny Plowright. Gul Khan had been the backbone to Ilford's batting and had spent most of the innings there, he was eventually out for 56.

There was a good crowd there that day, Brentwood had brought a lot of support and so had Ilford. There was a lot of the Essex staff there and the Essex coaches and selectors and a lot of people from Mobil, who were sponsors of the event.

In fact one of the Essex senior players had pointed out there had been more people watching that day than for some of the county games. Ilford reached 130 in their innings and so Brentwood felt confident going into lunch. 130 for a 40 over match was not really enough. We started quite badly losing Paul Collier who was one of our key players and shortly after Danny Hazel who was our best player.

I remember walking out towards the middle and listening to all the Ilford players, they were so pleased they had just got Danny out and they thought the game was going to be a easy and they made their feelings quite clear to me.

I didn't like people taking the piss out of me and I didn't like being wound up. I walked towards the crease with an even more determined mind. Most of these players were two years older than me and so I did feel a little intimidated.

I was batting with Dave Elmore and we put on a partnership of 67, I managed to hit a few good shots round the ground, I knew I had to do well because I knew all the coaches and selectors were watching and I desperately wanted to impress.

I managed to get 28 and help my team get back on course. It was Dave Elmore and Ben Cocklin who finished it off for us.

It was a great day and Ray East, who was head of coaching for the Essex Youth teams was presenting the trophies, he made a speech on the game and it was also his responsibility to pick the man of the match, he mentioned the performances of key players including myself, but it was Gul Khan from Ilford who won the trophy, he had bowled well and batted well.

Danny was presented with the main trophy and the whole team had photographs taken in front of the main pavilion.

I had done quite well in that game and a few weeks later I received a letter from Ray East asking me to attend indoor coaching sessions with the rest of the Essex players.

So Brentwood had won, we were the underdogs and we had beaten this great Ilford team. We made our singing voices heard that day, and the drinking began in the changing rooms. It was a great memorable day and everyone was euphoric. Brentwood Cricket club received a cheque for £1000, which we would eventually buy new cricket nets for the whole of the club.

The whole day was a great moment for us and also for all the members who had travelled with us to support. But throughout that whole day I felt the absence of my father, he had brought me up with cricket in the background, he had coached me and introduced me to this wonderful game. He should have been there.

His meeting with Yocasta Ferra that day had gone extremely well, he went to her house for dinner and met her boyfriend William, and he studied The Album and the one page report that Josephine Day had produced. William was actually studying graphology and looked at a few of the words in The Album and agreed they looked very similar to Hitler's writings. But he looked at the one page report and told my father that it was a joke, that this one page report meant nothing and that he would have to acquire a lot more evidence if he was going to get anywhere with it. He suggested my father went to Zurich, he said he would find the right people there who would be qualified enough to take on this kind of work. He had to have forensic scientists to look at this to examine the age of the ink, the age of the paper and to see if there were any fingerprints on The Album and to have the top Graphologists to examine the writing and for them to compare The Album against original Adolf Hitler writings.

William knew this was going to take a lot of money and Dad had been honest with them telling them that he had recently been made bankrupt and had little money. And so Yocasta Ferra had a friend called Bernie Cornfeld, he was at one point one of the richest men in the world, he owned a company called Investors Overseas Services (IOS) which was based in Geneva, he had built up this company which was worth 2.5 billion pounds before it collapsed in 1970 and he had spent 11 months in prison on fraud charges.

Yocasta suggested my Dad get in contact with him and in fact she phoned him that evening at his house in Los Angeles and explained to him about my father. Bernie Cornfeld took my Dad's phone number and told Yocasta he would phone him later that evening.

Both days were going quite well, I was having my success with my cricket and it looked like my Dad was having success finding someone to back his project.

I spent the evening back at Brentwood Cricket Club enjoying myself. My Dad had spent his evening back at the house in Dagenham sitting in the lounge waiting for a phone call from Los

Angeles. He finally phoned and after a long conversation decided that the Adolf Hitler affair was not for him. I guess Bernie Cornfeld probably thought to himself being involved in one fraudulent project in his life was more than enough.

I'm not saying my Dad's work was fraudulent but that was the attitude of a lot of people, they thought my Dad was a con man and a crank. Most people made their judgement without even consulting the experts.

So my Dad was hugely disappointed, the whole day had been built on hope; the only good thing to come from that day was the advice from William suggesting he goes to Zurich.

What I'm trying to get over is from that point there was this pattern, whereby my Dad would miss out on my brother and me growing up and would miss so many memorable days. He had become totally focused on this album and would not let anything get in his way and by now cricket meant absolutely nothing to him, it was unimportant. To me it was the world and meant so much. He had missed one of the most memorable days in my life due to that album.

The cricket season was drawing to a close after that game and was basically the last game for me.

I started spending more time with my friends from school. My friends had been going out a lot during the summer to discos and parties. I hadn't really joined in I was more interested in cricket, it didn't really appeal to me I wasn't into drinking or smoking.

But the end of the season came and one of my friends Antony Matthews invited me to a disco at St Helen's Cathedral. Brentwood. The Cathedral ran the disco every Friday night.

We all met up at Shenfield railway station, this night was the first time I would be purposely going out to get drunk. It was always my responsibility to get the drink for everyone from the off licence; I was the tallest and also looked the eldest. I was never asked for I.D. and would always pass for an eighteen-year-old. The drink we all favoured at the time was called Thunderbird; it was quite a strong drink, it did the job but tasted awful.

We jumped on the train and got out at Brentwood and walked up Rose Valley towards the Cathedral and as we walked up the road we would all start drinking our Thunderbird, it was a short walk to the Cathedral so we had to drink fast.

It was a great walk to the Cathedral. We were all drinking, laughing and joking; I was looking forward to the disco and looking forward to finding out what the feeling of being drunk was like. We got to the party and there were loads of kids our age. Due to my intoxication I was full of confidence that night and had no fear or hesitation getting on the dance floor. But I also remember talking to three or four girls that night who I had taken a fancy to, normally I would of shied away but again due to my drinking I had no fear and approached them one by one and was able to spend time talking to them. It seemed I could talk for England.

After that party, I had enjoyed myself so much, it would become a regular thing that on a Friday night we as a group of friends would go out. We would either go to a disco organised by the church or Keys Hall disco in Warley or house parties we had been invited to.

So the winter had come and I would still go out every weekend concentrating on my car cleaning round and I had the money to go out every Friday, I didn't smoke but buying drink was not a problem. I became more interested in what I was wearing. For a fourteen-year-old I was earning good money and it become important to me what I was wearing and how I looked, I would go to Romford regularly to buy clothes.

Some nights we wouldn't even go to parties we would spend our time just walking up and down Brentwood High Street.

Those days were good fun and it took my mind off a lot of things, I still had the same attitude towards school though, the attitude where by I thought I was just about to become wealthy and so nothing mattered. It was always about living for the day, did I have enough money for the day? What was I doing for the day? It was never worrying about the future because the future was taken care of, I didn't have to worry about that so I didn't.

My behaviour started to deteriorate more so in the fourth year, I began to slowly lose friends I had become slightly arrogant, the influence of this album had affected the way I conducted my whole life, I became big headed.

I look back now and can understand why, I was this fourteen-year-old boy who played cricket for Essex, was very popular with everyone at school and also had more pocket money than anyone else and to top it off I was just about to become rich, so I guess it was natural it all went to my head.

I used to have regular visits to the headmaster's office and he would ask me the reasons behind my behaviour, I never told him the truth but it would soon become clear to them what was going on.

My Mum used to be called to the school regularly regarding my behaviour, in fact once Al's Mum and mine were called at the same time to discuss our behaviour, as a pair they decided it was a good idea if we were put in separate classes. And after what was just about to happen with Dad and I, the school were losing patience with me. I was moved out of my class just before the end of the year.

My belief in my Dad's work strengthened over the next year and so I became even less worried about my GCSE's and my future. Alister's sense of honour and laid-back attitude towards school didn't help either. We were not the most favoured of pupils in our teacher's eyes.

It was also in the 4th year that I was reunited with my old friend Scott Douglas; we had played football together for Warley All Stars. His father Ian was in charge of the team and we would meet every Thursday night for training. Scott's Dad took the football very seriously and I remember playing one Saturday morning against a team from Romford and on one side of the pitch was Ian completely going mad, jumping up and down shouting at everyone but as he was doing that my Dad on the other side was also doing the same thing, it seemed they were trying to out do each other.

I used to play on the left wing, I scored a few goals but my main responsibility was to supply Scott with crosses.

We'd lost contact until we went to St Martin's but even then he was in the higher class so we didn't see much of each other until the 4th year when the higher class and middle class would share Geography together. I sat next to Scott and we would start to get to know each other a bit better and after a while he became one of our regular Friday night crew.

Joking apart though I had met Scott at such an early age and through life we would go our separate ways but fate would always bring us back together.

It was because of Scott that in 1995 I would sit down with the nephew of the Chief Editor, to the London-based Jewish Chronicle to discuss the findings that had been discovered regarding Adolf Hitler.

My Dad was slightly disappointed with the Bernie Cornfeld episode but had still been given some sound advice by William, Yocasta Ferra's boyfriend.

52

It had become quite clear now that no one was going to invest huge amounts of money for such a project, it was totally unbelievable and of high risk and so he became tired of asking people for backing and decided he would find people who could invest very small amounts. He contacted one of his old friends Bob Flain who invested £300. Dad had still got some of his Indian jewellery left over from when he was trying to sell it. He managed to sell the rest of it for half its value and so with Bob's money he had enough to buy an airline ticket to Zurich and a few days stay in a hotel. He flew in and booked himself into the Hotel Leoneck put The Album into a safety deposit box and opened a bank account with the Bank Verein. He would also give the bank my details so I had access to the box.

He opened these accounts so he could have funds from sponsorship put in there and eventually the money from the sale of The Album would also be transferred into that account.

He contacted two people, Professor Dr. Wulf Listenow who was a forensic scientist and a graphologist who taught at the University of Zurich and Elisabeth Klein who was a leading Graphologist.

They met at the bank and held their meetings down in the vault. Both experts examined The Album and witnessed the photocopying of it; they both received copies of the handwriting in The Album and copies of handwriting taken from Hitler's Letters and Notes and a book called *Young Hitler* by August Kubizek, they then went away to start their initial reports.

Young Hitler is the English version of *Mein Jugendfreund* by August Kubizek, Dad had first seen this book in the Imperial War Museum when making copies of Hitler's writing for Josephine Day. He would take this book out on loan from the Dagenham Library five days before it burnt down.

After five days Elisabeth Klein was the first to respond, they held a meeting in the bank and after another look at The Album, she handed over her report and told Dad The Album was written by Adolf Hitler when he was sixteen.

Dad knew the total authentication of The Album was going to take a lot longer and would need original documents by Hitler, that were stored in the Bundesarchiv in Koblenz. But this was a good start and he could build on it.

Professor Dr. Wulf Listenow returned with his reports and sat down with Dad in the bank.

After studying the English in The Album, which in all his previous research of Adolf Hitler he had never seen before and then checking once again the writings in *Young Hitler*. He looked up in some confusion with what he could detect within the English, it could also be detected in the German, now there was English writing to compare it with. What he was looking at had contradicted all his research and at the time there was no reason for Hitler to have written in English and he was finding it very hard to explain why at the age of sixteen Hitler was writing English freely.

What he was suggesting began to frighten him, he could not understand.

The findings of this album would change history but not in a way England would appreciate, it would turn the entire world against us.

He agreed he would continue with the authentication of The Album but insisted on working with Lotha Michel an expert from Mannheim University in Germany. Lotha Michel would arrive after the weekend and they would continue at the bank on Monday.

The Album would be put back in the safety deposit box every night and Dad would return to his hotel. Walking back that evening it had become clear to Dad that The Album was not only immensely valuable but it could also be used to uncover a possible conspiracy behind Adolf Hitler.

Why were the people of the world told he couldn't understand English or write it when he clearly could at the age of sixteen?

Dad became slightly nervous of what he had been told by a top expert, The Album contained the most powerful revelation. Dad would tell me on a train going down to Melk in Austria a month later, I totally dismissed it as complete bollocks.

Dad's money by this time had completely run out, he was living at the hotel without a penny on him; obviously it didn't appear to the hotel staff that way. Dad was very clever in that way, putting on a front, his appearance was always very smart, he spoke very well and gave the impression of being wealthy, he would make sure all the staff were aware of his meetings in the nearby bank. So the last thing they must of thought was Dad was just about to walk out without paying.

He booked into a nearby hotel and would soon learn that if you have just knocked one hotel in a city it was best not to use the same name in the next one.

The police arrested him and he spent a week in a Zurich prison for nonpayment of hotel bills, he was eventually deported via plane back to England.

This was obviously leaving one small problem; The Album was still in that safety deposit box in Zurich. He was not allowed to return to Switzerland for another five years and if caught in the country would face a five-year prison sentence.

I had just got in from school and decided to take Max out for a walk, after an hour of walking round the woods, I returned to an empty house, Mum had popped down the shops. As I cleaned Max's paws I could hear the phone ringing in the background. I left Max and headed for the hallway.

I picked the phone up and said "Hello."

It was Bob Flain, he explained to me who he was and that he had given Dad some money to go away with. He told me he had received a phone call from the Zurich Police telling him Dad had been arrested for walking out of a hotel without paying.

Obviously this was quite a big shock to me, I didn't even know my father had gone away so hearing this surprised me and I began to sense the initial stages of panic.

Bob didn't need to speak to my Mum or Gary; it was just me.

I thanked him for phoning and put the phone down.

I was determined to track my Dad down and speak to him. I had no idea where Zurich was, I didn't really know what he had done and I didn't know how long he was going to be in prison for.

I picked up the phone and dialled 153 (International Directory Enquires). After a few attempts I managed to get through to the Zurich police department. And the chap on the other end, who could speak very little English, tried to explain what had happened and why he was in jail. I asked him if I could speak to my father and he said no, but he would let Dad know I had rung.

I can't remember if I told Mum or not about Dad, I guess I must of, but my Mum even at that early stage had lost patience with my Dad. He had gone round telling his friends and my Mum's friends all about this album saying it was Hitler's and asking everyone for money, my Mum had become embarrassed by him.

I didn't hear anything for a couple of weeks. Dad got deported, he had made friends with a drug smuggler in the prison and they were both escorted to the plane and given £100 each and flown out of Switzerland.

I was itching to hear from Dad, making sure he was O.K. and generally wondered what had happened to him and why he was even in Switzerland.

I got back in from school one day in early December 1989 and the phone rang and it was Dad. I was over the moon to hear from him, he was phoning me from the phone box round the corner. So I walked straight round there, he was standing holding his briefcase.

He would rarely knock on our front door he respected the fact Mum was unhappy with him.

He went through his trip to Zurich with me and if I had any doubts about The Album then they were surely quashed when I read the report from Elisabeth Kline. It was a translation and I will quote parts of it. (Blue refers to The Album and yellow refers to Hitler's writings from textbooks).

"The left side in blue indicates a young writer, 16 years old. This handwriting is identical with the later handwriting (in yellow) of Adolf Hitler.

They exhibit one and the same identifying characteristics and peculiarities. The identifying characteristics of the two handwritten entries have remained unchanged and show no difference resulting from maturity or intellectual level.

Hitler could not move onward to full maturity after his seventeenth year of age, because a pathological component was also influential. Since childhood, he suffered from latent epilepsy."

She goes on to conclude after much technical explanation.

"In the course of the detailed technical analysis, the documents of A. Hitler were compared and examined. In the process, it proved that the combination of idiosyncrasies and characteristics of the handwritings (in blue and yellow) in The Album of J. Davey emerged with sufficient, with a certainty bordering on the very highest probability, that this is the personal handwriting of Adolf Hitler."

The most important aspect that has come out of Elisabeth Klein's report and is something not documented anywhere in our history books is that, Hitler suffered from epilepsy, Klein had detected it in his writing and so he must of hidden it from the public and kept it very close to himself but that information has a critical importance when later on linking Adolf Hitler to a member of our Royal Family.

He told me The Album was in a safety deposit box in a bank in Zurich and he had given me access to the account. He told me that he had been deported and was not allowed back in the country for another five years.

This immediately began to worry me, the thought of not getting that album for another five years filled me with horror. Five years I would have to wait until there would be an auction, I would be nineteen. Well that was far too long for me I was coming up to my last year at school and the sale of The Album had to be done quickly. I wasn't going on to do A-Levels and I sure as hell wasn't going to University, so I needed that album sold, I needed the money. And that's the way I thought about the situation.

Money played a big part in my life back then and apart from playing cricket it was all I was interested in. I would do anything to earn a little extra, I obviously had my car-cleaning round but I was always looking for other ways to earn money. One of my customers Malcolm Harrison owned a company called Space Maker and every year he would ask me if I wanted to work at the Ideal Home Exhibition and I would jump at the chance anything to own an extra bit of cash. Gray-Nicolls a cricketing manufacture sponsored me, due to me playing for Essex, they must of thought I was a good investment and I would order numerous amount of cricket bats and equipment and take it to the Cricket Club and sell it. What else did I do? I used to sell trainers at school, supplied to me by one of Dad's old customers. Half my year were wearing the same trainers. So I was always thinking of ways to earn money, but I knew there was only one big time moneymaker for me and that was The Album. So The Album being in a Swiss bank was no good, it had to come out, it had to be returned, it had to be authenticated and had to be put up for sale, it was as simple as that.

Dad had told me I had access to the box and he wanted me to go into Zurich on my own, crossing the German Swiss border by train to retrieve The Album and then we would fly home. He said we would be gone for three days which I stressed was essential as I needed to be back by the weekend because on the Friday night it was Brentwood Cricket Club's dinner and dance and I was receiving an award for colt of the year, which was being presented by Barry Hearn. So it was very important to me to be back, I was looking forward to that evening. Brentwood had had a good season and I had played well through it, I was looking forward to receiving my award.

Dad could not run the risk of being caught in Switzerland he would get five years in prison and that would have been the end of everything. He wasn't telling me do this he was asking me, he knew I knew The Album was real, he knew I had sat with Josephine Day, I knew it was real, so for me to agree to such a thing surely meant

The Album was a hundred percent. I was just about to do something that was shrouded in secrecy, he asked me not to tell Mum or discuss it with anyone.

He gave me a bundle of string, I asked him why I needed it, he said I should pack a bag and lower it from my bedroom window that night ready for me to pick up in the morning. He said walking out of the house in the morning with a big bag looked suspicious. He asked me not to tell Mum or discuss it with anyone. If Mum, Gary or Michael found out the whole operation would be cancelled.

He said he would wait for me in the morning at Martin Jocelyn's flat; Martin was one of Dad's friends from cricket. He lived in a tower block near Brentwood railway station. Dad also told me if I changed my mind he would understand.

So I went back to the house and up into my bedroom, Mum was making dinner and my brother was in his bedroom doing his homework. I emptied my squash bag and filled it with clothes and schoolbooks. I took all my books from school because I had mock exams coming up and I needed to revise. So in the madness of the days to come I would bury my head in my textbooks and try to maintain some kind of normality.

The kitchen was right below my bedroom and if my Mum had been washing up that evening she would of seen my bag being lowered from my bedroom window. I lowered the bag to the floor and went downstairs and started watching TV as if nothing had happened, not doubting at all what I was just about to do.

I woke up got showered and dressed in my school uniform, went downstairs and said goodbye to my Mum. I loved my Mum but I knew she was wrong about my Dad, I knew I was right, I knew what I had witnessed in Chelsea and so there was not much going to stop me unless Mum or Gary would find out and manage to stop us before we reached Dover. I gave her a kiss and a cuddle knowing what I was just about to do would devastate her with worry and anxiety. But it would only be for a few days she would get over it.

I walked out of the back door picked up the bag that I'd lowered the previous night and got on my bike and instead of riding through King George's playing fields towards my school I turned left into St John Rd and rode down toward Brentwood Station and the tower block. I left my bike in the reception area of the flats and padlocked it. I got in the lift and Dad invited me in, the first thing that hit me was the amazing view of Brentwood. It was a nicely decorated flat, which kind of surprised me because from the outside the tower block looked awful. I got out of my school uniform and changed into something else. My Dad told Martin to ring my Mum at 4.10pm to tell her what had happened. It gave us enough time to get out of the country without anyone being alerted. I remember saying to my Dad before we walked out of the tower block that I wasn't sure about leaving my bike there, he assured me it would be O.K..

We jumped on the train at Brentwood and headed for Liverpool Street, London.

Dad had to go and see Brian Baker, another friend of his from the Cricket Club, he was going to lend Dad £400 to recover The Album. Dad had promised a good return on his money. Brain worked at the Baltic Exchange near Tower Bridge, he left me at the green at Trinity Square and went off to see him. Dad had left me there because it was a risk taking me to see Brian, he may have got suspicious and thought twice about lending the money. Taking your fourteen-year-old son on a trip to Switzerland to retrieve a book belonging to Hitler, while in school time was a little odd.

Dad returned with the money and we got the Circle Line round to Victoria and boarded a train to Dover. At this time I had no problem with what was happening Dad was in a good mood, I guess in the back of my mind I was a little worried about my Mum but at that stage of the day she was unaware.

We stopped at Canterbury because it started to play on Dad's mind that he had taken me off; he thought he should be the one to tell my Mum. So we got off the train and found a phone box, he rang Mum, she was engaged so he tried his sister Evelyn but she was also engaged. All of sudden Dad got very angry he thought Mum and Evelyn were talking on the phone discussing him and what he had just done and talking about his mentality and whether he was in a good state of mind. This really annoyed him he smashed the phone down and stormed off toward the station.

We arrived at Dover and got the ferry across to Calais, France. The only thing I remember about the crossing was when I went up on deck and watched the cliffs of Dover get smaller and smaller.

We arrived at Calais and it was getting late so we booked into a small hotel. We woke up the following morning; Dad paid the bill, which in itself was quite bizarre.

Dad also paid for two one-way tickets to Paris. We boarded the train and I sat down.

By this time I knew my Mum would of known I was gone, hopefully she knew Dad had taken me and not some strange man and by now no doubt the police would have been alerted.

The phone rang at 4.10pm; my Mum answered it and was speechless to what she was hearing. She put it down and phoned Gary at work, he told Mum to ring Brentwood police station and he immediately came home. Within minutes of her phoning them a police car pulled up on the drive, two uniformed policemen got out and knocked on the door. Mum initially was so angry with my Dad for what he had done and the police had to calm her down. They realised quickly the seriousness of the situation so Mum was taken down to the station. She was introduced to Inspector Delamain. He was in charge of the whole station, and so a fourteen-year-old boy being kidnapped from Brentwood would become his responsibility. Dad had told Martin we were flying to Germany and then would go onto Zurich; Martin passed that information onto my Mum. Mum also knew about The Album and what Dad's intentions were for me.

Inspector Delamain asked my Mum lots of questions about myself, Dad and the strange reasons for the trip.

Inspector Delamain was quick to contact all the major airports, he was trying to stop us leaving the country he knew things would become more complicated if we managed to get into Germany.

Paris was a good two hours away and to take away my concerns for my Mum and my worries over her reaction when I got home I decided to take out some of my schoolbooks and start revising. I was sitting on my own trying to concentrate and after a while Dad joined me and what he was just about to tell me would slightly change my opinion on him. I trusted my Dad through anything and if he told me that it was raining cats and dogs I would have believed him and he had never lied to me up until that point.

He sat down and told me we weren't going to Zurich and The Album would be picked up at a later date. Obviously I was slightly confused and could feel the anger building up inside me which would grow more so as my Dad told me his intentions.

He told me we were going to be away for a lot longer than three days, he said we would eventually get The Album but first he had to raise the whole issue with the German press and not until then would I get The Album, he said we would be away for as long as it took.

I became hysterical and began to cry, I couldn't believe he had lied and tricked me and at that point I was travelling against my will and I told him when I got to Paris I would get on a train and come straight back. Again I began to feel angry, it all of a sudden dawned on me that I was going to miss my dinner and dance.

We got to Paris and Dad tried to calm me down, he took me for walk outside the station and we sat down and had tea and cakes at a café. He tried to explain to me how important I was in all this and how important it was for me to be a witness to his work. He told me where we were heading, it was a place called Melk in Austria.

We headed back to the station and in the ticket room I began to get hysterical again, this whole journey had gone badly wrong. Dad picked me up off my feet and told me to shut up and get a grip, he again told me how important this trip was and his work regarding Adolf Hitler, he told me I would be coming whether I liked it or not. He walked off to get the train tickets and I sat on the edge of my seat so tempted to run off to find a police station, something was holding me back though, I don't know why I didn't do it, I knew I could find a police station so it wasn't the fear of not knowing where I was.

We boarded a train for Austria.

The reason Dad wanted to go to Melk was because of something that happened to him in Zurich. Dad had become intrigued with Professor Dr. Wulf Listenow's curiosity in the book *Young Hitler* by August Kubizek. While he was making his comparisons between the writing in The Album and the writings in *Young Hitler* he would start to act strangely and start looking through all the pages of *Young Hitler*. He wasn't interested in any of the other textbooks there apart from that one. So with that Dad started reading *Young Hitler*.

During one of his days in Zurich Dad had to go to the library and he asked a young man for directions, the young man was kind enough to take Dad personally to the library. When they got there the young man, before saying goodbye told Dad of a journey he had taken with his Mum and Dad to a place called Melk and the main memory he had of the place was the magnificent library in the abbey. Dad thanked him for his help and said goodbye. That evening Dad returned to his hotel room and carried on reading *Young Hitler* he couldn't believe it when he started reading about a journey that Hitler and his friend August Kubizek made to a place called Melk.

My Dad doesn't believe in coincidences never has, he believes in signs from God and so after that young man had mentioned his trip to Melk and then reading about Melk in the evening he knew at some stage he had to go to there.

We were on the train heading towards Vienna; it was an overnight journey and was going to take a long while to get there. We had our own carriage and beds would fold down from the wall. I remember walking up and down the train looking around, I began to relax on the train I thought to myself that I couldn't do anything to stop what was happening, I at the end of the day was not going to get into any trouble, Dad was the one who was in trouble. So I just started to go along with it, I tried to relax and enjoy it, I didn't know what was going on, I didn't know why we were going to this place called Melk, I had obviously never been there and so I didn't know what to expect, we had little money by this stage we had spent most of it on train fares and so I laid back with a sense of anticipation and fell asleep.

I was deep in sleep when Dad woke me; he wanted to explain to me why we were going to Melk. So I sat up and began to listen. He said, " I know for a fact that Adolf Hitler was educated in England and so the reason we are going to Melk is so I can find evidence to prove Adolf Hitler was a member of our Royal Family." I looked at him with complete disbelief. I hadn't paid much attention in my history lessons but I knew Hitler was born in Austria and he went onto lead Germany in a war against England. So therefore there was no way he could have been part of the British Royal Family, so what my Dad had just told me went straight over my head. My Dad didn't elaborate on his comments and I asked no questions.

The reason he had even thought this, is again something that happened in Zurich. In the bank when Professor Dr. Wulf Listenow was studying both sets of writings, in certain words he could detect traits of Anglo Saxon. He then suggested the man who wrote these writings; Adolf Hitler must have been educated in England at the highest level.

My Dad while in prison had a lot of time to think about what had happened in the bank. He decided then that all this regarding Hitler didn't add up, firstly The Album being written in English and then this expert telling him he must have been educated in England. How could that possibly be, Hitler had gone on to rule Germany and nearly the world, he was an Austrian, growing up in Vienna, he became head of the Nazi Party, fighting Europe and was on the brink of invading England, he was also responsible for the slaughter of millions of Jews. How could it possibly be true that Adolf Hitler was an Englishmen?

Dad had no evidence at the time regarding Hitler being a member of the British Royal Family, he knew Hitler could write English and it appeared now that he was educated in England. To suggest to me such a thing meant he had a strong feeling about it but in reality he didn't know. He was guessing at the time, he knew Hitler was an extremely clever and powerful man who nearly controlled the world, he knew Prince Edward had dealings with Hitler before the war and so Dad thought that if Hitler was in anyway connected to England it had to be through our Royal Family. Also the findings in the Klein report referring to Hitler suffering from epilepsy made Dad wonder about one particular member of the Royal Family who was born in the early 1900's.

Dad has never told me exactly why he initially thought this but I guess he may have had a spiritual experience.

On the train Dad didn't make a big deal of it and to be honest it was a strange thing to even mention to me. I didn't force the subject, due to me not believing it. I remember lying back and going back to sleep.

That conversation wasn't brought up again; I knew why he wanted to go to Melk so I didn't get in his way. Professor Dr. Wulf Listenow was not the only handwriting expert to suggest these findings, two-years later Dad would sit down with a man from the Berlin Police Department and he also made the same conclusions. Over the years Dad kept this subject regarding Hitler being educated in England to himself, he rarely spoke to me about it. I was despondent regarding the subject; I was just interested in the sale of The Album. It would not start to sink in until I met a lady called Eva Maria Brunner in Vienna five years later, who spent four hours in my hotel room explaining to me in a scientific way that there was no doubt Hitler was educated in England. It was only then I started to understand the conspiracy that was unfolding. There was still no concrete evidence though regarding Hitler being a member of the British Royal Family. That evidence would have to be enormous for me to believe such a thing.

It had been twelve hours since Inspector Delamain had put the airports on alert and so his hope of catching us had faded. Mum was informed there was a high probability that I was in Europe. Interpol were informed of a kidnapping of a fourteen-year-old boy by his father, they were informed we were heading to Zurich via Germany.

My Mum was then asked whether she wanted media coverage of this case, she immediately said no. Interpol put the Swiss police on alert and the German Swiss border was also informed that there was a fourteen-year-old boy from Great Britain trying to enter Switzerland.

The train pulled into Vienna; the journey had seemed to take forever. I wanted to ring Mum, to let her know I was O.K., but Dad refused, he had become concerned again over security, he knew that one phone call to England could put the whole operation in jeopardy.

There was just one short journey left. We boarded another train and after a short time we arrived at Melk. We picked up our bags and got off the train. It was snowing and there were a few inches on the floor, I looked up and the beauty of this magnificent monastery stunned me, it was enormous and set back high, overlooking the town, it was beautiful.

We left the station and started walking into town; it was a beautiful town with many old buildings and of course the monastery, which was the main attraction. Christmas was drawing close and the whole place with the help of the snow, felt very festive.

Dad left me in a café while he went off to find a hotel, he found one called the Melk Town Hotel and so he booked us in.

I eagerly watched out of the window for his return and when I saw him in the distance I walked out of the café, he stopped when he saw me and bent down and started making a snow ball and then threw it at me, so in return I started making snowballs and we started having a snowball fight in the middle of the street. And for a brief moment I had forgotten all my worries, worries about what I was missing in England, worries about my Mum, it was like the old days again having fun with my Dad. We eventually stopped and he came over and told me he had found this hotel and that we would be staying there for a few days. We walked into the hotel and received a nice welcome, it wasn't a very big hotel but it was nice, it was a warm hotel with a log fire burning in the background, nice wooden beams everywhere and it felt comfortable and cosy.

We had a twin room with a TV and a mini bar, I unpacked my bag and tried to relax, I began to read my school books, it was probably the most amount of revising I had ever done. As I've said already reading my books kept me sane throughout the whole trip. After, we got showered, it had been a long day, and we dressed ourselves and went down for dinner. I had my favourite, prawn cocktail for starters and steak and chips for my main meal and as money was no object because we didn't have any and we weren't going to pay the hotel bill anyway, we just had what we wanted.

Back in 1989 in small towns, especially like Melk, they didn't have computers; all details were recorded from passports or driving licences and put onto cards and then filed away. We weren't going to be traced to that hotel and quite frankly there was no reason for anyone to look for us there, Interpol weren't looking for us in Austria they were looking for us on the Swiss German border. Dad felt at ease being there.

The following day we got up, got dressed and had breakfast, it was still snowing and we headed up towards the monastery, which was a good walk up into the hills.

We went on one of the guided tours and we were part of a large group that day, we went through the main rooms including the famous library. We were walking behind the tour and then Dad decided to break away from it and go on our own separate tour, heading through corridors and into other rooms. I didn't know what he was doing at the time but later it became obvious, he was searching for his evidence that he suggested to me he needed. But it was all good fun for me; it was obviously something I hadn't experienced before and after a few hours searching we returned to our hotel.

On the other side of the monastery was the Danube river and there were some caves at the bottom of the hill, that Dad had found, he was determined to find this evidence that he had come all this way for, he knew there was some reason why he was here.

He went to the caves during the day but not wanting to draw attention to himself decided it would be best to search them during the evening. That evening he explained to me what he was going to do, he was at midnight going to go out, with his recently bought hard hat with a torch taped to it and a broom and go off into this cave. He was going off to look for something but he had no idea what. And so midnight came and he said goodbye to me, by that point I was slightly concerned about what my Dad was doing but I had seen my Dad mentally ill in the past and he wasn't acting in that manner and so I kept calm, I said goodbye and rolled over and fell asleep. He went out for the night leaving me in this hotel on my own.

He returned in the morning, woke me up and we went down for breakfast. After breakfast he took me round to the caves and we walked in. He explained to me what he had done; using the broom he had swept away all the dust off the walls and swept all the leaves

65

to one side. Obviously I was slightly worried about my Dad's behaviour, it was an odd thing to be doing, but then what was normal in all this, finding a book belonging to Hitler wasn't exactly normal.

He had spent hours in the cave looking for something and finally gave up and while he was heading towards the opening, he noticed some writing on the cave wall.

He pointed to them. The writing was in thick red ink and there was only one letter and it was K and then four digits. Dad said to me he had found what he was looking for, it meant nothing to me and still to this day I'm not sure what the whole episode was about. Dad was happy though. He told me K symbolized King and the four digits was a date of birth. Dad thought Hitler had been to that cave many years ago when he lived in Vienna as an unknown, and drawn those figures on the cave wall.

I walked out of the cave, I hadn't got too exited about it and it wasn't the concrete evidence I was hoping for. I think deep down Dad knew it didn't mean too much and it wasn't going to prove anything but it kept him happy.

We went back to the hotel and Dad started preparing a document for Lotha Michel. The document contained the writings from The Album and the writing from *Young Hitler*. Lotha Michel was the man who was attending the bank in Zurich before Dad got arrested. Dad sent him these document through the post and wrote him a letter apologizing for his absence and he would be arriving in Mannheim within a few days. We went to the Post Office and sent them; they would hopefully arrive before we got there, giving Lotha Michel time to study them.

After he posted the documents, he turned round to me and told me it was essential we left Melk. He said we had been there for three days and may of created unwanted attention and the posting of these sensitive documents with the Melk postmark on them worried him and also by then he knew the police in general were probably looking out for a man and his fourteen-year-old son.

This was a little strange to me because we had no money to pay the hotel bill and where and how were we going. Dad told me we would be heading towards Germany, which would take us quite a while. I asked him how we were going to pay the hotel bill he said we weren't. He said we would be long gone by the time they realise we hadn't paid.

We went back to the hotel; it would be the following day we left. We had our last supper at the restaurant, once again I had prawn cocktail followed by steak. It was a strange feeling sitting there knowing the following day we were going to walk out without paying. The staff at the hotel had been great, they had been very friendly and so I felt bad at what we were just about to do. Dad assured me everything was going to be alright and once The Album was sold, the hotel would receive their money.

That evening I also had thoughts of back home, it was the night of the dinner and dance, I thought of my Mum and how worried she must have been by that point.

We woke up had breakfast and came back to our room. Dad stopped me packing my bag and told me to leave a number of books on the table and a number of clothes in the wardrobe. This was to give the impression we were still at the hotel. I wasn't too happy about leaving my clothes there, I had worked hard for them and the schoolbooks weren't even mine. I refused to do it and so he aggressively responded by saying how important it was to do so and did I want to get arrested. He stressed it was important to create an illusion to suggest to others we were still in town giving us enough time to disappear.

I was the first to leave the hotel, I walked to where the caves were near the Danube River and waited for Dad. We couldn't leave together it would have looked too suspicious. About twenty minutes later Dad turned up and we had successfully walked out without paying. We had stayed there for about four or five days and so the bill must have been a fortune.

We had absolutely no money on us and somehow we had to get to this place called Mannheim in Germany, where we were going to meet Lotha Michel who Dad thought was going to be responsible for raising the subject of The Album in the German press, Lotha had good contacts within the media including Stern Magazine.

We started walking alongside the river towards the motorway it was freezing. We walked for twenty minutes until we came upon it, we walked onto the slip road and eventually on to the motorway, and we were walking along the hard shoulder.

And so we just started walking in the freezing weather conditions towards Linz, within fifteen minutes of us walking, a grey 7 series BMW pulled up along side us and the man lowered his window and started having a conversation in German with Dad. We weren't thumbing for a lift, he just pulled into the hard shoulder, I was also quite surprised Dad could even talk German. We got in and headed towards Linz.

This was unbelievable in my eyes we had gone from walking along freezing to death to being in the luxury of a warm BMW. Dad made a few comments to the man driving which I had no understanding of. The man dropped us off, ten minutes from Linz, we both said "Thank you."

It was a short distance into Linz, we just had to make a steep climb over a hill passing a cathedral and into the town. We walked through the town and over the bridge and booked into a hotel. Dad had to be extremely careful now because obviously the Austrian police would have been informed of our activities at the other hotel in Melk. I'm not sure whether Dad used false names for that hotel but again it would have been difficult for the police to track us down there, unless they actually phoned the hotel to enquire and that would have been a long shot because there are a lot of hotels in Linz. Computers and technology wasn't as good as it is now.

We stayed one night and boarded a train for Nurnberg. And I witnessed another side to Dad I hadn't seen before, he became a brilliant actor. Due to us having no money or credit cards we couldn't buy tickets for the journey, but when the ticket inspectors came up to us on the train, he pretended that he had lost them. He would go through the same routine on each train, whereby he would begin to look in his wallet for them, then his coat, then his bags and then finally he would ask me if I had them. This whole act was performed to perfection and in most cases the ticket inspector would issue Dad with new tickets and they would send the bill to his address in England.

But this was a different side to Dad I hadn't seen, he seemed to have perfected the act of lying.

In Nurnberg he booked us into two hotels. By this time he had become very worried about our safety. He knew the Austrian police were looking for us, he knew Mum must of set the police onto us and he was also conscious of the fact that he owned a album belonging to Hitler that proved he was educated in England, he was positive certain organisations would do anything to destroy that album and the revelations, putting everyone's life at risk.

We stayed at the first hotel in Nermberg and at midnight Dad got me up and we left and went to the other hotel. That was a strange moment for me, I didn't ask too many questions but again he was paranoid over security.

We left that town in Germany the following day, knocking both hotels and not paying for the train fares. We were starting to leave a trail of debt.

We arrived at Mannheim, which was not far from the Swiss border and so if Interpol were doing their job properly, they should have caught up with us, instead it took something from me days later, in a completely different country for them to cotton on to where we were.

The whole purpose of the trip to Mannheim was to see Lotha Michael. So firstly we booked into the Holiday Inn and then made our way to the university. A young lady who then introduced us to Lotha Michel's secretary saw us. She told us he wasn't in Mannheim at that particular moment but she had received Dad's documents and would pass them on when he returned.

Dad wasn't too impressed with that and he knew we couldn't hang around for one week. So the whole journey to Mannheim had been a complete waste of time. Dad was beginning to get angry about everything and I started to wonder about the whole trip in general, even though I was having fun and it was adventurous there seemed to be no point to it. Initially it was all about retrieving The Album, then it was to find evidence that Hitler was a member of the Royal Family and then it was to see Lotha to raise the issue in the German press. So now we sat in this hotel without really knowing what to do. We thought about going into Switzerland to recover The Album but Dad decided against it, he didn't want to send me in alone and he knew he couldn't go in because he would face a five-year prison sentence. Dad decided we would head north towards Hamburg, the home of Stern Magazine.

Stern Magazine had been made hugely embarrassed when they paid £2,460,000 for sixty volumes of fake Hitler dairies.

Dad thought if he showed Stern his album and they decided to take the whole story on and fully authenticate it; it would start to heal their embarrassments from a few years earlier. He was going to do them a favour.

Hamburg was a good five hours away by train and it seemed to go on forever, this was mainly because we spent the good part of the journey in a toilet cubicle. Dad wasn't feeling too well and he didn't have the energy to go through with his act to the inspectors, so we were going to try and hide in the toilet the whole way. This worked for four hours of the journey but the inspectors finally cottoned on to what we were doing. They tried to open the toilet door but we managed to keep them out but they persisted and Dad turned round to me and said "Whatever I do next I'm completely acting, so don't worry."

With that the door was forced open once again and Dad let it open this time and he fell out onto the carriage floor. This shocked me; it looked like Dad was having a heart attack. The three inspectors immediately bent down to help him, they were concerned over his health and to be honest I was. They helped him to the canteen area and sat him down. He looked awful and sat there shaking I was quite worried. They brought us a drink over and some sandwiches. They asked me how long he had been in the toilet for, I said, "Since Mannheim, he was feeling sick."

Hamburg was approaching and by this time the inspectors hadn't even asked us for our tickets, they were just concerned about Dad. The train came to a halt and the three inspectors helped him off the train and said goodbye to us.

We walked along the platform and the train started to leave, I looked up at Dad with concern and asked him if he was O.K.. He looked at me and started to grin and said, "I'm fine son, now lets go and find a hotel, I'm starving."

It was quite a relief for me because Dad's acting had even convinced me, even though he had told me beforehand what he was doing.

Dad had been to Hamburg before and knew his way round; we booked into the Garden Hotel.

He gave them our details and they required Dad's passport for a kind of deposit, it was put in a safety deposit box behind the counter.

We got in the room and I immediately asked Dad why he had given them his passport, we needed that to get out of the country and back to England. He assured me everything would be aright.

We got freshened up and went downstairs for my normal prawn cocktail and steak.

The following day we spent time at The Atlantic Hotel near the river where Dad put together some documents for Stern Magazine. We delivered them to their building and made our way back to the hotel.

We sat down for dinner that night and Dad told me we would be leaving in the morning. I asked him about his passport and he said he was going to sort it out after dinner.

Dad sent me up to the room while he tried to get his passport back. I had bad feelings about this and thought to myself it could be the end of the road for us.

He walked in five minutes later and flashed his passport at me, I was so surprised, and I asked him how he had done it. He told me he had asked the girl behind the counter if he could see his passport for a minute, so she unlocked the box and gave it to him. As she turned her back he swapped the passport with one of their restaurant menus, they looked very similar to a passport.

I couldn't stop laughing; he was pulling off stunts you would only see in a James Bond film.

After I settled down, I sat on my bed watching TV; Dad once again was packing our bags. I sat there and started wondering about him. Dad had changed over these recent weeks; I had seen him do things that I was unaware of. I started to reflect upon the whole trip and I started to wonder about Melk and whether he had actually gone off that night for secret meetings and the story of the cave was just a smoke screen for me? I wondered about that man who had picked us up on the motorway, had it been organised? The conversation in German also made me wonder. How come the police hadn't caught up with us by now, we had walked out of so many hotels and surely Interpol should have tracked us down also by now? His acting on the trains was also a new thing for me to witness. I started wondering about the whole Hitler affair as well. Why was he involved in such a thing? Why was I being dragged into it? And then I thought back to the day I knocked the shed down and the moment we had found The Album, I started to wonder if in fact Dad had planted it in my pathway, knowing I would pick it up and pass it to him. If that was the case whom was he working for? And why was I being involved?

Years later I asked my Dad whether he had planted it and he turned round to me and said jokingly " That's funny because I thought you planted it."

The one thing out of this whole affair, which remains a mystery, is where that album actually came from. We have theories but no evidence to suggest exactly how it ended up in the garden shed in Dagenham.

There are five theories:

My Dad's uncle owned an antique shop in Holborn, London and he had often visited Europe buying stock for his shop. So maybe he bought The Album somewhere and gave it to my Nan as a present.

That same Uncle had a partner called Joe Banot and he used to live in Heidelberg, Germany which is very close to Speyer, which was the town mentioned in The Album. So maybe he found or brought it from there.

Is it possible my Nan, while in Germany before the war, had been given it as a present, but never dared mention it to anyone? Is it possible my Dad was working for MI5 and had planted The Album for me to find?

If I told you this theory, you would probably put the book down and not read another word, this theory makes more sense towards the end of the story, but again it is only theory.

We began the same routine where by I would leave the hotel first and Dad would follow. It was time for us to go home, we were heading for Flensburg, which was on the German border of Denmark and then he wanted to head up to Esbjerg in Denmark to get a boat back to England.

So we boarded another train from Hamburg. Dad was quite happy with his work there; he thought it was a good idea to show Stern Magazine the documents regarding The Album. He had also let them know that the handwriting expert Lotha Michel at Manniem University had also received the same documents.

I remember sitting on the train as it pulled out of Hamburg, thinking of what Dad had done with regards the passport and I would have loved to have seen their faces when they opened their safety deposit box to find, not Dad's passport but one of their menus.

The thought of us heading home made me feel happy, my birthday and Christmas was approaching and I wanted to be home for both occasions. I wanted to see my Mum. I didn't know what I was coming home to, I didn't know what kind of greeting I was going to get.

We arrived in Flensburg, we booked into another hotel and we basically had something to eat and left. Dad didn't want to cross the border; he didn't want to go through the procedure of showing his passport to the officials. He knew after walking out of so many hotels that the police must have been looking for him. He didn't want to get arrested in Germany; he thought if Stern Magazine had invited him back to Germany it would have been hard for him to come back if he got deported. Also leaving documents regarding Hitler with a few organisations in Germany may have sparked interest within the

German Secret Service so crossing the border through the official way was not a good idea.

And so we started walking up into the hills through woody area through rough ground and into Denmark. It was getting quite late now and the night was getting darker, we found a main road and started walking along it. We didn't really know where we were but we just keep walking. It was getting cold and I had walked for miles that day and I begun to feel weak, I had to stop. There were quite a lot of cars on the road and I told Dad to lie down and pretend to be ill on the floor while I thumbed a lift, but no one stopped. We kept walking into the night and then all of a sudden a man in a blue pick up truck pulled over and gave us a lift to a hotel in a small town just outside Esbjerg.

So once again it seemed someone or something had saved us, this kind of thing happens a lot to me and my Dad throughout this whole story, without it we would of both been dead. I sometimes consider these events as miracles from God, other times I'm sure that MI5 are just looking out for me.

It was a strange feeling again that night sitting down in a warm restaurant, eating my prawn cocktail but also thinking an hour or so ago we had been stranded in the middle of nowhere.

The following day we made our last journey together to Esbjerg. Dad had finished his work now he had done what he wanted to do; we hadn't got The Album back, which was my main objective of the trip so I was disappointed. He had done his work in Melk and was happy with that and his work in Germany with Stern Magazine and Lotha Michel. So now it was time to go home. We made our way to the port town of Esbjerg. On the way there we come across a Bang and Olufsen shop, which I was very interested in because that was the model of TV's and stereos I was going to have in my house, so I went in and had a good look round. While I was doing that Dad noticed a church opposite and so he went over and started talking to the vicar and began to preach to him regarding the church doors. I found this quite ironic really because it was only a few hours ago that we knocked another hotel and there Dad was talking to this vicar. Dad's attitude was that he was carrying out Gods work and the fact he didn't have any money wasn't going to stop him, he made a note of everyone he owed money to and once he had sold The Album he would repay them.

We booked into a small hotel in Esbjerg that was run by Chinese people, we got up into the room and Dad told me it was time to call my Mum. We needed money to get on the boat to get home and there was no way Dad was going to be able to blag his way through that one. So we went into town and found a bank, we walked in and asked if it was alright to transfer some funds. My Mum picked up the phone and said hello. She was so glad to hear from me she asked me where I was and I told her we were in a bank in Denmark, she took the details of the bank, but refused to send any money, she became upset because the only reason I had phoned in three weeks was to ask for money.

We left the bank and Dad told me "Whatever happens in the next few days don't let it frighten you or concern you, you will be perfectly alright."

I wasn't too sure what he meant but within hours I did.

We had dinner that night and went to bed early. At about 6am the door to the hotel room was smashed down and four policemen charged in pointing their guns at us. I jumped up in terror, they aggressively told us to get dressed, and refused to leave the room while I put my clothes on. We were both escorted out of the hotel and into a car and taken to the station. I was put in a cell and Dad was put in one next to me. I remember the only thing that annoyed me in the cell was the whistling I could hear from my Dad. He seemed happy to be there.

Within hours I was taken out of the cell, Interpol had informed the Danish police of the situation, I was put in a police car and taken for a two hour journey to Copenhagen airport, where there was plane waiting to take me back to England.

While Dad was still in the cells I boarded this small plane with only a few people on it, I had no luggage because I had to leave it in all of the hotels along the way.

It was couple of hour's flight to Heathrow and as we taxied in the pilot thanked everyone for flying and told everyone to have a safe journey. I was so glad to be home, it had been a long trip. The pilot come back on the mike and said, "If there is a Thomas Davey on the plane can he remain seated while everyone leaves. Thank you."

The air stewardess came up to me and said there were two policemen waiting for me at the exit of the plane. I remember her saying to me how much older I looked for my age and she was surprised when the police had told her that I was fourteen. She said if she had known that she would never have let me on the plane.

The police greeted me and asked me if I was O.K.. They said I had to follow them through customs because I didn't have a passport.

Then I was shown into a room where two well-dressed gentlemen were waiting for me. At this stage I hadn't seen Mum or Gary and I felt a little nervous. I sat down, they didn't introduce themselves but they were quite friendly and gentle in their questioning. They asked me questions about my Dad and questions about the trip. After a short while the policemen came in from outside and I was free to go. As I left the room I remember turning round looking at these smartly dressed people, they were standing there waiting for me to leave. The Security Services had entered my life.

The police escorted me to arrivals and I saw Gary standing in the distance waiting for me, I had never before been so glad to see him. He asked me if I was O.K. and I said I was fine. I asked why Mum wasn't there he told me how bad she had been feeling over this whole episode and she just couldn't face coming to the airport. He told me how lucky I was that the trip was for three weeks and not just for two days because I would have been in a lot more trouble but as time went by Mum's anger at me had turned into worry.

I got home and Mum came to the door, she opened it and burst into tears, she couldn't face me and she walked away. That night I had one of my Mum's cooked dinners, it tasted lovely. Mum explained to me at dinner that Dad was still in prison in Denmark and that he would be deported within a few days. She also told me I had to go to Brentwood police station in the morning to be interviewed by Inspector Delamain.

I went to bed that night thinking about the weekend ahead. Friday, the following day would be taken up with interviews at the police station but I knew at the weekend I had to go out and clean cars, I had to earn enough money to re buy all those clothes I had lost and to replace the schoolbooks.

I phoned James in the morning and he asked me where on earth I had been, I didn't tell him, but he told me everyone at school thought I was ill, that was fine by me, I preferred it that way, it was only the head master and the head of year Mr Forkenbridge who knew the truth. Brentwood police had put the school after that trip on alert, just in case my Dad decided to try and take me again.

James also informed me he hadn't once gone out and cleaned our customer's cars while I was gone. This infuriated me and I shouted a load of abuse at him and sacked him.

I put the phone down and started ringing all my customers, hoping they all still wanted me. That weekend I earned over £90 and I was able to not only replace my clothes but all of my schoolbooks.

Inspector Delamain spent time with me the next day, asking me questions about the reasons for my trip and he asked me whether my Dad had kidnapped me or not. I was vague in my answering towards the first set of questions but I insisted that Dad hadn't kidnapped me; it was my decision to go. He told me my Dad wasn't going to get arrested when he returned to England, after what I had just said and also the fact Mum didn't want to press charges, there wasn't a lot he could do.

Inspector Delamain did make it very clear though that I mustn't ever do it again, he said next time Dad and I would be in a lot more trouble. I assured him I wouldn't.

I walked out of the police station feeling quite pleased with myself, it seemed I wasn't going to get in trouble for anything and the only thing Dad had to go through was being deported from Denmark. He was going to get away with taking me off to Europe for three weeks and also away with knocking all those hotels. It seemed a little too good to be true.

Dad arrived back in the country a week later and he immediately tried to see me but plain-clothes policemen surrounded our house at the time, they had anticipated his move. The house was also fitted with panic alarms that were connected to the police station. Dad walked up the hill from Brentwood railway station and when he saw all those undercover police he turned straight round and went home to Dagenham.

Mum, Gary, Brentwood Police and my school were all concerned over my security, not because of the damaging Hitler revelations (due to them not believing them) but because of my Dad. Mum knew that we hadn't got The Album and she thought I might attempt to get it again.

My first day back at school, after my three weeks away, was approaching. I walked down to Brentwood railway station and back to the tower block where I had left my bike. While walking there I was convinced someone must have stolen it. I walked into the reception area and there it was, just as I had left it. I stood there smiling to myself and remembering the words that Dad had said to me before we left all that time ago, he had assured me that my bike would be alright. Not only was my bike alright but I was alright too, I wondered if he was O.K., I hadn't spoke to him since Denmark, I quickly reflected on our trip and then jumped on my bike and rode off to school.

I rode back into school and I was greeted by all my friends, they all thought I had been off sick, no one was any the wiser. Apart from the headmaster and Mr Forkenbridge, who I had to have a brief meeting with before lessons started. They asked me if I was alright and they told me the school were going to keep a good eye on me. They said I should try and make the effort to get to school on time because otherwise my Mum would be immediately informed. They also said I could go to them if I felt I needed to talk to anyone. How could I possibly speak to them about anything that was floating around in my head? But it was a nice gesture.

There wasn't much time left before we broke up for Christmas and so I was just about to have another two weeks off from school. I was quick to replace my textbooks and my friends helped me catch up with the work I had missed.

My Christmas that year was spent with Mum, Gary and my brother, it was a typical family Christmas and by Christmas Day it seemed that everyone had forgotten the chaos I had caused earlier on in the month.

Dad was also happy at Christmas, he had managed to go back to Zurich and get The Album. He had gone by train all the way and he had torn the deported stamp page out of his passport so that the inspectors didn't see it, it was still a risk because they only had to notice the page missing and he would have been put in prison for five years. So Dad spent Christmas in Dagenham with his Mum and The Album and with the thought that Stern Magazine might call.

The year of 1989 had ended quite well really; it had obviously been a dramatic year for myself. I had experienced a helter skelter of emotions and being only fourteen I think I dealt with them quite well; I had experienced happiness, sadness, excitement, anticipation, worry, anxiety and fear. If there was a path set out for me when I was born then it was truly destroyed in that year and this power had put me on a different one. Whatever power there is in the world whether it be super nature, God or a human power, then that power surely moved me that year, from living in Brentwood to end up living thirteen miles away in Dagenham so I could knock my Nan's shed down, to find The Album and therefore giving my Dad a purpose to his life. This power had used me to fulfil its plan and my god it was sometimes very hard for me. I remember the numerous times I sat on the bus home from school listening to Led Zeppelin on my personal stereo and I would sit there so unhappy and get upset because I couldn't understand why my life had changed so much.

There's obviously been a number of different circumstances and coincidences that have occurred throughout those fourteen years to bring me to that point in life, where I asked my Nan if I could knock her shed down. But no matter how hard it was for me and my family and going through everything that is coming up in the story, I honestly believe it was all meant to be, I don't understand for what purpose and still don't to this day. I just live my life day by day, I'm enjoying writing this story and I hope while I'm doing it I can figure things out a bit clearer and it will also give my close friends and family an insight into my life and my way of thinking. There is so much more information to this story that covers the next fourteen years of my life, there is a lot more adventure, there are also more revelations regarding Adolf Hitler but there is also in my life a big cloud of mystery that becomes clearer as time goes by, I will never truly be able to get on with my life until certain questions are answered. This story may seem damaging towards certain people but it's those people I believe that hold the key to my enlightenment. I sit here writing this story and sometimes wonder if I'm doing the right thing, I wonder who will eventually read it, I find it hard to believe that any organisation in their right mind will print this story, the Daily Express are looking at it at the moment but I don't expect anything from them. Like I said in my introduction, I never wished to stumble across that album and I didn't wish to know the things I know now. I'm positive there is a good ending to this story but I can't see it yet, I know, what I've been through is important and not for nothing and so I will keep on typing towards the unknown.

During the 4ᵗʰ year, the school had organised a trip to the River Rhine in Germany. Most of my friends were going on the trip but I wasn't too sure whether my Mum was going to let me go. It had been a hectic few years for me and I guess my Mum thought a school trip abroad with my friends might have done me some good.

My friendship with Al was still growing and we had spent most of the year causing terror for our teachers, there was also this split down the middle of the school whereby half the kids liked us but the other half hated us. We had a loud, funny, winding up and sometimes arrogant personality that people either liked or didn't. We would also take the micky out of everyone, it seemed everyone in our year had at least ten different nicknames. I had this great freedom at school and I enjoyed it, I didn't have the pressure like everyone else did whereby they needed to work hard because they needed to gain exam results, my attitude was, I didn't need exam results because I was just about to become rich.

The only subjects I did well at school were Geography and Maths. Geography because I liked the subject but also liked the teacher who took the class, his name was Mr Forkenbridge. He was head of the year and had shown my family great support through some of our family crises. He also played cricket for Hutton and so we had that small thing in common but he was also the kind of teacher who you knew exactly how far to push, he was a funny teacher but he also easily gained your respect.

I quite enjoyed Maths as well and I enjoyed working different sums out but I hated the teacher with a passion and so through the years I tried my hardest to disrupt her class. In my GCSE mocks I got an F for maths, which was totally unaccepted by my mother, and so I started receiving private tuition. I was determined to do well at maths because my teacher Mrs Hall continually told me I was going to fail. I never told her I received private tuition so she must have been so surprised when I got a C in my final exam. (The highest grade possible in that particular class) Maybe if all my teachers at school told me I was going to fail, I would have done a lot better.

I was regularly put on report card and my behaviour was closely monitored, the school and the teachers must have truly wondered what was going on in my little world. I was this nice popular kid who played cricket for Essex but had recently been kidnapped by his father and had also had his name mentioned in the national newspapers. But I was also this kid who went about school without a care in the world and I tried to create as much mayhem as possible.

My Mum agreed to let me go on the trip which surprised me somewhat because it had only been recently I had come back from my adventures with my Dad, so her letting me go must of taken her some consideration.

The German trip lasted three days; we went by coach and travelled through France, Luxembourg and into Germany. The whole trip was a chance for me to be with my friends and to get away from any influence my Dad may have had on me at the time. But if my Mum had intended the trip to help me with my general behaviour at school then it had failed. Al and my behaviour on the trip was quite bad, we generally messed around on the coach eventually being split up, and I was taken from the top deck to the lower. In the hotel, Al got in trouble for throwing the complementary sandwiches out of our hotel room window; they went crashing down on the glass above the restaurant where our headmaster was sitting. We were also caught in a local bar while being quite intoxicated, which again didn't go down well. The funniest thing that happened though, which made everyone laugh including some of the teachers, was when the whole group went to visit the town's main attraction, the castle. It was set high up on the hillside and the only way up was to walk a steep winding road. Everyone gathered at the bottom and our teachers handed out a drink and an orange to everyone. Al and I lead the way followed by our friends and teachers, halfway up I stopped and the both of us placed our oranges on the road, next to the curb and let them go. The sight of those two oranges going down the hill, passing everyone was hilarious. What made it funnier was when some of the others also placed their oranges on the road. Everyone stopped and just watched these oranges go down the hill reaching the bottom where the headmaster was waiting to pick them all up, he wasn't impressed.

The German trip was very memorable and drew our group of friends a lot closer and still to this day I have some of those same friends, in fact we have just all come back from another overseas trip to Prague, but the less said about that the better.

But if there was any doubt left in my teachers' minds about splitting me and Al up during that year, then the short trip to Germany made it clear for them. They must of thought I was the main culprit because it was me who was moved class for the last remaining months of the year. I don't think I was terribly disliked by my teachers but I think they were concerned over my potential they could see and fulfilling it. They could see I had certain gifts like my cricket and I was generally a nice kid but I think they could also see the previous years antics with my Dad had affected me. The school tried its best with me but to no avail.

I was still determined to play cricket for England, I tried my hardest at the indoor school and Ray East (who was in charge of Essex youth at the time) spent a lot of time with me changing my technique and my approach to batting. I think this held me back a little though, I believe if you start to have too much coaching in any form of sport you start to lose your natural flair for the game.

I knew if I played well in the next five years there would be a good chance Essex would offer me a contract. So I was so determined and focused. That was until midway through the season when I played for Essex against Yorkshire at the Shell ground in Corringham, Essex.

There was England U15 selectors there and our organiser Jim Boden made us all aware of it. We all wondered whom they were here to see, there were some good players on either side but I knew I had been in good form through the season and had good reports from last. Jim Boden had thought a lot of me; he had me playing for him the year before (a year above myself) including one game against a touring side from South Africa. So I was determined to do well in this game and show these selectors I was good enough to play for England.

I scored a hundred that day, I batted like someone inspired by a greater force, I smashed the ball to all corners of the ground and reached my hundred with a six, the ball went high into the nets (nets that stopped the ball from going out of the ground). I tore the Yorkshire bowling apart.

I walked off the field that day after entertaining everyone and felt sure the selectors would approach me and ask me to play for England, if not that day then in writing. But instead I didn't even receive a "well done" or acknowledgment for my innings. I knew I had done well that day and also previously in the year, so if those selectors were there to see me then what on earth did I do wrong?

Well maybe it was the fact I didn't go to a public school and my Dad didn't earn over £100,000 a year. Or was it the fact that the Establishment didn't want someone playing for England whose Dad was involved in something politically damaging. Or was it so MI5 made sure the selectors didn't pick me because they didn't want my cricket career to develop too far because it would jeopardize the mission?

My attitude towards playing for Essex slightly changed after that, I felt if my efforts were not recognised after such an innings then deep down in my subconscious I knew a career in cricket wasn't for me. I still put in the effort and enjoyed playing for Essex but something felt different.

I still played for Essex that year and the following year, but when the Essex U19 trials came along I refused to go, so it was then my Essex career ended. It was also in that period Ray East retired and Alan Lilley took over as head coach and development officer at Essex Cricket Club. We didn't see eye to eye with each other from the start, he gave me less time than the others and I also tried to avoid him, he also was in charge of the U19 team so playing under him was something I wasn't going to miss.

After the game at the Shell ground, don't get me wrong I was still interested in cricket but other interests started to develop for example: going out with my friends and girls.

I remember playing for Essex U15's one Friday during the summer. And during the whole game, I was really looking forward to going out with my friends in the evening to the Keys Hall disco in Brentwood. My focuses after the Shell game had slightly changed, I enjoyed being with my friends and enjoyed the feeling after I had a few drinks inside me.

The Keys Hall disco was organised by a family from Harold Hill, Romford and I used to like going there every week because I liked the DJ's sister, her name was Fay.

A lot of girls generally seemed to like me and so it wasn't hard for me to make new girlfriends, but the girls through my teenage years that I actually liked, didn't seem to like me in the same way. I think it was more the case of me being too shy towards girls I liked and the fear of rejection from them. A lot of the girls thought I was unapproachable, because sometimes I would stand back in pubs, clubs and discos and observe from a distance, sometime summing up the situation before making my moves.

The main two girlfriends I had in my life I did manage to build up the courage to speak to them. My first serious girlfriend was when I started college. So up until then, I had girlfriends but not serious ones and not long term ones. I was more interested in my sport, friends and going out having a good time, I didn't want to be tied down to just one person.

During the 4th and 5th year we started going out more and more and so we would make a lot more friends and so we got invited to a lot more parties. A few of our friends started smoking and experimenting with drugs, they were offered to me but I was dead against it. I liked drinking but I drew a line at that. My health and fitness meant more to me than finding out the different feelings drugs caused. It would not be until just before my seventeen birthday that I tried my first marijuana joint, I was at my friends house, Greg Connor, he had gone to St Martin's but I hadn't got to know him until I went to college. We were at his house and while watching the film *The Doors* I smoked my first joint. It was obviously a new experience for me but would it be one I liked? And if so was it the root because for some of my dilemmas in my early twenties?

My school progress suffered a lot in the 4th and 5th year due to my way of thinking regarding The Album, thinking I was just about to become rich. I had obviously seen Josephine Day and I also knew Dad was continuing to work at his project. I thought it was imminent, the fact Dad also told me The Album would soon be sold and we would be rich didn't help.

Going through school and later on in life I would always keep a close eye on the news, always waiting for something relating to my Dad's work to come on. Even as a fourteen-year-old boy if the news came on the TV, I would have a quick look at the headlines before turning it over. But it was early one morning in 1990 at 4.30am, I woke up unusually early, I sat up and checked the time, I used to get up at about seven to walk Max so 4.30am was far too early. I couldn't go back to sleep and thought I'll just lay there and listen to my radio. I used to listen to Capital Radio and enjoyed listening to their DJs and music. I switched the radio on and the news was on, I lay there waiting for the music to start, the news was ending and then I heard them say something about Hitler. I didn't quite hear what they were saying because I wasn't listening to the news but I was sure it was something to do with The Album. I jumped up and ran downstairs into the lounge, I put the main stereo on and waited for the news again. I didn't have too much contact with Dad at the time, I had been protected, guarded from him but I knew he hadn't given up and he was travelling the world perusing his project. The man on the news came on again and towards the end he said, "A book written by Hitler has been found in a garden shed in Dagenham," he went on to say that John Davey owned it and he had had the writings authenticated by handwriting experts. I was so excited maybe this was the beginning and the publicity my Dad needed. Shortly after my Mum came downstairs, surprised to see me up, I told her with a sense of satisfaction (because I knew Mum and Gary and in fact everyone we knew thought Dad was mad) that Dad's album is being mentioned in the news on the radio.

Within half an hour of us being up the phone rang, it was Mum's friend Alan Everard and he had rung to tell Mum, the whole story regarding Dad and The Album was in the newspapers. I quickly got dressed and rode down to the shop to buy the newspaper. It was mainly featured in The Sun; I bought it and went back home. The story was on page 3 next to a naked lady who funnily enough was holding a cricket bat. The article described how Dad had come across The Album and why he thought The Album was Hitler's and where he thought it had come from. The article also mentioned my name because I was there when he found it. I was quite excited by all this, the newspaper had written a fairly good account, it had been written in a fairly light way, The Sun had picked the story up from the Dagenham and Barking Post, a local newspaper that had taken on the story in a slightly deeper way. They had properly interviewed Dad and had taken photos of The Album and had featured the story by covering two pages of their newspaper. The Sun's story was not as convincing and it also doubted the English in The Album and where it was found. However Dad was quoted "It is not me who says the writing matches Hitler's, it is the handwriting experts"

I felt quite excited about all the publicity but felt quite nervous about going to school that day and fronting everyone there. But I knew I could cope mainly because of knowing Dad and I were 100% right. My brother and myself were taken to school that day; Mum was concerned there might be journalists hovering around wanting to ask me questions. On the way to school I put Capital Radio on, I wanted to hear the news again, I quite enjoyed my Mum having to listen to it, the news came on and the story was on the last slot, after the reader had finished Chris Tarrant started taking the piss out of the story in particular about where The Album was found, he joked "And of course Adolf Hitler took his holidays in Dagenham." He continued to joke about the story. I was shocked at what I was hearing, not even The Sun had mocked the story to this extent or previously on the station. If there was any seriousness left in the story then it was taken away by Chris Tarrant. My short journey to school that morning was now filled with dread, how many of my friends and other kids had heard Chris Tarrant, well quite a lot. It was the worst day at school I had ever had, I received strange looks from some, others laughed at me and others just took the piss, even my closest friends e.g. James Cooper and Amanda Hartman didn't know what to say to me and I could see their disbelieve written all over their faces. Thanks to me having a strong personality and also a 100% belief in my father's work, the whole episode didn't affect me too badly but ever since then I would be very careful whom I discussed the Hitler affair with. It would only be with people I became very close to and with people I felt I could trust. I hated the feeling of people not believing me because I knew it was true.

I had already been through a lot in my life and for someone like Chris Tarrant to come along and dismiss it in such a way, hurt me. After that I would never again listen to his radio show and if he ever came on the TV I would switch it over. I suggest to you and others like you to think very carefully about what you say because you never know whom you are offending or hurting.

Dad received a phone call from Thames Television that day, they had asked if they could come round and interview him for the evening news. This would have been a great opportunity for Dad to show everyone The Album and to put the record straight regarding the English and where The Album had come from. But after waiting in for a couple of hours for them he went out for a game of tennis and therefore missed the film crew coming round. When I heard what had happened I was disgusted with my Dad, he seemed to deliberately miss a great opportunity. I asked him why he hadn't phoned them back and he said if they really wanted the story they would come back round. Well that might have been alright for him but I now wanted the record put straight to prove to everyone they were wrong about The Album and my Dad. A news channel going round to my Dad would have helped that.

This was not the only time Dad had found himself in a great position and then pulled out at the last minute, it seemed to happen time after time, I couldn't understand why he was doing it and it used to frustrate me no end. Why was it my Dad got himself into a commanding position whereby he could have ended the whole affair but instead, pulled out and explored other avenues. Still to this day I'm not 100% sure but as the story develops it becomes slightly clearer and it means delving into the way my Dad thinks and an understanding into his beliefs and what he feels happened to Hitler after the Second World War. These beliefs (some of them proven) are beliefs I was subjected to for hours on end when I again moved to Dagenham to live with my Dad and Nan. But to start to understand I need to explain what my Dad was doing in his research through the years of the early 1990's for him to become to believe such wild beliefs.

I remember once while living at Hartswood Rd when me, Mum and Gary were sitting in the lounge, having a normal peaceful evening watching the TV and then my brother walked in. He had come rushing in from upstairs and was quite hysterical and crying, he was only thirteen. He stood in the middle of the room and my Mum asked him what was the matter? He said, "I'm really frightened because the KGB are coming to get me." I sat there and cringed, it was obvious Dad had been talking to him, he had said similar things to me over the years but I tried to ignore him and certainly never discussed those conversations with Mum or anybody else. Dad had throughout this whole story been concerned over the security agencies of different countries including MI6, MI5, FBI, CIA, KGB and Mossad.

The reason Dad was so concerned over the KGB was because during his recent research with the book *Young Hitler* by August Kubizek, the book had some writing in (which I will go on to explain) which suggested (when examined by experts) that Adolf Hitler was alive in 1953 and therefore it would have been impossible for the Russians to have his remains, that they reported to have found in the Berlin bunker in 1945.

Dad thought if the Russians cottoned on to such evidence, they would do absolutely anything to destroy it. Because the Russians believe they have the remains of Hitler and such an embarrassment (that they were fooled into thinking that the remains were Hitler's) would not be tolerated. Therefore, them having to make a few people disappear including the whole of the Davey family and anyone else involved, would not be such a big sacrifice for them to maintain their pride and spare their blushes.

Even before this whole affair started I remember Dad talking about satellites and bugging methods, he used to say in general conversation how a satellite could take a photograph of your car number plate and he used to talk about the different ways to bug phones and houses. He told me that technology was so advanced now (back in 1981 when he had just returned from America) that somebody could ring your home number, have a conversation with you, could be about timeshare or double glazing and after you put the phone down, thinking nothing of it, the person on the other end (Secret Service) would be able to listen into everything being said in the house.

I remember for ages after Dad told me that I had to get hold of such a device because I would have endless amounts of fun with it.

Still to this day I have never heard of such a device or technique for bugging homes and that's after reading numerous amounts of espionage books and after having conversations with certain people.

And so over the years I became used to his stories and his fears for our safety. Looking back now I can understand why he had them because at the time his discoveries were massive and without doubt damaging towards many countries. And if this was a film or a fictional book then yes I guess a few people would have been killed by now. But this is real life and I guess whatever power planted The Album in the shed then they had a much bigger plan for us.

Throughout the early years of the affair, I would listen to my Dad but certain things he said regarding security services I would tend not to take too seriously. I was only young but he used to try and warn me of their (in particularly MI5) involvement and how dangerous they could be. He used to try and make me more observant and to be more vigilant in my surroundings. He would try and make me understand that not all MI5 agents went round dressed up in suits looking like James Bond. Most MI5 agents would blend into a crowd, whether on a train or on a building site.

He would also try and make me aware and would frighten me by saying one day a car could pull up beside me, wind down the window, ask for directions and then when I was close enough, drag me into it. I would then have been kidnapped by MI5 and be used by them to blackmail my Dad with regards to The Album. He would say they would do anything to get their hands on The Album because of what it contained.

At the time things he used to say to me went over my head but subconsciously they went in, I was going through my teenage years and I guess if a security agency wanted to kill or kidnap me, then there was not a lot I was going to be able to do about it. I was enjoying myself growing up and so I wasn't going to let the small threat of MI5 affect my good times.

I sometimes think though that through all this I have been shown and experienced so much, I feel I have been trained to do something without me consciously knowing it. There have also been so many times throughout my life that I have been rescued, rescued from injury and on a number of occasions from certain death. Also the fact that I haven't been killed in a car crash or freak accident means to me that my life has not only been guided and protected but has an immense importance, which will become clearer as the story develops.

Throughout my life I have felt a presence, a sixth sense if you like that I have become to trust and respond to. I seem to have a good sense about people and different circumstances that I find myself in at times. I seem to sense danger ahead and if I feel deeply uncomfortable about a person or situation, I will react accordingly and if I don't the presence that surrounds me will force me away sometimes without me even knowing it or liking it.

My awareness of MI5 became stronger when I became slightly older and more mature and mainly when I was involved directly with my Dad. At first it made me paranoid, I used to worry about everything I was doing and worried about anyone who entered my life. I will go into more detail as the story develops. I look back at it as a learning curve, sometimes a harsh curve that taught me the importance of reality and also the consequences that can happen to you if you step out of line. I now lead my life with a great respect for certain things, I've gone through things in life that have taught me in the hardest way not to cross certain lines and so I don't.

It seems I have been privileged enough to go through a slightly different life and not just live the normal nine to five life. It's not always been easy but I have had many good and bad times and fascinating experiences along the way, not all has been easy I have been to the deepest depths of depression and despair and also to the highest points of mania and madness.

Today as I write this I can look back and sometimes laugh at certain points of my life which proves to me I've not only overcome them but I continue my life in a more positive attitude and outlook. Don't get me wrong and maybe it's too early in the story to talk about this but I'm allowed to live a fairly normal life today with my wife and two children. But I know deep down inside me, (mainly because it has been drummed into me for so many years), that there is something big and terrible around the corner, soon to happen to this world we live in. I have been and gone through and seen certain evidence to suggest otherwise. If it does come and it's in the way I think then myself and certain others become very important, The Album will play the key part in stopping it all happening again, not only The Album but this story and the way it has all happened, it becomes important. This needs more explanation and I will elaborate when I write about certain revelations regarding Hitler and a member of our Royal Family.

But I know if it does happen and I do keep an eye on the news to wait for the beginning, I thought September 11th 2001 was the start but after two days, I was told it wasn't, I felt sure during the 2nd Gulf war that Iraq was going to completely bomb Israel into the Mediterranean sea. But they didn't. It would be something like that that would indicate the beginning of the second holocaust. When it starts it will completely shock the whole world, but not me and not a few others who are involved in all this. I also know when it comes I will eventually have my date with destiny. I look forward to it and

I know it's coming soon because I know time is running out for a certain person. I know that if this is a possibility then it is the reason why I have not been killed and been allowed to carry on. I sometimes speak to organisations such as the newspapers regarding the revelations and my Dad goes round telling everyone his theories for the future, sometimes making himself look mad in the process. Newspapers, media and people like them seem to take no notice of the revelations but I'm sure MI5 made sure of that and put a stop to any media organisation printing anything about this, I believe there is an agenda being kept by organisations such as MI5 and the Royal Family and nothing nor no one will get in the way, they know Dad's research is important but cannot highlight the points because of the repercussions it would have from other countries such as Israel, Germany and Russia. But when the time is right the whole truth will come out, but first there has to be the beginning of the nightmare I truly believe the ending will create a new world that is filled with peace and love. It would have taken a lot of death and misery throughout the years but hopefully there is a great reason for it all. Sometimes this story reflects badly on organisation such as the Royal Family but I think their hands are tied and maybe being blackmailed by someone but in the end I believe they will overcome all their present day problems and resume their control and power on our world, power given to them by the grace of God.

The last year at school, being the 5th year, seemed to fly by, it was a year the school prepared you for your optional release on the world. It was a year everyone was preparing for their final GCSE exams. There seemed a lot of time allowed off by the school so everyone could revise. Some pupils even left early in the year, normally those who knew they wouldn't do well and wanted to get on with their chosen careers.

Dad's affair had not yet produced the riches it had promised and so I thought I better get my head down and try to come out of school with some exam results, so I could get a fairly decent job that would tide me over until it all begun.

During 1991 while I was still studying for my exams, my Mum and Gary split up. I am not sure of the real reasons but I guess my father's constant intrusion on their relationship must of taken its toll. He would constantly ring the house and would sometimes, out of the blue knock on the door. There would also be the numerous occasions when the police were called because of my father's behaviour. He would sometimes turn up at the house, Mum would never let him in and so he would scream and shout in the driveway, aiming his aggression and frustration towards Mum and Gary. Dad at the time was concerned over everyone's security and that included Mum and Gary's. So when they continued to ignore him it made him angry. The fact also that I supported my father 100% didn't help and also my Mum over the years had shown a small degree of loyalty towards him, which again didn't help their relationship.

Gary had entered our life when things were fairly normal but as time went on it all became a lot more complicated. The intrusion from my Dad and the subject he was involved in and the constant wondering that every time the phone rang or when the doorbell went it could be him, I believe finally drove Gary away.

Gary had seemed to come into our life at just the right time, my first impression of him, when I met him at the house in Billericay was a good one, he treated my Mum well and didn't seem to worry about her having two kids.

The fact he knew of my Dad as well must have made it slightly harder for him. He was able to get on well with all of my Mum's friends and had easily been accepted by my Mum's Mum and Dad.

It was because of Gary we moved back to Shenfield where all my friends were and school was. So I was always grateful to him for that, he had also properly introduced me to squash and again I thank him for that. He basically treated my brother and me like his own sons and for a while the unit was perfect. It must have been at the time really hard for him; he was only young and he had kind of adopted this family and taken on this great responsibly. I have so many memories of him and his influence in my life will always be remembered. He took me and Mike to America for three weeks which was such a great and wonderful time and I still to this day reflect back on that trip, I would like to thank him personally for it and also thank him for being in my life.

There are no hard feelings on my side for anything that has happened in the past and in my opinion what ever did was meant to.

Gary remarried and now has two children of his own; I have visited him in recent years and am pleased he had found happiness in his new family.

When Gary left in 1991 it did not affect me at all, Gary was a fairly strict guardian and so without him around I started to get away with murder. I learnt later that Gary had given Mum maintenance money for bills and food etc, for Michael and me; he didn't have to and had no legal requirement to do so.

I had now become man of the house and made the point of telling everyone by mowing the word TOM into the lawn, in the back garden and every time somebody went upstairs they had to pass a window which would give them the perfect view of what I had done. It was a strange thing to do and my Mum wasn't too impressed by it.

So once again it was the three of us, my Mum again did well to keep things together. Gary was still paying the mortgage but Mum knew eventually the house would have to be sold, she also knew she had to go and get a job.

She eventually got a job in the Docklands, London, selling luxury flats for Ideal Homes. The building was called Prospect Wharf and had been built by Trafalgar House the big construction company, the same company in fact that built the QE2 Bridge.

In a strange way it was because of me she got the job. During my school days at Woodlands I had become very good friends with a girl call Amanda Hartman, we spent a lot of time together and so naturally the two sets of parents were introduced.

We would spend time at each other's house, I particularly liked going to hers because there was so much more to do there. She had a massive games room that we spent hours in playing pool and table tennis. She also kept horses, which I liked, and so again we would spend time riding them. The main thing that I liked about going round there, don't get me wrong here, me and Amanda were not boyfriend girlfriend we were just very good friends, she was a very pretty girl but also had this tomboy attitude to life that appealed to me. As I was saying the main attraction of her house were the two quad bikes that she had. To get to Amanda's house you had to drive down this long country dirt track, she lived in Noak Hill, and so that's where we would ride the bikes, they were quite fast and most enjoyable.

Amanda went to Woodlands and then to St Martin's, she was in the same class as me right through senior school so we had, over time spent many hours together.

During senior school Amanda's father died of a heart attack and obviously Amanda was deeply upset and it was then my Mum and Amanda's Mum Sue became a lot closer.

When Mum had split with Gary the two of them started socialising a lot more and we would all go on trips and holidays together. Sue had also taken me on holiday to her timeshare apartment in Portugal with Amanda and Steve, Sue's son. So as you can see up until we left St Martin's the two sets of families were very close.

I think the fact that my Mum had lost two men she loved in her life and Sue losing the man that she loved made it easy for them to communicate with each other.

Sue had phoned the house one day and asked Mum whether she wanted to go for lunch in the Docklands. Sue was having lunch that day with one of her friends who happened to manage the recently built Prospect Wharf. During the lunch Sue's friend Caroline said she had to cut short their lunch because she had to go back to work to interview a women for the sales job that had come up. Mum and Sue decided they would follow her back to Prospect Wharf because they were fascinated about these apartments that were for sale. While Mum was in one of the apartments she noticed the women who had turned up for the job and after giving her the once over decided she would ask Caroline about the job. Mum had never had a job since leaving her hair dressing round some twenty years ago she was determined to do this and to do it well. Caroline gave her the job and within a year Mum had sold every one.

During that period it was either a time for playing cricket or revising. I used to spend hours in my room revising for my exams. I hadn't seen or heard from my Dad for a while, he was off travelling the world researching his project. The way I revised was to write everything down from a textbook onto paper, it was the way I could remember things better. I knew it was going to take a miracle for me to pass any of my exams; I had spent so much time messing around at school and the fact I had trouble learning and concentrating for any period of time wasn't going to help. I knew I was up against it. The exams were taken during May and June of that year and I always remember going into the assembly hall where the exams were held and whoever was sitting in front of me, I would ask them to hold up their paper when I coughed so I could double check my answers. All the exams eventually finished and I was quite confident I had done well. I knew if I achieved four to five C grades that I could get a job in one of the local banks and earn at least a couple of hundred pounds a week, I thought to myself that would tide me over until Dad got his project off the ground.

During those early years in the 90's, Dad and I had drifted apart slightly. He always kept me up to date with what was happening but I guess I didn't understand him or his work. I was enjoying myself growing up and he was travelling around exploring different aspects of Hitler's life that at the time didn't interest me.

Back in 1989 Dad had accidentally come across the book *Young Hitler* by August Kubizek, it was the textbook he used to get Hitler's writing from so he could have the writings in The Album compared with it. He had come across the book in the Imperial War Museum in London.

Young Hitler is again the English version of *Mein Jugendfreund*, obviously written by the same author. While Dad was in the library back then in 1989, he noticed the book contained a copy of Adolf Hitler's birth certificate. Even back then right at the start Dad noticed a few of the letters in the birth certificate looked similar to Hitler's writing. Dad didn't show this birth certificate to anyone, he had held it back, and he knew his work with The Album had to come first.

But in January of 1991 Dad visited Vienna. He was 100% sure through seeing a number of different handwriting experts that his album was Adolf Hitler's and now had become more interested in this cover up or deception if you like which was unfolding regarding Adolf Hitler's life.

Dad had spent quite a lot of time going back and forth to Austria, studying this book *Young Hitler*. He had read it word for word and had basically come to the conclusion the book was not true. Not only had he noticed the birth certificate but the book also contained postcards written by Hitler to August Kubizek. The postcards were apparently sent to August when Hitler was eighteen but when examined by a handwriting expert they were quick to discover that the writing on the postcards were of a man of 50-55 not eighteen.

So things about this book weren't adding up and he even started to study parts of the actual story in the book and go over the same grounds that had been written about. He discovered in this research that parts of the story would have had to have been impossible to have happened. E.g. the grand piano and the Melk Monastery. Hitler had had a grand piano in this flat in Vienna, but when Dad visited the flat it was quite obvious to him that due to the smallness it would have been impossible to have a grand piano in it. Another inconsistency with the book was when Hitler apparently lived in Linz but had never seen or heard of the monastery at Melk; Dad thought this was ridiculous because a man with such an interest for architecture would definitely of known of such a building that was only a few miles away.

When I heard of this kind of research Dad was participating in, I was quite concerned because to me it was going too far. He was retracing the footsteps of Hitler. He had visited his previous homes and other places mentioned in the book *Young Hitler*, I thought this was a bit strange and never asked him any details regarding that nor was I too interested in the revelations, I was just interested in selling The Album and becoming rich. Looking back I can kind of understand why Dad got involved in such research because at the end of the day he was following signs and following his instincts and if that meant him ending up outside the previous home of Adolf Hitler at no29 Stumper Gasse in Vienna then so be it.

Dad went to Vienna as I say in January 1991 and met a handwriting graphologist called Alois Schaffer who lived in the centre of Vienna, just behind the main shopping area but in a quiet part of the city. He was an elderly man and had studied graphology for many years. Dad had gone there to show him the birth certificate. Dad was quite sure by now that Hitler had written this certificate himself and he just needed to get confirmation from an expert. Alois Schaffer studied the birth certificate and it didn't take him long to come to the conclusion that Adolf Hitler had actually written his own birth certificate. Alois smiled and looked up at my Dad and told him there was no question the birth certificate that appeared in *Young Hitler* was written by Adolf Hitler himself.

I quote from his report: "I also analysed the "certificate of baptism," of which, however, only a copy was available, and I came to the following conclusion: In my opinion the handwriting on this certificate of baptism is the same as the one that was examined under the blue/yellow marking," (blue and yellow is the writings from The Album and Hitler's writing in the textbooks).

"Summary. All handwriting samples submitted to me, including the certificate of baptism, three post cards and various handwritten texts from the original album, like the handwriting samples marked in yellow, are with the greatest likelihood written by the same individual."

So while Dad was in Vienna, he already knew from when he first met Professor Dr. Wulf Listenow in Zurich the previous year, there was some kind of major cover up regarding the whole of Hitler's life. And with this book *Mein Jugendfreund* which contained fake postcards and a birth certificate written by Hitler, I think now after seeing Alois Schaffer and realising the massive deception that had obviously been put in place, that he became more interested in the cover up (that he had accidentally stumbled upon) than that of The Album.

And so the question is at this stage of the story, why would someone need to write their own birth certificate? In my opinion the only reason why is to give the impression to everyone that you are either younger or older than you really are and in this case it was done so Hitler appeared older. In fact sixteen years older. The birth certificate was suggesting Hitler was born on April 20th 1889.

I know this is not true but will explain why and how later in the story. If I told you now it would sound ridiculous, there is more detail to this story that needs explaining beforehand.

So again while Dad was in Vienna, it was being shown to him through graphology and forensic science that this book *Young Hitler* was not true and complete rubbish and it had become obvious to Dad that Hitler had written this book himself using the name August Kubizek after the Second World War. Don't get me wrong here August Kubizek did existence and still has family living in Vienna but he didn't write that book, he may of known Hitler as a youngster but Hitler wrote that book using his name.

So what we have is a book, *Mein Jugendfreund* by August Kubizek that was published by Leopold Stocker in Graz, put together after the war and was first published in 1953. Eight years after the war.

Dad over a short period of time had visited Germany and Austria numerous amount of times. A man called Ken McCullen who lives in Canterbury had financed him.

Ken hadn't put the money up for all his trips and so Dad had sometimes travelled around with no money, like when I was with him in Europe back in the early days. He used his skills and knowledge to travel around Europe for nothing, walking out of many hotels in the process.

Dad had come back from Austria and thought he had done his bit with Europe. He had a huge amount of respect for certain places and countries in the world and one of those was Austria (because of the obvious connection with Hitler) and so he thought he would give them the first opportunity to take this project on. After time things were not working out in the way Dad had anticipated and he had come to the conclusion that maybe it was time for him to go back to America to raise all these issues.

Dad had spent much time before all this started in America and seemed to easily get on well with people over there. With the money Ken again invested in him, he decided it was time to go back to New York.

His idea was to raise this whole issue in New York (via the media) using the birth certificate found in *Young Hitler*. So he packed his bags and flew to New York. While on the plane it dawned on him he had forgotten his copy of *Young Hitler*, which contained the copy of the birth certificate. It must have been an odd moment for him because it was the main reason why he was going and not to have the book meant he was going to land in America with no real purpose.

When he got there he was due to see a man called Osborne, he was a handwriting expert. But firstly he had to go to the New York public library to see whether they had a copy of *Young Hitler*.

And so what was just about to happen was a pure accident because of him forgetting the book. He went into the library, which is in Madison Ave, and asked if they had a copy of *Young Hitler* and they must of typed something into their computer and told Dad they had a 1953 edition and a 1954 edition.

But they were stored in the archives of the library and weren't allowed out for borrowing. Dad still asked to see them because he just needed the page with the birth certificate so he could photocopy it.

The man came back from the archives and gave Dad the two books and while he was looking through the 1953 edition he came across, probably on the third or fourth page, an introduction by August Kubizek and then the signature of him dated in 1953. Now this signature does not appear in every single copy of the book, it only appears in some of them for some peculiar reason and it was the first time Dad had seen this. Dad had taken just one look at this signature of August Kubizek and knew there and then in the New York public library that it was the handwriting of Adolf Hitler.

Dad wasn't allowed to take the book out of the library and so he went to one side and tore that page out and placed it his briefcase. He then gave the book back promising himself to take that page back to the library one day.

The signature in that book was dated in 1953 and the book itself was published in 1953 and so anyone who had written this had obviously been alive in that year. Dad had studied Hitler's writings and knew instantly that the signature of August Kubizek was in fact the handwriting of Adolf Hitler which suggests quite strongly that Adolf Hitler didn't commit suicide in Berlin in 1945 and was obviously alive and well in 1953.

Dad even right at the beginning in 1989 thought Hitler was still alive and after seeing that comet in the car park in Rose Valley and after asking the question about "You up there with everything you've got you bastard," which in his mind meant you're alive and dangerous somewhere in the world and so when the comet went over it just confirmed his thoughts. But how ironic a few years later Dad comes across this signature dated in 1953 which in his eyes and mine and anyone with any common sense meant he was alive in 1953 and therefore at the time wasn't dead.

And so this information now brings a major question into play; when did Adolf Hitler actually die?

Dad went to see this man Osborne but didn't spend too much time there, he hadn't shown this man the signature but instead The Album and quickly came to the conclusion he was not qualified enough to take on such work.

So in New York Dad went back to the library and got the names and addresses of graphologists and forensic scientists in Berlin and sent documents to them, which included the writings of The Album, the birth certificate and this August Kubizek signature.

I guess he attached a letter explaining he needed this album 100% authenticated and needed work done on other findings and would fly back to London to await their response.

He arrived back from New York and after one week he received a letter from two people in Berlin one being Peter Achmann who was a graphologist and the other being Fredrick Koppe who was a forensic scientist.

Not only did Dad receive a letter from Peter Achmann but also he continued to phone him to invite him over to Berlin to discuss these matters further.

Dad stayed at the California Hotel in Berlin and Peter Achmann had arrived at Dad's hotel one Sunday in late December of 1991.

Peter has spent twenty years of his life working for a publishing company called Springer and had been sacked because of a book he was writing. The book was about Martin Bormann and Eva Braun living in South America and he had received huge amounts of persecution from everyone for suggesting such things.

Martin Bormann, who was Hitler's right hand man and had apparently witnessed the suicides of the Goebbels family and of Hitler himself and according to history books, died soon after but there is mixed views on how he died. And years later he was apparently spotted in Italy and also Brazil and Chile and was rumoured to be living in Argentina.

Dad immediately got on with Peter, I guess the persecution they had both suffered over the years, had made good conversation.

Peter Achmann spent four hours with Dad that day, discussing the whole affair and how he had come across all these revelations.

Dad had The Album on him and he took it out so Peter could examine it and again this subject regarding the English in The Album came up. It seemed to catch everyone's eye and it caught their imagination and their general interest in the whole affair. Peter looked at the word Antwerp that is written in English in The Album and he looked up and asked, "Do you know where Adolf Hitler was educated?" Dad replied "Yes," he then said, "Therefore would you agree that he was educated in Austria?" My father said "no," and Peter Achmann agreed and Dad turned round to him and said, "Where do you think he was educated?" Peter replied "It appears that there is no other place possible other than England." Dad said that he believed Hitler was educated in England up until the age of thirteen and then continued his education in Austria.

After Dad was satisfied that Peter knew his album was authentic, he pulled out of his briefcase the page that had the August Kubizek 1953 signature on it and showed it to him. Peter studied it for a while and then looked up at my Dad and told him the signature was written by Hitler but of a Hitler that was older than the one who had written the last known writings in the Third Reich. He also said it was impossible for any other person to have written it. Peter was comparing the signature with writings from the book called Hitler by Joachim Fest. And just by coincidence Peter knew Joachim Fest and so probably confirmed with him at a later date whether or not the copies my Dad had given him were in fact from his book.

He then turned to my father and with great worry on his face told him, he was carrying a time bomb in his brief case.

Peter said he was willing to take on the work of authenticating The Album. He told Dad he would need to work with Hitler's original handwriting from Koblenz and would need the assistance of a forensic scientist to date the ink and the paper. He told my Dad he would come back to the hotel the following morning to draw up a contract.

The following morning as promised Peter turned up and sat down and had breakfast with Dad. He wrote this contract, basically saying he would work for a certain amount of money for each hour spent on the project. Which my father agreed to.

Dad was due to meet Fredrick Koppe that day, who was the forensic scientist and so Peter and Dad left the hotel at the same time and made their way to the train station.

As they both waited for their respective trains Dad turned to Peter and with hundreds of German commuters surrounding him said " In your opinion what would be the general reaction from all these people standing here if they all knew Adolf Hitler was English?" Peter looked at my father and I think it wasn't until that point, he realised the magnitude of the findings. Because then it became clear to him that what he had suggested in the hotel the previous day meant that during the Second World War (while millions of Germans were dying and the country was being bombarded by England) that the country was actually being controlled by an Englishman.

Dad never heard from Peter Achmann after that day and still to this day does not know the real reasons why but in my opinion there are two reasons; firstly the whole thing frightened him and he didn't want to delve any deeper; and the other was because it had only been a few years since he had put his whole reputation on the line with regards to his own book and he was not going to put himself through that persecution again.

Dad boarded the train and made his way to the outskirts of the city where Fredrick Koppe and his wife Helena lived. Fredrick Koppe was a former forensic scientist for the Berlin Police Department. He knew very little English so Helena was at all their meetings to translate the conversations. Fredrick had already had the documents for seven days, which Dad had posted to him from New York regarding the August Kubizek signature and so after studying them invited my Dad through means of several letters to his home. And once again one of the first questions asked by Fredrick Koppe was where do you think Adolf Hitler was educated? As I say Fredrick Koppe had spent most of his life working for the Berlin Police Department and had just retired. He agreed that the signature and birth certificate and the writings in The Album all matched Adolf Hitler's writings. He agreed to take on the authentication of The Album but first insisted that Dad got the age of the paper and the age of the ink verified. Dad agreed and went back to London and visited the Metropolitan Police to see whether they could take on the job but due to them recently moving offices and having to deal with police matters and not having time for private work they refused.

So Fredrick Koppe recommended a friend of his called Michel Ziegler whom was a forensic scientist working for the Berlin police department. The date was arranged for Dad to go into the Berlin police department with Fredrick to meet Michel. Dad was quite nervous at this point because he knew he had major revelations regarding Hitler including one that suggested he was educated in England. To cover himself he sent a fax to Rupert Murdock and a fax to his financier Ken McCullen making them aware he was going to the building to discuss those matters.

Dad entered the police department with just two of the postcards, Michel put one of them under a microscope and enlarged it onto a screen, he then took out from one of his files a piece of paper with original ink samples on it and compared them with the writings on the postcards. The ink from the postcard is an iron based ink, which dated back to 1907 and hadn't been seen on this planet for some 30-40 years, he was explaining to Dad that the pigmentation was the same on both documents and the age of the paper was dated back to the 1900s. Fredrick Koppe had already agreed the writings from Dad's album was Hitler's and therefore making it quite impossible for anyone to have forged that album. And even if Dad was clever enough to have faked that album the last thing he would have done was write it partly in English because as I've said it is documented that Hitler apparently could not write or understand English.

The following day feeling quite confident Dad went back to the Berlin Police department with the whole album. Michel Ziegler measured it, counted the pages, took scraping from the ink and paper, weighed it and photographed it. While he was doing this he was dictating the information onto his colleague Schmidt who was making a report, which was later going to be typed out and passed onto Dad and Fredrick Koppe.

Michel Ziegler then wanted to take out each one of the postcards to photograph and to examine them and Dad agreed. Then Michel asked for one particular postcard but Dad would not allow him to look at it. It was one of the postcards of the Notre Dame in Paris and

Dad told him it contained information on it which was personal to Hitler and therefore confidential. Michel instantly became unhappy and suspicious about it and constantly questioned my Dad over it. Still to this day I don't know what is written on that card and there is one other he won't show anyone, it also contains writings and a picture of the Notre Dame. Those cards from that day have always been kept separate from The Album for security purposes; Dad thought if any of this family were kidnapped or The Album was stolen he could use those cards as a bargaining tool.

That evening the four of them; Dad, Michel Ziegler, Fredrick Koppe and Helena sat round a table having dinner and discussing the affair and Dad was asked many questions about where The Album had come from and also about how he had come across all these other revelations. Dad answered their questions to their satisfaction.

Helena said on behalf of her husband they wanted to launch this whole affair and expose this conspiracy on the 1953 signature of August Kubizek. They had agreed it was impossible for Adolf Hitler to have died in 1945 and they felt the world had a right to know.

The evening had ended well but the following day when Dad went back to the Berlin Police Department to pick up his report Michel Ziegler said it was not fully ready and he promised he would post it on to Dad's address in England when it was completed.

Dad flew back to London after telling them he would wait for their report and fly back when invited by Fredrick Koppe. That was the last Dad ever heard from either one of those people in Berlin and I guess it's a time in the story to ask yourselves certain questions.

Who frightened or scared off those experts? Maybe they had their hands tied or maybe they just became suspicious over those held back postcards. Either way it doesn't really matter they had made their conclusions to Dad over their findings and they were positive, it was just a shame he didn't get his hands on that report, it might of made things a lot easier for him in the future. Dad had little support throughout this campaign financially or morally and now even the experts were backing off.

Other questions needing to be asked at this stage are;

Why was Hitler writing in English in The Album? If Hitler was English was it England's intention to go to war against Germany but didn't want to be seen starting it, but having the ultimate insider as in Adolf Hitler on their side to not only start the war but to direct it in England's favour. If that is the case why did England purposely start the Second World War? Was it maybe to sink the threat of communism from Russia? That may all be true but the question of the Jews and why that happened was personal to Hitler and I believe had nothing to do with the English Establishment and basically got in the way of England's objectives to the war. Therefore the war had to be stopped and strategies rethought. Again if that is the case where did England find someone so intelligent and so clever to pull off such a mission? Well read on I'll give you a clue.

The signature in *Young Hitler* dated 1953 obviously meant he didn't die in Berlin in 1945 and therefore could it be possible he his still alive today? Not forgetting that his birth certificate in *Young Hitler* is a forgery and therefore his date of birth is wrong.

And if that is a possibility where is he now and what on earth has he been doing all this time since 1945, surely not nothing but maybe planning something big before he dies.

If this were all true why would Hitler take the risk of having *Young Hitler* published and run the risk of being exposed? Well I think he had the book published because he wanted to remind certain people, in certain circles of our world, that he was still about and obviously still powerful. That book was first published in 1953, the same year his niece (which I was lead to believe) became Queen of England, was that book *Young Hitler* a gentle reminder to her that he was alive and well? And was it also a coincidence that Stalin died that year?

And one final question, what would the people of Germany and England and in fact any country think if they were told that Adolf Hitler was an Englishman? Well I can't answer that and I wouldn't even try to but I'm sure there would be many unhappy people out there.

The one thing that has kept me slightly sane knowing all this information is the belief that there must have been one hell of a good reason for it all.

During the summer of 1991 I seemed to have a lot of free time playing with my friends or playing cricket, Gary wasn't around so it seemed that my friends and me had the run of the house. Mum was working in London and it was also in that period, at the age of sixteen I started lying in bed until the late morning and sometimes-early afternoons, a bad habit to get into.

At that stage I had finished my car cleaning round, I was at an age where I was more concerned over my image, and riding my bike with a bucket and sponge was not suiting it, no matter how much money I was earning. Just by coincidence though a shop specialising in cricket and hockey equipment opened on Warley Hill just a short walk from my house and so I went down and asked the owner, Billy for a job. He was impressed with my cricketing achievements and gave me a part time job, which eventually became full time during that summer. It was a fairly simple job really just giving customers advice and dealing with the transactions and generally talking about cricket, which I liked. I needed that job obviously for money and to tide me over until I got my GCSE results.

One of my last ever cricket games for Essex came in that year, it was in a Texaco Trophy tournament game in the 3rd round against Middlesex. Middlesex were a very good side and had two players who were playing in the Middlesex adult team including one current England player Richard Johnson.

The game was held at Blackheath and my Mum had taken the day off to take me there. My attitude for playing for Essex had slightly changed due to that game the previous year but I still enjoyed it and still enjoyed doing well but deep down I knew cricket had no future for me.

We all turned up at the ground and all of the Middlesex players with their team tracksuits on were already out practising, that was always an intimidating sight for any visiting team.

The Texaco Trophy was a 50 limited over game and the winner went through to the next round of the tournament. We batted first and lost quick wickets, their star performers were mainly bowlers and very fast ones at that.

It was in that game I would wear a helmet for the very first time. My innings started slowly just trying to chip a few runs away off the bowlers. Wickets were falling all around me and then Jim Thornton came in and we started to develop a partnership. One of their fast bowlers came off and was replaced by a spinner. It was then I managed to start to get my eye in and hit a few boundaries including a few fours off of Richard Johnson. Richard was a huge menacing figure who was a very aggressive cricketer.

All of a sudden the crowd started clapping, I wondered what it was for and Jim told me that I had scored my 50, I was so surprised, it was one of the most controlled innings I had ever played, I went onto get 76 before I shouldered up to Richard. As I walked back towards the pavilion Richard walked passed me and said "Goodnight Charlie" I felt like reacting to his comments but I didn't and I carried on walking towards the pavilion, where I received a huge applause and my Mum took a photo of me holding my bat up to acknowledge the clapping crowd.

The side itself only scored 176 that day which really wasn't enough. We took tea and then we had a team briefing about how we were going to defend such a low total, as we all got up to go back on the field one of the managers pulled me to one side and said to me, that he felt that it should be my responsibility to up lift the team spirits while on the field. Well I did just that and we bowled and fielded excellently and managed to win the game. It was a great feeling and a great day beating a team that would have probably won the tournament.

We lost in the next round to one of the minor counties, which was played at Colchester Cricket Club, and not knowing at the time was the last game I ever played for Essex.

While working at the cricket shop there would always be long periods of quiet spells so I would listen to Kiss FM and on one particular occasion they were doing a competition where you had to ring in when a particular song came on, the competition that day was for two tickets to an all night rave organised by Kiss FM to the Astoria in Charing Cross, London.

Well the song came on and I rang in and won. The tickets were posted to me via Royal Mail's recorded delivery so I received them the following day. I was going to take Stuart Barnes (who I had recently met up with at a party and started hanging round with him again) but his Mum would not allow it because he was only fifteen. So I went with Steve Ferber a recently found acquaintance. Steve had joined St Martin's School in the fourth year, his parents owned a masonry company in Forest Gate, London. And due to its success had moved to Brentwood. Steve and I had a fair bit in common, he was the same height as me being 6ft 3ins and we had the same sort of features and we made good companionship when we went out clubbing.

So we both got prepared for our first proper London nightclub, we got dressed up in our smartest clothes, making sure our shoes were well polished.

We made our way up to London by train and underground and how shocked we were when we arrived to find everyone queuing up were wearing just jeans and t-shirts, it made us feel slightly intimidated and also knowing we were under age didn't help. But we did manage to get in and it was an experience I will never forget.

The place was a massive old theatre that had been turned into this nightclub. There were all different kinds of people there from all walks of life. Everyone was enjoying themselves, people were dancing everywhere including on the tables and I guess this is when I became aware of drugs and the problem that that scene has with it. I wasn't into drugs but it didn't stop lots of people asking me whether I wanted to buy them. We were offered Ecstasy and LSD on a regular basis and I'm quite sure that most of the people in the place were on something, everyone was drinking water and I'm not sure they even sold alcohol.

But Steve and I still enjoyed ourselves; I was high on life anyway at that point so I didn't need drugs to get even higher. We danced throughout the night, we bumped into some girls we both knew from Brentwood so we spent most of the night with them. Yes it was great, the music was great, and I've always liked that kind of music including music from the Prodigy, Moby, Felix, Sweet Harmony and Bizarre Ink.

We danced away into the early hours of the morning and it was a good experience. We must have got the night bus to Stratford and then a train home.

I always remember while walking home that morning from the station, thinking how strange it was that it was already daylight and the birds were already singing. I spent the whole of that day in bed.

The whole experience got our little group into clubbing and Steve and I were keen to show them what they were missing. From that point a few of us including Steve, Stuart and Paul Barnes, Elliot Everard, Anthony Kinnear and eventually girls such as Hannah Bentley, Susanna and Julie would follow.

We would often visit London during the weekends mainly for clothes or to buy records from shops such as Black Market Records and Boogie Times, we all loved our music and Stuart was a keen and up and coming DJ.

Stuart's family had moved from Middleton Rd and bought a much bigger house in Hall Lane, Shenfield next to St Mary's School. Barry had bought the house to redevelop and it took some time for it to take shape but in the end the house looked magnificent. He put a tennis court in the grounds and an outer house for guests to stay in and an indoor swimming pool with a sauna, obviously the whole inside of the house was immaculate and Barry had even built a big games room for his children which included a pool table, TV, video and games console but the main attraction of the room was the DJ equipment that was there. Stuart had Technics 1210's and a mixing system and all the other equipment needed to perform his wonders. Stuart not only had all the equipment but also was very good at it.

I guess it was a natural progression after that event at the Astoria and the fact that all our friends liked that kind of music meant we would soon be visiting clubs such as the Café De Paris, Limelight, Legends, Astoria, Garage City, Mr B's of Southend, Berwick Manor of Rainham and of course clubs such as the Ilford Palais and Hollywood's of Romford.

By this stage my Mum was getting quite concerned over the amount of clubbing I was doing and my general attitude to life, with regards to my sleeping in during the days and going out in the evenings. I wasn't into drugs by this point but my Mum would always drop questions relating to them into our conversations, trying to catch me out but in the end she was quite convinced that I wasn't on drugs.

I think she was just hoping my GCSE results would be good and I would be able to go and get a job in the City. But that day came when the exam results were issued and I remember riding my bike to the school to pick them up. I wasn't really sure what I was going to do in my life after getting those results but I was fairly confident I had done quite well.

Everyone else from the year was there in the reception area of the school, opening their envelopes, which contained their results, and I noticed many people were happy and laughing and the girls would stand there hysterical. Others would just walk away without saying too much, so I decided to take my envelope and get on my bike and open it in private. I rode back towards the house and about halfway there the intrigue got the better of me and I stopped riding, I was on the Thiftwood Estate in Hanging Hill Lane in one of the many ally-ways the estate has. I got off my bike and opened the envelope and I was fairly disappointed really, I got three pass grades, which was in Geography, Maths and one of the Sciences. And I knew to get any kind of decent job I needed four or five passes which would ideally include English, which I received a D in.

I rode back home wondering what I was going to do. Mum was in her bedroom and I remember going up to discuss it with her, she said she was proud of me for passing even three exams, she would repeatedly remind me of the learning difficulties I had when I was young. She tried to make me feel better about everything and we came to the conclusion I would go back to the sixth form and retake some of my exams. It would hold up whatever career I was going into by a year but deep down that didn't bother me, I wasn't ready for work then and there was more fun to have and I used to think that hopefully Dad's affair would break in the meantime and then I wouldn't even have to work.

In the sixth form at St Martin's you didn't have to wear school uniform but just smart trousers and a shirt and tie. There was a good social feeling about the sixth form we had a big hall so everyone could meet and see each other.

I always remember the joy that came across Louise Ferguson's face when she saw me walk into that hall for the first time. She wasn't sure whether I was going back to sixth form or not.

Louise and I met in the 1st year in a H.E lesson, we would sit next to each other and she would help me get through the lesson. H.E was about cooking etc., and so we would have great fun making different kinds of cakes. H.E was always at the end of the day and at the end of class we would both head for the exit of the school and we found it quite strange on the first occasion when we found ourselves walking in the same direction home, Louise lived on Hutton Mount and I had to walk through it to get to my home.

Like Amanda, I was very close to Louise we spent a lot of time together at school, we both knew deep down we liked each other but rarely did anything about it. Louise was in the highest class possible at school and was immensely intelligent, not that she always came across like that, and she was also great fun to be around and easily made you laugh. If we ever saw each other out at parties both sets of friends would know they wouldn't see us for the rest of the evening

Mine and Louise's relationship was a little bit like mine and Scott's really, whereby she came in and out of my life, I did like her and if circumstances had of worked out differently I may of ended up being with her but that wasn't to be, I actually left the sixth form after only being there for a few days and so we went our separate ways. I went my way and she eventually after completing her A-Levels, to my surprise when one of my friends told me, went to Cambridge University. As I've just said she would come in and out of my life and a little later on in the story I will write an episode about Louise and the period we spent together for a week discussing the Hitler affair and how she was going to approach Cambridge University with the findings.

As I say I didn't last long in the sixth form, as I said before you had to wear a shirt and a tie and the last thing I was going to do with my money was go out and buy a load of ties, I wasn't into that, I was more into fashionable clothes and ties were not part of my wardrobe. So I think for the first couple of days I must of worn one of Gary's ties he left behind but that was it, I wasn't going to buy any ties and I wasn't going to search for them. I remember finding the classes quite boring really, it was stuff we had already been over the previous year obviously, but there was something about that little period that didn't seem right and what happened on the fourth morning just confirmed that to me. I had walked into the sixth form area in the morning without my tie on and the head of the sixth form Mr Marshall, was standing in the hall with most of the sixth form and upper sixth form surrounding him. As I walked in through the main doors, he spotted me straight away, I know I'm tall and stand out I guess, but I must of caught his eye straight away and in front of everyone he told me to "Get out and don't come back until you have found a tie!" The entire sixth form just stared at me some laughed but I turned round and never again entered that room. No one was going to talk to me like that, no one was going to belittle me like that, who the hell did he think he was. So I left, I walked out and said goodbye to St Martin's School.

Once again I got home and spoke to my Mum about what I was going do, I could have got a job I guess but not the sort of job my Mum wanted me to have. She wanted me up in the City working in a bank or something like that.

She phoned my private maths tutor who lived in Cricketers Lane, Ingrave and after they discussed my options he asked to see me. I went to see him with my Mum and sat down with him and had tea and biscuits and chatted about what I wanted to do for a living and what I wanted to do now. We just went through the different options I had and we came to the conclusion that the best option was for me to go to college and study some kind of Business course.

He said he had gone to college and they were the best days of his life and so he highly recommended it. After several phone calls to different colleges, trying to get into a business course, it was eventually Thurrock College who gave us the greatest hope.

Thurrock College was in Love Lane, Aveley, which is on the outskirts of Grays, Essex. The college was an old secondary school, not the most attractive building but had all the necessary rooms and sports facilities inside. That particular college in Thurrock dealt with Business Studies and Travel and Tourism.

My Mum arranged for me and her to have an interview with the head of Business Studies, Mr Stone. He was a fairly young man for someone who held such a position; he owned his own company but also got pleasure from teaching. We arrived at the college and it seemed like we were in the middle of nowhere. He greeted us at the reception and took us through to one of the study rooms, where we all sat down and discussed the different courses on offer. He explained that the course on offer was a two year BTEC Business and Finance course which if completed was the equivalent of two A-Levels and would give me access to certain universities. To be accepted for the course you needed a minimum of four GCSE's, I had three so I needed to impress this chap for him to accept me. We discussed my exam results and my intentions for the college and what I hoped to achieve from the course.

Now I knew I was going to have to come over quite well if he was going to give me a place on the course, the course had already started by a few days but there were still some spaces left, so I knew I had to perform in that interview to give me any chance of a place. Then to my disbelief he started talking about how he wanted to improve the sports facilities at the college but mainly he spoke about wanting to develop a cricket team that would represent the college. I thought right, yes, I'm in now. My Mum quickly brought up my cricketing achievements and told him I was currently playing for Essex and playing cricket was my number one hobby. That impressed him, he wanted to know more about me playing cricket for Essex and so I went through some of the games with him and mentioned a few of the players down at the county ground and basically I had this man hooked. And so at the end of the meeting he offered me a place, he said it would be great to have me, he wouldn't worry about the fact I only had three GCSE's but would monitor my work throughout the two years. He said I could start the following day.

Excellent, I thought this was great, at college you didn't have to worry about what you were wearing you could just turn up in jeans, shorts or whatever, you know, it was like very casual and very laid back. Everyone was easy going, the teachers weren't on your back, if you didn't turn up for class then that was down to you, it didn't concern them as long as you caught up and got your assignment in on time was all that concerned them really.

There was one problem though, I remember sitting there thinking how on earth was I going to get there everyday. He told me there was a regular coach that picked students up from Brentwood and dropped them at the main college which was six miles away and then I would have to get on a separate coach from there to the business college at Aveley.

I wasn't too happy about that, it was quite a long trip everyday and a lot of messing about but anyway who was I to complain too much?

A two-year course, great I thought it would keep me entertained for two years, it would stop me having to go to work and it gave Dad another two years to get his project off the ground. I knew it was going to happen it was just a case of when. So the two-year course would keep me happy and it would also keep my Mum very happy indeed.

As we all walked out of that room and started to say our farewells and goodbyes, something happened and not knowing at the time, would change my life and the direction of it.

As we stood there this student came up to Mr Stone (which is not his real name because I don't know what the fuck it is), he was the same height as me but with long blonde hair, blue eyes and was slightly older than me. He interrupted Mr Stone and eagerly asked him some questions about his own course work. Mr Stone asked him to hang on a minute.

As he stood there it dawned on both of us that we both knew each other. His name was Greg Connor and he had gone to St Martin's school but was two years older than me. He had been thrown out of the sixth form for admitting to possessing drugs. He had taken the blame for one of his friends and so had to leave St Martin's. He spent time after that working in a clothes shop called Yankee Doodle's in Lakeside, Thurrock and then in Victoria Jewellers in Epping. But after a while he became bored and he knew if he wanted to achieve anything in this world he would have to go back and get some qualifications, he was very intelligent but that's why he was at Aveley college, he was doing exactly the same course as me and had just started it a few days ago.

Greg was eighteen at the time, he was two years older than me, his birthday was also in December and he was driving to college everyday in his bright yellow Suzuki jeep.

I also remember Greg from school because he was one of the older kids I used to wind up and he would chase me all over the school he never caught me but he tried.

But he was one of the outgoing kids of the year, he was one of the personalities of the school, the party goer, the lively outgoing person who entertained everyone and made everyone laugh, he was someone to know if you like.

And so when he came up to us that day, I started talking to him while my Mum was talking to Mr Stone and I asked him about the course and he said it was great, he mentioned a few people there that I knew and he made me feel at ease about the prospect of starting there. And it was there and then that I asked him if he had room in his jeep for one more, he told me he was already giving two people a lift everyday but could squeeze another one in, he said he was charging a pound a day for petrol and said he would pick me up first in the morning and then go on to pick up a chap called Paul Mason who I didn't know but came from County High School in Brentwood. Paul was a year older than me and also celebrated his birthday in December, in fact the three us celebrated our birthdays within days of each other. After picking Paul up we would drive towards Grays and while driving through Ingrave we would pick our last person up a girl called Natalie Smith who I already knew from my school days, she was in my class.

So I left the college with my Mum feeling confident and felt right about me going to this college for some reason. I don't know why, maybe it was for me to take this course and succeed, I had walked in and spoken to this man about cricket, I'd met Greg and he was going to give me a lift, he was also picking up a girl I knew and so everything just felt right and fell into place. And so I was actually looking forward to the following day.

I remember bumping into Scott later on that day and he was quite fascinated in why I had left the school a few days earlier. I went through it with him and he agreed about the teacher being totally out of order. I told him I was going on to college and he said everyone back at the school was talking about what had happened and a lot of people thought it was shame I had left, but he wished me luck. He had a record bag on him at the time; you could buy these bags to hold your 12in records. There were CD's around in those days but most people of our age were into records. And he gave me the bag and said this is for you, you can carry your coursework and pens around in it. I said thanks and that become my bag throughout my college days. I would eventually give the bag back to him and he would go on to use it while he was at Leeds University. It was one of those items that holds a lot of memories between us two.

I got prepared that evening for my first day at college, sorted out what I was going to wear and packed some notepaper and a pen. As promised Greg picked me up outside my door the following morning, we then drove down to Brentwood railway station where I was introduced to Paul Mason. The one thing I remember about Paul's personality was he was such a funny person, he cracked jokes at just the right time and made everyone laugh he was that kind of person.

So we picked him up and then we headed to Ingrave where Natalie got in. Natalie was surprised to see me sitting there in the back. There wasn't much room in the back of Greg's jeep and what with me having a bad knee (from my squash days) didn't help. But there wasn't a lot I could say about it at the time, I was just grateful that Greg was giving me a lift. Natalie asked me about school and why I had left. It was nice to have someone to talk to, I knew Greg but didn't know him well, you know when you first meet someone and it's an effort to try and make conversation and Paul I didn't know at all.

The thing I do remember about that journey that I wasn't happy about, apart from being squashed up in the back, was that Paul, Greg and Natalie all smoked, even though the windows were down there was still this massive cloud of smoke around me that I didn't like. I didn't think it was healthy for me at the time but again couldn't really complain.

We finally arrived at the college after a good half an hours drive from Brentwood. Paul Greg and Natalie were all in the same class. There were two classes for that particular business course and I wasn't sure which one I was in. So I got to the college and Greg introduced me to a few people and I sat around in the canteen for a while having a cup of tea. Then Mr Stone came up to me and said hello and said he was pleased to see me and asked me to follow him to his office, we sat down and had a little chat. He told me I would be in the other class, separate from Greg, Paul and Natalie. That being because there was no room in Greg's class and so I had to be put in the other class. That was fine I didn't mind, but what it did mean was I didn't know anyone in that class and it also meant, more importantly, my timetable was different to Greg's which meant that I had to sometimes take that awful coach journey home because on occasions Greg's lessons would finish earlier than mine, it also meant that later on in the course I would bunk off the last lesson so I could catch a lift with Greg.

Mr Stone took me up to the class and introduced me to the teacher and to all the students, which was quite daunting for me and I guess anyone who has had to change schools or started a course late would surely appreciate.

I immediately spotted a space at the back of the class, which was great, I always liked sitting at the back not because I was naughty but I could easily assess the situation that I had found myself in.

So I walked to the back of the class took my jacket off and sat down next to a chap called Tony Riley, he was a few years older than me and was taking the course so he could eventually take over his family's business which was in Rochford, Southend.

I introduced myself and we seemed to get on quite well straight away, which was good for me because I didn't know anyone in the class. Tony also spent time with me that morning going through the work I had missed in the previous days, fortunately there wasn't much but I was grateful to him.

I also remember sitting there on that first morning having a good look round at my fellow classmates and checking out if there were any nice looking girls there. There was one, her name was Jo, she was tall, had long brown hair and had this cute face and an amazing body, she came from Grays she was nice girl and we got on well but she wasn't quite the sort of girl I went for but we were quite good friends throughout college.

Tony the chap who I had made friends with, after getting to know each other a bit better, we found out we had a similar interest in squash. And so we had a couple of games down at the sports centre in Southend. The whole class actually had a bet on who was going to win the first game we ever played. Jo had organised the bets, the bets were meant for our class only but the whole college seemed to get wind of it and Jo found herself taking bets from everyone. I hadn't told anyone I used to play squash for the county and that I was obviously quite good at it and so I would encourage people to bet for me and I would also put some money down for myself. The game took place in Southend and a few people turned up to watch and I won the game fairly easily and made a fair bit of money in the process.

Because of our interest in squash, at the college in the sports centre, they had a badminton court and so during our spare time we would normally be found there.

Badminton is a great game it's obviously slightly different to squash and requires more skill but I did enjoy playing it. And Tony and me were more evenly matched when it came to that game.

After being at the college for two or three weeks I had got to know most of the people there as I've said it was quite a small college and in the end everyone knew each other. The courses on offer there were either Business and Finance or Travel and Tourism and therefore there was an awful lot of girls at the college and so I had come to the point where I thought it would be nice to have a girlfriend, don't get me wrong I had had girlfriends in the past but only very brief encounters. There were two girls at the college that caught my eye and both of them were called Nicky funnily enough.

One of the girls was from Danbury, Essex she was a stunning looking girl with blonde hair and blue eyes. I had mentioned to Greg that particular morning I was going to approach this girl. I always found it hard to approach girls especially beautiful ones, especially if I liked them as well; I found it hard to know what to talk about and I also hated the thought of being rejected. But I spoke to Greg about it that morning and he funnily enough had the same views on this particular girl and so he then asked my permission whether he could approach her first and if he had no luck I had the go ahead but he did ask me first and I said yes, no worries, cool and I guess me not being that worried about it meant I didn't fancy her that much. I gave him permission to talk to her first and so he did. He approached her and they got chatting and he actually gave her a lift home that day but he was suppose to have picked me up in the evening to go out and so he let me down and the following day he explained that he spent most of the evening with that girl and had got on really well with her and they had started going out with each other. I wasn't that worried about it; I was more concerned he hadn't picked me up that evening. I was ready and waiting for him but I remember that was the one thing that upset about the whole episode, not that he was seeing this girl I initially liked but he had not even rung me to let me know he wasn't coming round to pick me up.

But there was this other girl also called Nicky, she was from Leigh-on-Sea in Southend. She was a year older than me and also celebrated her birthday in December. She was studying Travel and Tourism.

It wasn't so much her looks, which appealed to me even though she was a nice pleasant looking girl but it was her personality that appealed to me. She was the most out going, loudest girl in the college and there was something about her I liked. I hadn't spoken to her at all by this point but I just used to remember seeing the way she went about her daily routine and how she was with her friends and yes I did like her.

And the way we got together was all quite bizarre really. During one of the weekends in that period probably in early October of 1991, Stuart and I visited a record shop in Romford called Boogie Times, Stuart was buying some records and I used to buy some as well, and kept them round his house. It was at Stuart's house that the whole of our group would meet, it was our meeting point before we went out, and was also the focus point of our spare time and what with the facilities at his house it was just a nice place to be.

So we had visited this shop in Romford and at the counter, there were a number of flyers that were advertising clubs and raves taking place in the near future. Now none of us had ever been to a proper rave before we had only been to clubs.

One flyer took my eye it just said Telepathy. I picked it up and it looked like a very impressive event taking place in North London in the next week or so. I can't remember all the details but I think the tickets were £15 -£20 each and so I picked a handful of the flyers up and spoke to Stuart about it and the rest of our group. And we came to the conclusion we would go. Now this event at the time was massive and was probably one of the biggest rave events London had held, it was being advertised on all the pirate radio stations including Pulse Fm, which we all listened to. We gathered this large group of people from Brentwood who were also interested in going, there were about fifteen to twenty people including Hannah and Suzanne.

I liked going out in big groups, it made me feel secure, I guess deep down the worries my Dad had over the Security Services had affected me subconsciously. Even though I wasn't really taking too much notice of what he was saying at the time but what he was saying obviously went in and so going out in bigger groups made me feel a lot more confident, it also gave me the opportunity to talk to a range of different people, which I liked.

The opening page of The Album with an example of one of the postcards.

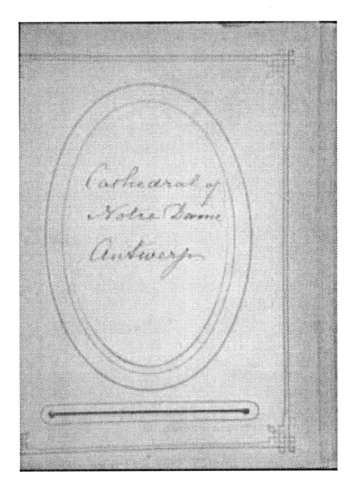

**An example of the English written by
Hitler in The Album.**

While at college on the following Monday, I started handing out some of these flyers and leaving them about the college and as I walked from the canteen and up the stairs to my lesson, Nicky was walking down and she must of noticed me holding those Telepathy flyers because she stopped me and asked me if I was going to the event. I said yes I was going with a few of my friends from Brentwood and she said, "That's funny because I'm also going with a few of my friends and my boyfriend."

I said "That's great, wouldn't it be funny if we bump into each other up there?" knowing there wasn't much chance of that because this event was going to be massive and thousands of people were due to attend.

It was being held in a sports centre in Holloway and so the likelihood of us seeing each other without making a prior arrangement was slim. We spoke a little more but that little encounter on those stairs that day was the first bit of communication we had, it was nice and also coincidental, it was also coincidental we were both going to this same event I had planned for all my friends. And so we had a small chat that seemed to flow easy, it wasn't one of those conversations where you are racking your brains out to know what to say, it was just pleasant. The fact that she had a boyfriend obviously meant there wasn't much hope for me, she had made the point of telling me about him and so I didn't think too much else of it.

Another event that took place during that period that would change my direction in life and also my views on certain subjects was my first drugs experience. My short time at college was so eventful and I couldn't possibly write every memory down but I would recommend it to anyone, not so much because of the course work but the fun I had there was immense.

At the time I was dead against drugs and shied away from it whenever it was offered to me, I felt that I didn't need them but one day Greg, Paul and I decided to take half the day off from college and go home. Greg dropped me off at mine and while saying goodbye said I was more than welcome to come back to his to watch a film, I said thank you but decided against it.

Greg's Mum worked at Lloyd's in Brentwood and his stepfather worked as a driving examiner and so they were rarely at home during the day. Greg's real father had died a few years previous in a tragic car accident. I think the fact that we had both lost our Dad's in different kinds of way, made our friendship more solid, I guess whatever differences there were between us that was the one thing we kind of had in common. My Dad had obviously not died but sometimes the man who called himself my Dad, I hardly knew. I would rarely see my Dad at this stage but he would always ring the house to speak to me and update me on his progress. He would always have this great way of giving me hope and would always say to me that he was so close in bringing his affair to an end, his classic saying was "It's just about to come down," he would say my life had a great importance and I had a role to play in it after the so called "nightmare".

After getting bored at home rather quickly I phoned Greg and told him that I would be there in five minutes. Greg lived on the Thiftwood estate and so I jumped on my bike and rode through King George's Park and through the East Ham Estate and on to his house.

Greg had some similar tastes in music to me including Led Zeppelin and Jimmy Hendrix; he was also into The Cure and an American band called The Doors.

The film we were going to watch that day was called *The Doors*, it is a film about Jim Morrison, with Val Kilmer and Meg Ryan in it and is directed by Oliver Stone.

I had no interest in this particular film at the time and had never listened to The Doors. After about an hour, Greg stopped the film and said he was going into the kitchen to roll up a joint. I followed him fascinated in how that was achieved, Greg had obviously done this many times before because he was masterful at it.

We all walked in his garden and they began to smoke it.

Greg had this amazing personality, he was two years older than me and so I guess I looked up to him but he also had this great influence over me, which no other person had.

As I watched them smoke it, I remember the nice smell it generated and I made a comment on it, Greg seized on the opportunity and suggested I try a little. After him trying several attempts to convince me it wasn't going to kill me, I said O.K..

And so I took this joint and tried to smoke it, without much luck at first, I had never tried smoking before and so had no idea how to inhale. Paul showed me and so then I managed to have a couple of lugs on this big fat joint. I just remember feeling instantly tired and I had to go in, I also felt dizzy and just collapsed on Greg's sofa and started watching this film *The Doors*.

The film at the time seemed to have this hypnotic affect on me, the film was at the stage when Jim Morrison jumps on a car outside the nightclub in LA and the film starts with the song *The End* and the film goes from the car scene into this scene where Jim and his friends are taking LSD in the desert. The song *The End* is a very powerful and deep song and while listening to it and watching these amazing scenes my mind just seemed to drift. I was also fascinated to see Red Indians in the film, my Dad had spoken a lot to me about his experiences with Indians in Arizona and his beliefs regarding Hitler and Indians, it's a bit deep but will explain later. Anyone who has seen the film *The Doors* will surely agree that that part of the film especially when you see Jim through the Indians eye on the stage at the Whisky-A-Go-Go, is the most brilliant piece of film work, it was mind blowing. "I lied, I am afraid."

I remember lying on Greg's sofa feeling quite stoned but feeling very relaxed and chilled out and also realising that I had found two new fascinations in my life, one being Marijuana and the other being Jim Morrison and The Doors.

We all instantly heard the base the rave was generating as we came out of the tube station at Holloway Rd. We all headed in the direction of the music and basically just followed the crowds. As we turned the corner to the sports centre we were all quite shocked to see the amount of people queuing. It was a large event and the security had to search everyone before letting them in and so it was taking time. The sports centre had told the organisers of the event that there was a maximum amount of people allowed in but they had sold a lot more tickets than expected and I guess they were hoping that everyone wasn't going to turn up, they were wrong.

We didn't realise this at the time and so we made our way to the back of the queue, we seemed to have to walk for ages until we reached the end of it.

After an hour of queuing, which had disappointed us all because the last thing you want when you visit a club or rave is to have to queue for hours. We hadn't made much progress towards the entrance and I had spotted a burger van across the green and made my way to it and bought a burger and a drink. I had also noticed at that point the extreme lack of police about, for such a large event I expected more. As I walked back towards my friends I noticed a girl running towards me, it was Nicky.

She said she had seen me from the queue walking over towards the burger van and thought she would come over and say hello. She seemed so pleased to see me, she told me they had also been queuing for quite a while but had managed to get quite near the front. She suggested we join them at the front of the queue. I said thanks and said I would discuss it with my friends. She then said to me, it would be nice if we bumped into each other inside, she said she would try and find me. I thought that was a bit strange because she was with her boyfriend but here she was telling me she was going to try and find me, so there was obviously some kind of problem going on between them.

I got back to where my friends were and they had hardly moved any nearer to the entrance and so they had spoken about leaving, they thought that there wasn't any point spending the whole of the evening queuing. Most of them had decided to head into London and go to Limelight, the nightclub in Shaftsbury Ave where we had been a few times before. They had asked my opinion, but they had already made their decision and I said to them that there was no way I was leaving, even if it meant me staying on my own, because firstly, I had organised this, I had paid my money but mainly because I was intrigued by this rave, I had never been to one before, I had heard a lot about them and so I was going to stay because I wanted to see and experience what was going on inside this building. I made my point clear to them and said goodbye, as they were all leaving Hannah turned round and said she would stay with me. So we were the only two out of the massive group to stay that evening and the rest made their way into London.

After being in the queue for a further half an hour, I began to feel slightly awkward about the situation, I have always summed up different situations quite well and had always noticed what was going on around me and at that particular point of the night I had noticed unpleasant characters walking up and down the queue scrutinising everyone. I didn't make an issue out of it to Hannah but did suggest to her we should try and make our way to the front of the queue and if we couldn't join it and get in rather quickly, maybe it was time for us also to go.

We walked along and made our way right to the front and basically pushed our way in, which we managed to do. As I stood there for a while I turned round and to my complete surprise two old friends from Woodlands were standing literally next to me. Jamie Tingle and Jonathan Owen. Jonathan had completely changed since school and I didn't recognise him at first, he had long hair, bony face and his eyes were bulging out of his head, he was on a different planet that night and I don't think he recognised me but Jamie seemed perfectly well and normal. It was a bizarre conversation really because not only were we in the middle of London at this rave where there were thousands of people but the last time we had spoken was at this privately run primary school which in fact was owned by Jamie's Mum.

As like any conversation you have when you bump into someone you went to school with, you talk about what you are doing at the time and what you have been doing but it was just bizarre because we were just trying to conduct this normal conservation while in the background there were all these people around us and the noise that was pumping out of this building didn't help and by now also there were security people everywhere surrounding us in the queue protecting us from local muggers, who were trying to get people's tickets. Within ten minutes we were inside, Hannah and I were both searched, our tickets were taken off us and we were allowed to go in.

As we walked through the double doors into the main arena, it was a scene that is quite difficult to imagine if you have never been to such a place, it's quite difficult to explain. Basically when we went through that door the first thing that hits you is the vast amounts of people everywhere, wearing all different kinds of colourful outfits with whistles hanging round their necks, some blowing horns, everyone jumping up and down to the music and dancing in unique ways and everyone obviously seemed happy probably because most of them were on drugs. But the music was like this kind of trance garage kind of music, which with the affects of all the lighting including lasers and strobes, seemed to have this kind of hypnotic affect on everyone. The whole experience was something I hadn't seen on this scale and I guess if an everyday normal kind of person was there, they would have surely thought the Devil was at work. At the time I liked it, I liked the music, I liked the people around me, I wasn't into the ecstasy or the LSD but I did enjoy dancing the night away with Hannah. Hannah had become quite a good friend in the past year and so we felt quite comfortable in each other's presence, but I did feel very responsible for her that evening, she had made a point of leaving the rest of her friends to be with me and I think she probably had the same views on it as me with regards to wanting to get in.

I never saw Nicky again that evening but the following Monday at college she said to me that she had had a good time and had searched the whole place for me but without any success, she said that she wanted to be with me that evening, she said that she was having trouble with her boyfriend and just wanted to spend time talking to me.

That evening Hannah and I stayed until about three in the morning and then we left. We had to make our way over to Stratford to catch the train back to Shenfield, and I remember walking out of the sports centre, there were no buses around and so we just had to walk and it was quite a frightening walk really, Holloway is not the most pleasant of areas and its not recommended for walks in the middle of the night. We were easy targets for anyone that evening, just the two of us wandering the streets looking for a bus stop but we eventually found one and had to wait there for a good half hour and had to witness numerous strange people walking past us, winos, drug addicts and cars flying up and down, it was frightening experience but fortunately nothing happened to us and we got on the bus and got to Stratford, we had to wait there for an hour or so, so we both fell asleep in one of the waiting rooms and we eventually got on the train which took us back to Shenfield.

We walked back to Stuart's because that was where we were all staying but when we got there we found no sign of life and so we made our way down to their guest house, the house was still being renovated at that point but we managed to get up into one of the rooms and so we both fell asleep there.

The whole event was an interesting experience for me as I say it was the first time I had witnessed a proper rave before and was actually the last as well. It was also nice and coincidental that Nicky and me had spoken that evening and she had made it quite clear she liked me and so in my eyes the night was a success. I had also seen two of my old friends I hadn't seen for years and so I was pleased I had arranged the whole evening and pleased I went. It was a shame though that my friends hadn't witnessed the same event but then that was their fault for not following out the evening. I was always one for staying in it until the end making sure I didn't miss anything.

Now the next three to four months leading up to the end of 1991 were quite dramatic months for me, I would experience things I hadn't done before in my life and I began to be influenced by people that had just entered my life, for example Greg and this girl Nicky.

They were two people that came into my life at the same point and had a great effect on the direction my life would subsequently take. They also changed me, changed my views on life and changed my personality as well I guess. Greg came alone and he had introduced me to smoking joints but we were also very close, I guess you could say he opened my mind with regards to the way I was thinking, he got me more into The Doors, he lent me a book about Jim Morrison, he bought me a book by Jim Morrison on poetry and would lend me numerous amounts of their CDs. I was intrigued by that side of life, I guess the outrageousness, the wildness and the anti-authority approach to life he had appealed to me, I think also his relationship with the Indians and the occult is also very important but did also intrigue me at the time.

I think that period just opened my mind a little and opened new doors and new interests. I spent a lot of time with Greg, we used to go out in his jeep and plot up in a country lane and sit there smoking gear and listening to music and talking about our dreams that we both had. Greg knew nothing about the Hitler affair at this point but he did also have great plans for his future and would always talk about how rich we were both going to be. I hadn't known Greg that long at that point and so I didn't tell him about the Hitler affair, as I've said before it was only people I became very close to and people I trusted.

I'm not sure whether my marijuana taking period was a good thing, I know it took me off route for a while and took me down another road in life, it differently changed my direction but then I sit here today and feel it was obviously meant to be. But at the time and if you look at it from my mothers point of view then I guess it wasn't such a good thing.

But with regards to Nicky, she had come in to my life at the same point and we started to spend time together, we got back to the college on that Monday after the rave and we sat in the canteen talking and she said that she had finished with her boyfriend after that night. And so we made an arrangement to go to Colchester Zoo and that was our first date, she took her friend Sarah so I took my friend Stuart. We drove up to Colchester Zoo in Sarah's black XR2 and even then during that early stage of our relationship I noticed this outrageous side to her that I liked, she wasn't the normal kind of girl really, as I say she had this extremeness about her, which I liked in people. She went round the zoo like a big kid, she loved it and I loved seeing her enjoy herself. And from that point we would start seeing each other properly and she would regularly stay round mine and I would regularly meet her from her work in Leigh-on-Sea and we would go out and I would stay at her house. When she was on her own with me she was completely different, she was quiet and so we could have long deep conversations but it was when she was around other people that she had this complete change in her personality which was quite bizarre.

She was my first real girlfriend but if you ask me while I sit here today whether I loved her or not, I'm not sure. I know we were quite close and so I did enjoy having her company at the time. We spent a lot of time together going out etc, she introduced me to all her friends and vice versa but as I say she had this influence on me with regards to drugs, she was quite heavily into the rave scene and into ecstasy.

And there was this one occasion when we had arranged to go to this club in Rainham called Berwick Manor. Berwick Manor was a rave club in the middle of nowhere but was the place to be for our area. It was a pub that had been transformed into a club

We used to go there all the time but on this one particular occasion it was me, Nicky, Sarah, Stuart and a chap called Nick Brett. Nicky had discussed with me about trying one of these ecstasy tablets, she had convinced me they were alright and I guess she just wanted me to experience what she thought was a great thing.

We all met at Stuart's and as we all sat in the car before leaving for the club we all took these tablets, I'm not sure how much the others took but Nicky suggested I only took half to see how I got on and so I did.

The journey to the club that night was a nervous one for me and filled with mixed emotions, I was quite looking forward to the night and the anticipation that taking this drug had caused but I also remember worrying slightly because of the obvious dangers that come when you deal with drugs.

We arrived at the club and Stuart, Sarah and Nicky went instantly onto the dance floor and looked liked they were enjoying themselves but I had stepped back from that, and was observing from a distance with Nick Brett. We both looked at each other wondering what the big deal was with regards to these ecstasy tablets we had taken because the effects had not taken their toll yet. They weren't doing anything to us and to be honest the whole period of the night was not enjoyable. I knew I had taken this drug and nothing seemed to be happening so I felt kind of let down by the whole thing really.

Nick and I walked out into the garden area leaving the others on the dance floor. The garden area was quite large with lots of benches available for all the clubbers that needed a break from inside or just wanted some fresh air. Nick said to me about taking some LSD and I asked him what it was all about and he said he could quite easily get hold of some, so I said yes why not. I got to this stage in my life where I had been reading quite a lot about drugs and it kind of fascinated me a little and I thought yes why not I'll try it and at least I can say I've tried it. He came back after twenty minutes with these two little square bits of paper and so I took it and within half hour of me taking it the beginning of a frightening evening began.

I must of sat in the garden for an further thirty minutes and after feeling quite disappointed about the effects of the ecstasy tablet, which was quite a big thing back in those days and lots of people had spoken highly of the drug but it had disappointed me and I sat there waiting for the effects of this LSD trip I had taken and to be quite honest I started to wonder what the whole fuss was all about.

As I sat there talking to Nick he all of a sudden turned round to me and said his trip had started to kick in and his face lit up with delight, I guess at whatever images he was seeing and then he just suddenly got up and left, leaving me sitting there on my own. And I sat there wondering what on earth that was all about.

By this time I still hadn't seen any of the others and they were obviously unaware of what I had just taken and I know if I had of discussed it with Nicky she wouldn't have agreed.

But as I sat there, I looked off towards the left and there was this big tree and as I sat there staring at it, it all of a sudden turned bright pink and then pink round devil like faces appeared at the end of each of the branches and as I was staring in disbelief the branches all at once swooped back like a catapult and then headed very quickly in my direction. I turned away quickly to avoid being hit but when I looked back the tree was its normal self again. Well fuck me, it was a frightening sight seeing those devil faces heading towards me and it did rock me severely. I then obviously realised that what ever I had taken had just started to have its affect on me and to be quite honest I didn't like it. And after what I had just seen, I felt a sense of panic set in because if I was going to spend the next 6-8 hours looking at images that turned into evil fucking things then I didn't want to go through it.

I jumped up quickly and headed for the bar, I had read somewhere that drinking orange juice had a numbing effect on the

126

drug and so I ordered two of them and downed them in front of the bar girl who looked at me quite strangely as I ordered another couple. I took these drinks off into this room called the chill out room, which people go off into just to talk and chill, it was a quiet room with no music but there were loads of people in there and as I entered it appeared everyone was looking at me. I couldn't look at anyone for too long because their faces started to change. I hid myself away in the corner of that room and crunched myself up and finished off my drinks. I just remember not being able to look at one particular thing for too long because it would start to change shape and turn into things that were not nice. And so I tried my best to control the situation, I tried to control my mind over this drug but I think the mixture of drugs that I had taken that night, LSD and ecstasy started to have an awful affect on my brain. I jumped up and in my panic I went out the front door of the club where all the security and bouncers were standing and I remember saying to one of them "I need an ambulance," and as I said it the rest of the bouncers stared at me with disbelief at what I had just said. They asked me why and I told them straight out I had taken this LSD drug and it was affecting me really badly and I needed to get to a hospital. Well as I told them two police riot vans pulled into the club car park. So if my paranoia wasn't paranoid enough then the two riot vans pulling in didn't help the situation at all.

By this point the owner of the club had appeared and the last thing he wanted was trouble at his club and an ambulance pulling up outside the club that was already renowned for its drug problem was the last thing he wanted.

As these riot vans made their way round to the entrance, the owner of the club came up to the bouncer who I was talking to and told him to take me round the side of the club.

Looking back at that point of the evening, I think I was very lucky to have got away with what I had said to the bouncers and plus the police turning up, the owner didn't want me anywhere near them and so when he said to take me round the side of the club, I think I was lucky not to have been knocked out by this bouncer so that I wasn't able to cause a scene.

But that wasn't the case, in fact this particular bouncer started to talk to me quite sensibly and he tried to control the way I was thinking and feeling. He spoke about his previous experiences on drugs, in fact he told me one story about how he had woke up, after an evening of drug taking, in a ditch and not knowing where he was.

I found it quite funny but I was just pleased I had found someone who appreciated the situation I was in. By this time I still hadn't seen the others and quite frankly I wasn't concerned about them, I was just concerned about myself and the effects these drugs were having on my mind.

As this bouncer spoke to me, I think he noticed I was controlling myself a bit better than ten minutes previous and so he told me he was going to take me back inside the club and introduce me to a couple of his friends who he said would spend the evening with me making sure I was alright.

This was all unreal really because this club had such a bad reputation for the way the bouncers treated anyone over drugs and I had heard some horrific stories of what had happened to drug dealers who were caught in the club. And here I was telling them I had taken drugs and telling them I needed an ambulance and there they were treating me with great respect really, they didn't just leave me or throw me out of the club instead they took me back in there and tried to help me enjoy the rest of the evening.

So he introduced me to his friends, he explained to them what had happened to me, I remember them looking quite shocked at the amount of drugs that I had taken especially being my first time. Anyway they started talking to me and the bouncer went back outside, his friends were saying to me that I should just try and go along with it because there was nothing I could do about it, so they said try and enjoy what is happening and they also made the point in telling me, that if it appears that everyone is staring at you, they're not its just you being paranoid. They took me back to the dance floor area and I just started dancing.

It was a strange feeling, like I was actually floating; it didn't feel like dancing on wood, it felt like I was dancing on a bubble and everyone around me was jumping so high in the air. I was surrounded by friendly monsters jumping up and down. Obviously I wasn't but being on these drugs it just gave that illusion.

I started to relax a little mainly due to the bouncer and his two friends who didn't leave my side the whole night, I also felt quite relaxed about the whole situation with the security because they could have easily have thrown me out but instead, looking back they had also protected me from the police that evening because if the police had got wind I was taking LSD they would have arrested me and asked me all sorts of questions.

Then as I was dancing Nicky, Stuart and the rest of them came up to me and asked me where on earth I had been the whole evening and by this time Nick Brett had told them what I had taken and I told them I was having a bit of a rough time dealing with all these drugs that I had taken. Nicky said we were all leaving. I said thank you and goodbye to my newly found friends and walked out of the club and back into Sarah's car.

While being in the car the feeling of paranoia quickly came over me again and I remember Stuart looking at me and it appeared that he was constantly laughing at me and making stupid comments, I told him to shut the fuck up and told Sarah to get us home. Nicky was staying at mine that night.

My head on the way home just seemed to be buzzing, there seemed to be something inside that was flying around it and making this high pitch kind of noise constantly going round and round, I was still seeing images while I was going along in the car and I was just trying to go along with it, remembering what those two people in the club had said to me.

Just as we got back to my house, we stopped for some reason at the woods and we all got out of the car and for some reason Nicky and Sarah started running round the woods in a continuous circle. And as I stood there watching them running round their bodies turned into lights and I found myself standing watching this light show in the woods, it was the highlight of the evening.

As we headed for the front door I was just hoping that my mother wasn't up because she would have instantly known something was wrong with me and I know I wasn't in the right frame of mind to have been questioned by her.

Fortunately she wasn't up and so I said goodnight to Nicky and went into my own room (we always stayed in separate rooms when staying over each others house). The feeling of being alone in my room quickly came over me; throughout the whole evening somebody had been there for me. I started to feel scared again because of the visions I was having and so I went into Nicky's room and spent the rest of the evening with her. I didn't get any sleep and spent the night trying to control these drugs that were messing with my mind, it was a battle, a battle I'm not sure I won.

I spent the whole of the following day in bed while Nicky was downstairs with my Mum. Nicky eventually went home and then I decided to go downstairs and confront my Mum as to what had happened to me. I didn't tell her the truth, I lied about the whole event, I didn't want my Mum thinking her precious son who in her eyes was perfect basically doing well at college and who played cricket for Essex, I didn't want her thinking I had deliberately gone out and taken drugs. So I lied to her, I said my drink had been spiked at the nightclub and I was having an awful time getting over the effects from whatever was in my drink.

She made some dinner and we sat down at the table in the kitchen and in a way she sort of understood and told me that maybe it was a harsh lesson for you with regards to drugs and hopefully the experience will make you never want to go near them in the future.

I couldn't hide the fact to my Mum that I wasn't right and I was acting rather strangely so I told her what I thought I had been spiked with. It meant nothing to her, I could have turned up at the house with a bag of grass and she wouldn't have even questioned me.

But the effects of these drugs seemed to last, not just for that evening but all the following day and through to Monday as well. Whatever I had taken that night was a powerful drug something that I don't advise anyone to do.

Monday morning came about and Greg picked me up as usual and I told him what had happened. He was quite disappointed that I had taken this LSD without him; he was upset that I hadn't enjoyed my experience and was concerned I had seen the wrong side of LSD.

We got to college that day and I still wasn't feeling 100%, I hadn't spoken to Nicky the night before and for some reason I was feeling quite nervous about going to college that day. I had this paranoia that the entire college had found out what I had done and were going to persecute me for it. I remember walking into the canteen that morning and it appeared to me the entire college were in there and as I walked in it appeared to me everyone just stopped what they were doing and stared at me. With that I began to feel frightened again and paranoid, I started getting concerned that this drug I had taken on the Saturday had not only not worn off yet but I was wondering whether it had affected me permanently, I had heard stories before of how drugs can brain damage people and so it started to concern me a bit.

I went straight home and spoke to my Mum about the situation and she suggested that maybe I went to see the doctor.

I fed the doctor the same lines as I did my mother with regards to my drink being spiked, I'm not sure he believed me but he prescribed me some tablets that he said would help me to relax and help stop the feeling of paranoia. He also went on to say that maybe this unpleasant experience would make me think twice about taking drugs in the future.

I remember walking out of the surgery agreeing with him. I took these tablets and I remember feeling better a short time after, I don't know whether it was the effect the tablets were having on me or me just thinking I had swallowed something that was going to take all the bad feelings away.

I guess after such an awful experience and feeling so frightened at times and having to see my doctor about the whole episode, you wouldn't believe that within three days I would be back out with Greg and Paul experimenting with LSD again.

As I've said before Greg was quite concerned I had had a bad initial experience on LSD and I must of told him I had gone to see my doctor and I was feeling quite rough but him having that knowledge still didn't stop him from trying and persuading me over the next couple of days to go out with him and Paul one evening and do some LSD. He said it would be a totally different experience, he said I would be with two people who had done it before and would take care of me the whole evening. I dismissed it at the time but Greg had this great influence over me and had a great way of persuading me to do things, and in the end he must of sold me the idea and so I accepted.

And coming back from the Gray's area, where we had picked up this LSD, we all took it in his jeep heading back into Brentwood. We decided to go back to my house first and I told my Mum we were going to see one of Greg's friends in Havering and I would be gone the whole evening, I told her I was going to spend the night studying for one of my college assignments.

What we did then, we all got back into Greg's jeep and by this time we had all begun to come up on this LSD, we drove round the corner and left his jeep in one of the side roads near mine. We then spent the whole evening wandering round Brentwood. It was a bizarre night really. First we headed towards Warley where we bumped into some old friends, and they had instantly noticed that I was on drugs and so we quickly went our way. Being round normal people while you are on drugs is not a good thing.

We made our way from Warley to Ingrave, a small village just outside Brentwood, Greg was heading for The Halfway House, not because he wanted to go in the pub but because in that area there is a big roundabout for the A127, which you can either take for Southend or London, but on a previous LSD trip, Greg had made this same journey and when he finally got to the roundabout, he started to have visions of Jim Morrison being crucified on a cross and he wanted to take us there to see if we could see the same vision.

It was slightly different for me that evening from the previous one, I guess because I was surrounded by people I knew and thought I could trust, I felt a lot more secure but I was still fighting the effects the drug was having on me because I didn't particularly like what it was doing to my mind, I didn't like seeing things change shape and turning into different things, I didn't like that and so again I spent the whole evening fighting it, I didn't say a word to anyone the whole evening, I was just using all my energy to control my mind again. Totally in contrast to my friend Greg because he seemed to get off on the fact he was high on this particular drug. He walked beside me the whole of that evening making sure I was alright but also letting me know his thoughts and visions. And so as we approached the roundabout at the A127, Greg became excited at the prospect of seeing Jim Morrison again but I couldn't even look at the roundabout I was beginning to become frightened of the images my mind might allow me to see, I looked away and didn't force the issue.

We got to the roundabout and Greg had been disappointed, he never saw Jim that night and so I guess the day he did, he must have been on even stronger drugs. We all decided we had walked far enough that evening and it was time to go home. By this time it had turned extremely cold it was the middle of winter and there we were walking around in it. We had also attracted the police by this time the same police car had passed us about four times on the road that evening and Greg suggested that we cut through the woods to get back to mine, he thought if the police saw us anymore that evening they would stop and question us, which neither of us were in the right mood for.

We got back to Greg's jeep and it was totally frozen up and Greg had to drive it with his head hanging out the window to see where he was going and thank God the police didn't see us at that particular point.

We pulled up on my driveway and we got out of this frozen car shivering, my Mum opened the door and knew there was something not quite right. Greg instantly took over the situation and told my Mum the jeep had broken down and we had to wait for hours for the AA to turn up and that was the reason we were so cold.

My Mum followed Greg into the kitchen and he made tea for everyone, this was great because he diverted my Mum's attention away from me and therefore allowed me and Paul to go into the lounge.

We all stayed in the lounge that night and the last ever images I had of taking LSD was seeing all snakes and spiders crawling over the floor and so with that I went into the kitchen and took one of those tablets my doctor had given me and went upstairs to my room and went to sleep.

Well that was the last time I ever took LSD, its not a very nice drug, I don't recommend it to anyone, unless you want to be close to the devil that is, because that's all it is, fuckin evil shit. Apart from one other occasion when I went to a club in London with Nicky and tried Ecstasy again, I never again touched those kinds of drugs. LSD was not for me, it frightened me and with Ecstasy I just couldn't see the point of it and I came to the conclusion I could quite easily dance all night without having to take them. At the time they did fascinate me, I enjoyed clubbing and so the drug scene that came with it begun to intrigue me but I was lucky really because I didn't like those drugs so basically that was my only ever experience with Ecstasy and LSD. Thank God.

If anything positive came out of that evening then it was that Greg and me had become a lot closer. I could see he obviously liked me a lot, he had spent the whole of the evening with me not leaving my side and trying to make me have an enjoyable time, I guess some people would disagree and would say he wasn't a friend in the first place for making me take it again. But it was different, it wasn't like that, we were quite similar in personalities whereby we would both try anything once and if you are like that then drugs are going to be something you try in life. I don't ever regret doing it because I don't think you should have too many regrets about what you have done in life, I think you do certain things and go through events in life for a reason, for a purpose, not saying I would do it again because I wouldn't. I do sometimes wonder now though after going through my mental illness whether the LSD I had taken on those two occasions had opened up some part of my brain that would sometimes in the future make me very paranoid. Because on the two separate occasions when I became ill there was a huge amount of paranoia involved caused over certain organisations I was concerned about at the time. But as I sit here today and have overcome those periods in my life I do wonder whether it was the LSD I had taken that did actually cause those paranoias to come again later on in my life.

(16/02/04 I have just finished reading "A Royal Duty" by Paul Burrell, the main reason I read it was to see whether or not Princess Diana had ever mentioned or hinted anything at all to Paul about the direct connection between Hitler and a member of our Royal Family, I also wanted to read his stories and accounts while dealing with different members of the family and in my opinion he has painted a fairly decent picture of the main individuals. The book reflects well on our monarchy and gives the public a welcomed insight into their lives and personalities. His book mentions nothing about Princess Diana knowing anything regarding the Hitler affair, apart from maybe on the last page of the book when she writes to Paul Burrell and in the letter mentions a secret "What a secret?" and that is how the book ends, with the end shrouded in mystery over this secret. Well if Princess Diana knew about the biggest secret of all that being the one about a member of the Royal Family who was kept hidden from the public and then went onto rule Germany. If it was Princess Diana's intention to expose that secret and therefore bring down the House of Windsor. Then it is in my opinion that that secret, (maybe learnt from Prince Charles,) was the real reason why she was killed by our security services in Paris in 1997. It is also probably the reason why Paul Burrell's trial collapsed because it appears Paul Burrell also knows that secret and therefore the Royal Family could not risk such information coming out in his trial, therefore the Queen put a stop to it.

It would also not surprise me if Paul Burrell actually works for British Intelligence; he worked very closely to Princess Diana and worked all the hours under the sun, for not the greatest amount of money. He was privileged to be in the company of Princess Diana for many hours and had access to her private life and seemed to be trusted by her, so don't tell me the likes of MI5 never approached him and offered him money etc, to pass on information about her and her contacts, it all make sense really, because if the Establishment don't want things to happen then they don't. His book was apparently an embarrassment to our Royal Family and so they could have easily put a stop to it but I believe MI5 have used Paul Burrell and his memories to basically portray an image of the Royal Family that suits them and the monarchy.)

I became to trust Greg a lot more and we would often go out and have deep conversations about our beliefs in the world and our theories on different things. Greg was very ambitious and wanted desperately to be a worthy person and so did I and so we also had that in common.

I was doing quite well at college and Greg was also doing well. So we carried on at college but I always remember as I was going through college in those early months thinking I couldn't see myself at college for the next two years studying for that business diploma. It felt like I was being held back on the world and I didn't like that feeling. There was also nothing I could do about it at the time because I had no other options and so I did stay there for a while. I completed my course work, which to my surprise I was doing alright in.

But I also remember thinking I knew I didn't really have to complete the course because I knew my Dad's project, the Hitler affair was just about to explode into the spotlight of the world's media and so I would be taken out of college for more important purposes.

This same pattern of thinking, like when I was at school, once again cropped up, in fact this way of thinking dominated my life and my decision making until I reached the age of 21, when finally reality started to kick in and the gradual realisation of my situation began to frighteningly sink in, it then took me a few years to come to terms with the reality of my life at the time, it took so long because my brain had been brain washed and set to a way of thinking that controlled my life and so when my subconscious decided it was time to come to terms with reality and prepare me for the future, (which would be a very different future to the one I had imagined,) it took time to adjust and to be honest I have never really 100% adjusted, but going through what I have witnessed and was responsible for starting, it is hard to forget and hard to now try and live a normal life.

The time had come in Greg's relationship and mine when it was time to talk to Greg about what I was involved in. He had come round one evening while my Mum was out; he had brought a big lump of gear and after a few joints Greg again started to talk about his ambitions and the money he was going to make and how he was going to take me with him, he said it would be a great partnership. I remember listening to him but it all went over my head because I thought it was all bollocks because there was no need for me to go down those working roads because my empire was already in the making and it was just a question of when.

So while outside smoking these joints and after listening to Greg's dreams, I decided to tell him. I gave him the whole bit, I told him everything (apart from the royal connection because at that point I knew very little of it and Dad had also not really started that side of his research)

He took it all on board quite well but was still quite shocked that his newly found friend was involved in something so great. I could see the same excitement in him I must have shown to others when I first found out and he instantly started seeing pound signs and he wanted to know more, he questioned me all night about The Album and the other revelations and he wanted to get involved, he wanted to know why nothing had happened and I explained it was a difficult subject for most people to accept. He suggested to me we both went over to my Dads in Dagenham.

Obviously I was pleased at Greg's reaction to what I had just told him. In the past I had seen people react a lot differently, I had seen the side where people thought my Dad was mad and would joke and laugh at him behind his back but that was the reaction you got, people either laughed at you or they were very serious about the whole thing.

And it was fortunate Greg took it seriously because that would probably have been the end of our relationship.

I was quite surprised at his reaction, I had been with Nicky a few months now and had not even told her what I was involved in, at the time I didn't want her involved in it I didn't want to risk our friendship which had developed, she didn't need to know at the time, I guess I would of told her if the subject was going to hit the newspapers or if the auction was going to go ahead but at that point of our relationship there was no need to rock the boat, we were enjoying ourselves going out and being together and it was nice being with someone who knew nothing about my background.

I hadn't seen my Dad for quite a while. Throughout this affair we had a relationship where we would see each other for a while and then we wouldn't. It was down to both of us really, we were very similar in our personality and I guess sometimes we just clashed and what with us both being stubborn there would be long periods of silence between us. And at that present point we were going through one of those periods, I had broken away from Dad because he had gone off in a different area of research that I wasn't concerned about and didn't interest me, I was only interested in The Album because I could see that as something that could be sold and money be made from it and so he had gone off in this different direction, I had seen him a few times during those months but they were never meetings of what a Dad and son should be like, he would sometimes come round to the house trying to smash the door down, he would ring the house all the time, trying to reach my Mum and convince her of his beliefs and all sorts of shit like that.

But it was because of Greg that one night we went over to see my Dad and it was good really because it put an end to that particular silence. And so from that point me and my Dad began to communicate again.

I knew obviously about The Album but knew little of the other revelations, so as I sat there in his house in Dagenham watching him go through everything with Greg, I became fascinated. And it was also interesting to see my Dad perform his magic on Greg, I could see Greg was totally absorbed by the subject and totally blown away by my Dad's personality and his energy that he showed for the subject.

We were there for three to four hours and I was slightly nervous because I knew what my Dad was all about and taking my good friend round there was a risk, I was wondering what Greg's reaction was going to be after we left my Dad's house. Greg could have easily have been exaggerating his interest in front of my Dad and he could have mocked my Dad once we had left but he didn't, he was genuine and fascinated by it all, he also began to think like I did, we would thereafter have lots of conversations and dreams about what we were going to do with all the money which was coming our way. My Dad had given Greg the whole story and had sold him the dream. Dad was always looking for people to invest in his project. Dad always had a plan to what to do next but it normally involved needing money. So if he could convince (which he did very well) anyone to invest money in him then he would.

Dad quickly cottoned onto the fact that Greg had a bit of money in his bank. Greg had inherited some money when his father had died a few years earlier, he had spent most of it on cars but did still had five thousand pound left. Dad knew that I would not allow one of my friends to invest money in him because I had seen people previously invest their money into Dad but his promises were never delivered and I couldn't bear to see one of my friends lose their money.

But my Dad did ask Greg to withdraw money from his bank and leave the cash under his bed. Dad told Greg he was concerned over the security of the family because of the threat of the newspapers leaking the story. Dad told him if he got wind of that ever happening he would have to get his immediate family out of the country. Greg saw where my Dad was coming from and agreed to withdraw the money on the understanding it would only be used for an imminent escape of the country because of the shit hitting the fan.

They both agreed.

Over the next few months or so, I would spend a lot more time with Greg discussing the Hitler affair, we were still into smoking cannabis and of an evening we would go out in his jeep and plot up in some country lane and sit there smoking joints and talking about our delusions for the future when we had all this money around us.

My whole life at this point was surrounded by fantasy really, I still went to college and was still involved in the cricket set-up for Essex but there was this other side to my life that was totally taking over and now Greg was now involved and also had the same visions at my father with regards the money side of things, it made everything seem so real. I also think the drugs I was taking at the time gave me a heightened sense of fantasy; I think they opened my imagination to unrealistic ambitions and dreams, which in the end would cause me to do such outrageous things.

My relationship with Nicky had started to suffer a little due to me spending more and more time with Greg and also my relationship with my father started to develop again just before Christmas. I do remember spending time with her when it was her birthday, which was early in December. But we were slowly drifting apart and I was becoming tiresome of her continuing route down the ecstasy road, I also wasn't sure whether I could 100% trust this girl and to be honest my plans I had made with Greg for after we became rich, did not include her and so at that point I was not too concerned over which way our relationship was going.

One of the final memories I have of college was when it was mine, Paul and Greg's birthday, all at the same time within a few days of each other. It was also the last few days at college before the Christmas break and everyone wasn't going to see each other for a while because straight after Christmas we all began our three week work experience.

So everyone decided during the lunch break, that we would go down to The Plough, a local pub in South Ockendon, to celebrate our birthdays and generally have a fare well drink.

Everyone from the business studies seemed to be in the pub and half of all the girls from the travel and tourism as well, they had all come along to celebrate our birthdays and to have a Christmas drink.

The lecturers did not welcome our attitude towards college by then and it had also rubbed off on a few of our fellow colleagues. And so the drinking began and it got heavier and heavier as the day went on and was mainly orchestrated by Greg, he had a great way when entertaining everyone and so most people stayed until it was time to go back to the college for the last lesson of the year.

Greg started buying rounds of Jack Daniels and by that time I didn't care what I was drinking and as I drank one there would soon be another replacing it. It was the first and last time I would drink whisky neat and after a while everyone in that pub that day was slaughtered. But it was a funny day and we celebrated our birthdays in style.

The stupid thing we did after the pub was Greg drove back to the college. He was in no fit state to drive and if the police would have seen us we would of definitely been pulled over because Greg was driving at stupid speeds and going all over the road. We were lucky that day to have survived but Greg would never learn his lesson and he picked me up once drunk a few years later and on that night we would not be so lucky.

We all got back to the college and everyone went back to their final lesson, everyone was drunk and the whole of the college became very rowdy. I was the most drunk and I decided to participate in Greg's lesson rather than my own, I'm not sure I meant to or whether it was just me following Greg. But while being in the lesson that afternoon I began to feel horribly sick inside, my whole stomach felt like it was on fire and I quickly ran out of the class and made my way down the stairs towards the back exit of the college. I managed to reach it and opened the door and was violently sick everywhere and I just remember sitting there with two girls who had followed me down to make sure I was alright. Greg once again took over the situation and got me home safely and made me numerous amounts of coffee, which sorted me out.

My birthday and Christmas came along and I remember the best present you could possibly wish for when you turn seventeen, that was from my Nan and it was driving lessons.

I hadn't seen too much of Nicky over that period, I had seen her briefly to give her presents but I chose that year to spend Christmas eve with my friends at the Eagle and Child, our local pub. Everyone knew each other in there and it was a nice place to spend the evening but Nicky obviously didn't think so because the following day (Christmas Day) she phoned me from a pub, she was drunk and all I could hear was blokes voices in the background and she tried to make me feel jealous regarding them. I told her there and then that I didn't want to see her anymore and I didn't appreciate the way she was behaving.

That Christmas was spent with my Mum, brother and Nan, Amanda Hartman and her family came round and of course Greg was there to entertain everyone. It was a nice Christmas but it was a shame about me and Nicky and the way we had split up but we weren't meant to be together, it was nice at the time and she showed me a few different things in life but there was where it was meant to end. I liked to be surrounded by people I could trust and unfortunately Nicky in the end wasn't one of them.

I knew I was going to have to see her again because she went to the same college as me and so it was inevitable, but she made the whole situation a lot worse. She would continue to phone me afterwards and would say the most horrible things to me, she would say she was pregnant, which I didn't believe and had one of my friends find out and it turned out to be a total lie. She also said she had had an AIDS test and that the result was positive, which was a horrible thing to have to listen to but again I didn't believe it. Yet when someone says something like that no matter how ridiculous it sounds at the time, after a while you do start to wonder if they are telling the truth. Subsequently I visited my doctor again in the New Year and asked him for a complete medical and he asked me for what reason. I told him the full story of what Nicky had said and he told me there was more chance of me getting run over by a bus in Brentwood High St than having the AIDS virus, he also said it was a horrible thing for anyone to lie about and suggested I chose my next girlfriend with more care.

The only positive thing that came out of this was in the future I would be a lot more careful about women and the risks involved, even though Nicky had lied to me about having AIDS it was still a frightening feeling thinking that maybe I did have it. In the future I would be a lot more careful with whom I was with and what I was doing and to be honest that experience stopped me many times in the future from risking my health.

I spent two weeks work experience at Scorpio's a health club in Warley, Brentwood and I spent those weeks working in the gym dealing with customers and doing routine stuff, it was good and I enjoyed it, I made friends with a few of the staff but I had got to the point where the college had set a massive assignment surrounding this work experience and I just couldn't see myself completing it. I just didn't want to put in the effort, I had a lot more important things going on in my life and so me wasting my time writing about some gym in Brentwood seemed pointless. I didn't have any other option at the time apart from just finishing this work experience, but at the end of the second week Greg phoned me at work while I was in the middle of wondering what I was going to do with myself. He gave me the option I was looking for which meant I could leave college and therefore not have to complete this assignment.

Greg was working for Victoria Jewellers at Lakeside and he had come up with an idea with regards to opening a shop in Lakeside. I listened intently to his ideas and he told me he wanted to use the rest of his inheritance to do something worthwhile, he also said he didn't wish to go back to college. He had come up with quite a unique idea whereby he was going to offer people the chance to part exchange their second hand Levi jeans for other bits of clothing in the shop and then re-sale the second hand jeans, which at the time was fashionable.

He offered me a partnership in the business and I immediately said yes, he had given me the get out clause I was looking for, not only could I leave college, I could also leave my work experience, I left a week early due to them putting me on ground work duty and because the weather was so cold at the time.

I had also learnt from friends from college that Nicky had been spreading rumours about me in the past two weeks and she had created a massive tension between her friends and mine, and had basically divided the college into two camps, one being people that believed her and the other being my loyal friends who basically thought she was mad. But I didn't really want to spend another minute of my time at that college and having to study under those circumstances made me cringe, so this idea by Greg had come up at just the right time.

Greg would come round regularly and we would discuss our ideas for the shop and make plans for it but the day was approaching when we had to go back to college and we would have to make a decision about our future there.

We got to the college that morning in late January, I hadn't completed any of the assignment and I had three options, one follow Greg's idea, two follow my Dad in his pursuits or thirdly stay at college for another 18 months. I had spoken to my Mum about it and she thought the idea of the shop was a good one, she thought I was destined to be in business one day and so if that opportunity had presented itself then she thought I should follow it, she even arranged for us to talk to one of her friends who owned a clothes shop in Coggeshall.

I walked into the canteen that morning with the pressure of not knowing what to do but as I walked in I immediately noticed the tension between my set of friends and Nicky's. I also noticed Nicky looking at me in a smug way, I stood there for a minute, I took one final look at everyone and walked out. It was the last time I set foot in that college and the last time I ever saw Nicky.

The realisation of what I had done quickly came over me when I got home. We had both decided to leave college and Greg had found himself in the same boat as me. It was a strange feeling really, I had got home and after a short time began to realise the predicament that I was in. I had just left college, had no girlfriend and I had no job and therefore no income. I knew I had come to an end of an era, my school and college days were now over and now I had to start my way in the working world. (The job that I had down at the cricket shop had also gone because the shop had closed down due to lack of sales over the winter period.)

But I do remember feeling very confident about the future, no matter what situation I found myself in, I would always have great hope, whether it be hope that I had generated or hope my Dad had given me over the prospect of his affair breaking.

In those days I never got down about the things I had done and never worried about the future or the consequences of my actions because I always seemed to have hope in my life. I was always a positive person anyway but this hope that was generated for me gave me the determination to carry on.

But it dawned on me I either had to set this business up fairly quickly or go out and find a job. My Mum was quite keen for me to set this business up with Greg and so she didn't get on my case too much over me leaving college but I also knew sooner or later she would require housekeeping money from me.

Greg and I put all our efforts into setting up this business at Lakeside Shopping Centre. We had arranged an initial meeting with Lakeside management to discuss the possibility of us renting a unit from them. Greg had worked previously at Yankee Doodle in Brompton Walk and so was quite experienced when dealing with this kind of shop. He had also made a lot of contacts within the business.

And so I did wonder why he needed me but never questioned him too much over that, I guess he just wanted to take me along for the ride and so I rode with it.

We had named the business GT's obviously after our first names and Greg was very positive about his plans for the shop and his plans of the future for GT's. Greg was never satisfied with having ample; he was always looking at the bigger picture.

I also had great visions for the future regarding our shop, we would both go along in his jeep talking about the chain of GT shops that we would one day own.

Greg had asked me to go into partnership with him, I wasn't going to lose anything and so I accepted, Greg was putting in the money and I was there just for the ride.

The initial meeting at Lakeside went ahead, we hadn't done much research into the shop by that stage, we hadn't contacted a bank, we hadn't done any market research and we didn't have a business plan, so we were just playing it by ear, I think we were mainly concerned over whether or not Lakeside were going to rent us a unit.

The meeting was held by two men, one was fairly old and the other looked as young as we were. And their main concerns over Greg and I was our age and our experience and also whether the shop was unique enough to survive at Lakeside. They were also quite concerned that there was already a number of clothes shops at Lakeside and therefore stressed to us the importance of our shop being different from the rest.

With concerns to our experience fortunately Greg had worked in Lakeside at Yankee Doodles and Victoria Jewellers and I also had my experience from working in the cricket shop, so all this in my opinion was sounding quite good.

Our age concerned them and obviously there was no getting away from that, I was seventeen and Greg was nineteen and so we stressed that people of our age had set up business before and so we argued on that point, I also pointed out to the younger manager that he was also quite young to have such an influential job, therefore age shouldn't be taken in to consideration.

Then they told us the only space available to rent was down in the market stall area. It was in an area away from the main shopping area but the market area was also well known for its original and individuality.

They took us down to show us the unit which was available, it was a fairly big unit compared to some of the others but still not quite what we had imagined and we both felt a bit dispirited.

But after thinking about it, we came to the conclusion it was a start for us and if we did well and created a good reputation then we could have upgraded our premises in the future.

We got back into their office and they were concerned we didn't have a business plan or any banking facilities and he also wanted to know the brands and the kind of clothes we would be selling in the shop. He told us he would like to see us again in two weeks and asked us to bring along our business plan and some samples of what we would be selling.

We walked away from that meeting feeling quite confident about the whole thing and it appeared if we played our cards right and gathered the information and the materials necessary then Lakeside would offer us a unit at their shopping centre.

This news was greatly received by my Mum and it appeared my decision to leave college was the right one.

We had decided Greg was going to take care of the business plan and the banking side of things; he was going to approach Lloyds (where his Mum worked) for help with the business plan and for an account but we were also going to apply for a business loan.

It was my responsibility to find and approach a supplier and try and get some samples of clothing that we were going to sell. Greg didn't want to use his contacts at that point because he didn't want the owner of Yankee Doodle finding out we were opening a shop only a few yards away and so he didn't want to upset them at this early stage.

The previous year I had ordered the Yellow Pages for central London mainly for the listings of nightclubs in the London area. But also for the numbers of car dealerships so I could phone up Porsche etc, and order brochures on the cars I was going to buy with the proceeds from Hitler's album.

144

So I used this book to track down clothing manufactures and suppliers and after numerous amounts of phone calls I found this man who owned a shop and a market stall in Brixton. I explained the situation and said he would be more than happy to help; he said I could visit his shop and take away a few samples with the intention of ordering larger amounts in the future.

Within a week of us leaving college things seemed to be moving at quite a pace. Greg had arranged the meeting with the bank and I had arranged a meeting with this chap in Brixton but unfortunately the two meetings coincided with each other. So I went to London and Greg went to the bank.

Greg's main objective at the bank was obviously to open up an account but also to apply for a business loan; he had money from his inheritance but still wanted a further sum of money to fall back on. He thought because he knew everyone at Lloyds and also his Mum working there that he had a good chance of getting the loan. The loan was for £7000 and therefore would give us enough capital to buy our stock and get us on our way.

Things seemed to be looking quite good. Sometimes when things are going too well I always wonder what's round the corner, always have done, not used to things going well but anyway my day was spent in London. I got the train and made my way round to Brixton, the journey seemed to take forever. I had to walk for about ten minutes through the high street until I found this chap's shop.

He owned quite a big clothing shop and I got dressed up to try and give the impression of someone who was in business. I met this chap, Paul I think his name was. He was a fairly trendy chap with long blonde hair. He was a very friendly bloke and a very trusting one at that. We sat down and I explained to him my plans for the shop and where I wanted to go with it and so I guess he could see I wasn't some idiot or wasn't there to rip him off because he told me I could walk round his shop and anything I thought was appropriate to show Lakeside management he said I could take. And so with that he gave me a number of empty bags and I spent time looking at different clothing and picked out what I thought would impress. It wasn't necessarily what we were going to sell, I just needed to get hold of some samples to impress Lakeside management, they had wanted us in but they wanted us selling unique and individual clothing.

It was a very strange feeling looking and selecting all those clothes and then putting them into bags and walking out the shop without having to pay for them.

And I must have walked out with at least five bags of gear from his shop. He was the most trusting person I think I have ever met because he didn't even know my phone number, he didn't know who I was and so I don't know what I had said to him but I must of come over extremely well for him to allow me to do that, I was walking out with a good couple of hundred pounds worth of gear. I told him I would be back within a week and that I would phone him to let him know the results from Lakeside management.

Greg picked me up from Brentwood Station and bad news was waiting for me. I put the bags in the back of the jeep and got in. Greg wasn't looking too happy and I asked him what was wrong and he said the bank manager at Lloyds was willing to set up a business account for us but was not willing to lend us at that point any money to help us start the business.

Greg took this quite badly, I didn't have any cash to put in, I was skint. What it meant for Greg was, he was going to have to use his £5000, which was left over from his inheritance to set the whole business up. £5000 was enough but wasn't a huge amount to begin with, it didn't give us enough working capital, it gave us enough to set up and buy us some stock but there wouldn't be a lot left over. And that worried Greg a little; it also worried him that he was using the last of his Dad's inheritance.

The day quickly came around when it was time for us to have our next meeting with Lakeside management. Greg had put together the business plan and we had put a demonstration of the clothing samples together. We were going back armed with the samples they wanted and the business plan and all the answers to their questions.

So we were well prepared for our final meeting and were quite confident the outcome would be positive. We got dressed up in our smartest clothes, Greg was wearing a suit and I was wearing black trousers and a shirt and tie and a brown jacket from Next that Greg had lent it me. We made our way to Lakeside in Greg's jeep.

The meeting was held by the same two gentlemen we had seen initially and their attitude towards us had slightly changed, it was a more reserved attitude and I could sense their scepticism about the whole thing. Greg had also picked up on this as well. They weren't as positive as the previous meeting and I guess they were having second thoughts about our ideas, our age and experience.

Greg sat back and I think came to the conclusion things weren't working out and so subsequently I took over the meeting.

They were mainly concerned by how many clothes shops there were already at Lakeside and another one opening in the market area meant there was a risk to us for losing our money and wasting out time and they seemed concerned over that.

I knew at that point I didn't have any other options open to me, Greg did, he could have gone back to work for Victoria Jewellers but I had nothing to fall back on, so I gave them a presentation of the clothing that even surprised myself.

I came across very confident about the products that I had got from Brixton and spoke in depth about each product and explained why they would be different from all other clothes sold at Lakeside and I also brought up the idea of Greg's unique plan for second hand Levi jeans.

But I was quite forceful over the uniqueness of the clothes we were going to sell in the shop and put my point across well and it was received well. I also made the point of how serious we were about the project how and we had both given up college to pursue it. So after a further ten minutes of discussing the whole idea, the head manager turned round to us and said that they would offer us a unit in the market stall area for a trial period of three months.

I felt when he offered us a trial period he was doing it to cover himself. He had given us this opportunity but I felt I had sold him the idea and without me actually doing that I don't think they were even going to give us a trial. But he was reluctant to do it, that reluctance made us feel quite aware of the situation.

We said goodbye, and we all shook hands, we told them we would think about it and get back to them.

We stopped at McDonalds for a coffee and discussed what we were going to do. Greg had come to the conclusion he was not willing to put his £5000 into a project that was a risk but was also only on a three-month trial basis.

So that was the end of that little project. I was fairly disappointed, I had seen a future for the business and the potential of it and I think Greg and me would have made a good partnership, I know the business would have been a success. We were two strong willed, lively personalities who would have been the front of the business and would of attracted customers and I know it would have been a success.

I guess looking back on that period, at the time you can't understand why certain things are happening, I can pin point why certain things happened and in this case I believe the setting up and the initial idea of the shop was to take me away from college, where I was obviously not meant to be. It was right at the time I had spent four good months there, I had met Nicky there and had met some good friends. But as I say that business idea took me away from college and it also took me away from Nicky and her influences and had now set me down a different road because now I was in a position in life where I needed to find a job.

My relationship with Greg also started to drift apart slightly from then on, we still saw each other now and again over the next few years but as I say we started to grow apart. His relationship with his girlfriend Nicky intensified and he also began his career in car sales eventually going onto work for Mercedes Benz. The last time I ever saw him was while I was in Warley Mental Hospital in 1996, he had come to see me to try and lift my spirits, I hadn't seen him for a while but he knew that I had been totally involved with my father and so thought he could get through to me. The last I heard he was living in France with Nicky.

During my stay in hospital in 1996, I in my paranoia would look back at different situations and different people and would wonder whether they were introduced into my life by MI5, so that they could steer it into a direction that would prepare me for the mission. I wondered if Greg was one of those people. He had come in and out of my life like a whirlwind and had without doubt affected the direction of it.

He introduced me to a more destructive way of life with regards to drugs and Jim Morrison but also steered me away from college but most importantly he took an interest in my Dad's work and therefore it was because of Greg that my relationship with my Dad continued. That I believe at the time was the main intention of MI5, so that what was just about to happen in the story was witnessed by myself, so it would give me a greater belief and a real feeling of importance and hope. If that was the case then Greg had done his job perfectly well and succeeded in his orders.

I took the samples back to Paul in Brixton and thanked him for his help and his trust. I had explained what had happened at Lakeside and he actually there and then offered me a job, he must of seen my potential and my ambition and he offered me this job at his market stall in the Brixton area.

Obviously I was flattered and considering I needed a job it was temping to accept but Brixton was miles away from Brentwood and also working on a market stall was not quite what I had in mind.

My Mum suggested that I went back to college to catch up on my course work and to finish the course, I told her I wasn't going to, she told me I would have to go out and find a job.

In the month of March in 1992 I passed my driving test, I had ten lessons, I was taught by a chap called David Leigh and I passed first time of asking.

My Dad had already taught me how to drive years ago, he would let me sit on his lap and allow me to steer the car and as time went by he would gradually teach me more and eventually let me drive his car on my own.

I had also been practising in my mother's car and she allowed me to drive whenever we needed to go anywhere. I also picked up many good tips from my mother's second cousin, Nigel Nunn's. Nigel comes from Wiltshire and is a keen follower of Rallying; he had previously taken my brother and I to a race meeting and had also demonstrated his skills to us through the winding roads of Chippenham.

He and his wife had come down for one weekend to see us and so it gave me the perfect opportunity to ask him many questions about driving. At that point I was having trouble going round sharp bends, I was O.K. going round them normally but had trouble going round them at speed and so Nigel took me out in my mother's four door Rover 216 and showed me exactly how to do it. It was just a matter of dropping down a gear and keeping the revs up just before you go round the bend. He also showed me a few other things with regards to the pedals and showed me some major points to watch out for when driving, he especially made me aware of a number of things when overtaking. Nigel in that afternoon taught me some driving skills that David Leigh would never have taught me, it was more advanced driving but I was grateful to him for that.

I had also picked up many tips from a man from the Cricket Club, he was a specialist driver for the police force and I believe today is a driver for the Diplomatic Protection Service. But on away matches I would always try and jump in with him and get a lift in his car. He was a fast driver but also a safe one and he would always point out to me the dangers that lay ahead and made me aware of things to look out for when overtaking cars e.g. he said never overtake a car when there is a right hand turn coming up because very rarely does a driver who is turning left out of that turning look left, he only looks right before pulling out and so wouldn't see you overtaking and therefore it would be very dangerous. And so he would give me all this different kind of advice, which at the time meant nothing but once I got behind the wheel of my own car all his advice came flooding back.

I remember the day of my driving test, I had joked previously to Greg's stepfather that maybe he could take my test so that I was guaranteed a pass but he said he wasn't allowed to test friends or family.

I do remember in the test that I did actually go up two curbs, everything else I did went perfectly well. I got back to the test centre and I was quite sure he was going to fail me but for some reason he didn't.

I had already arranged to go out with my friends that night; I was so confident I was going to pass that I had made arrangements to go out with Alister and his friend Phil Apicella in my Mum's car.

I remember getting home that day from the driving test and I was so excited, I rang my Mum and told her the good news and also phoned my Nan who had paid for the lessons in the first place and she was obviously pleased for me.

I didn't have a car of my own and Mum was at work with her car but I do remember getting on my bike and going for a massive bike ride over Thorndon Park. I rode for hours full of joy and excitement at what I had just achieved.

I spent that night driving my Mum's car around with Al and Phil in the car. I remember having my first race that night, I remember overtaking my first car and we spent the whole night just driving round, we clocked up hundred miles that night in my Mum's Rover.

I remember after I dropped Al and Phil off, it was the first time I had been in the car on my own and it was a great feeling. It was a feeling of a step up in life but a real sense of freedom came over me as I drove home that evening.

So now I knew I had to find a job, save up some money and buy a car of my own because unfortunately my father's project had not delivered the riches it had promised and the Porsche 911 that I expected to be driving around in was not on the driveway.

I was quite determined at that point in my life to get on. I had just passed my driving test, I had left college and my Mum was now providing for my brother and me. She was out working everyday and I did feel a sense of responsibility come over me and I did feel it was my time in life to crack on.

I remember sitting in the lounge one day in March 1992 racking my brains out, thinking about what I wanted to do. I thought about going up into the city and finding a job as a Stockbroker. I made a few enquires, I got my Yellow Pages out and phoned a few banks and they suggested I write in with my CV attached. But it didn't feel right; I didn't particularly want to spend the rest of my life getting on a train going up to London everyday.

I thought to myself I would start a valeting business. I had made quite a fair bit of money from it in the past and had been quite successful and I enjoyed it so I thought to myself that is what I would do. I would invest in a small van and buy a few bits and pieces and start up my round again.

The thought about the valeting just came to me from nowhere and the minute it came into my head I thought it was a good idea and went with it.

I immediately got on the phone to one of my old customers Malcolm Harrison, he had been one of my regular customers and had also helped me by recommending me to his friends and neighbours.

I phoned him at his office, he owned a company called Space Maker, which was a bedroom supply, and fitting company. I told him my intentions and he said he already had a car valeter, a man with a family and kids to provide for.

I think Malcolm must of picked up some kind of desperation in my voice and approach because he there and then offered me a job at his warehouse in Hutton, he said it would be five days a week from eight until five, working in the warehouse as a general odd job boy, he told me I would be on £100 a week.

I accepted his offer. I thought it would do me for now and it would also give me the opportunity to save a bit of money for my van. He said I could start the following Monday.

I was grateful to Malcolm for offering me this job but the money didn't seem that great and I needed a lot more to get my valeting business off the ground and so I went through the job section in the Brentwood Gazette that week. And there was a travel company in Brentwood offering part time telesales jobs. So I phoned them up and spoke to a lady called Jane Martin Philips, she said they were interviewing that day and would I be interested in coming down for an interview straight away. I said yes and asked her where they were and she told me they were in Warley Hill.

When I got there it was quite a strange moment really because the travel company was directly opposite where I had worked for the cricket shop and so when I stood at the window of the shop all those months ago and wondered what all those people were doing walking in to that shop, I was now ironically just about to find out.

The front of the shop looked like a travel agents with beautiful pictures of beaches etc everywhere but as you walked through the next door it was just one big room with about thirty phones in it. Jane met me and she took me through into the next room, which was her office.

Jane was manager of the Brentwood office and I sat down with her and she explained what the job entailed and explained what the company was all about. The company was called Tomorrows World Today International (TWTI) and they were a timeshare company selling timeshares in the Canary Islands. The company's head office was in Grays but this office in Brentwood was their marketing office. Its purpose was to get members of the public to go to exhibitions in either Grays or Rochester with the main aim of selling them a timeshare.

To do this, the marketing department in Brentwood employed some thirty people to randomly phone people out of the phone book and tell them they had been selected to receive a free seven-day holiday in either the Costa del Sol, the Algarve or the Canary Islands. And if the people on the phone answered yes to three questions, regarding their status to confirm whether they were homeowners and married then they were told they had won this holiday and told all they had to do was go to one of these exhibitions and pick up their travel documents. A letter confirming their appointment and also included details of their holiday was posted to them. It was all very professionally done. They were never told the exhibition was to do with timeshares but they were aware they had to go through a short holiday presentation to receive their holiday.

As you can imagine many people turned up to these exhibitions but hardly anyone took the holiday. That was because the holiday would very cleverly be arranged to be totally inconvenient to the customer. e.g. you could only take the holiday in school time or they would say you had to fly from somewhere like Liverpool and so these kinds of arrangements would put most people off.

152

Jane told me I would receive thirty minutes of training and then I would work on my own but with a script and with a question and answer page. The hours of the job were between 6-9 in the evenings and they would pay ten pound per shift, the minimum amount of shifts per week was four and the maximum was nine, being two shifts on a Saturday and two on a Sunday. She said I could start the following Wednesday.

Well I walked out of that building feeling quite proud of myself realising I had got the first job I had ever been for. I was told later that basically anyone who went for that particular job got it. But I still felt pleased with myself because within a very short period of time I had found two jobs.

It was also in this period of March/April 1992 that my relationship with my Dad started to re-establish itself, mainly from the day when I had gone round there with Greg. He started involving me more so in his affairs little by little probably sometimes without me even knowing it.

But my Mum did become aware of his continuous ringing of the house and the long conversations I would have with him.

It was also in this period that my father had taken me to Peterborough to get a passport. He was just about to hold meetings and plan certain operations and he felt it would be best if I were out the country while they were happening. My name on my Dad's passport had long expired and so he thought it was essential I went and got one immediately. My Mum was aware of my trip to Peterborough and came quite concerned over me and my intentions because she thought I was just about to go on another overseas trip with my Dad.

I never spoke to my Mum about anything to do with my Dad, mainly because I knew she didn't believe The Album was written by Hitler but also because she thought my Dad was mad. And so her attitude towards him would sometimes affect our relationship quite badly, I was 100% behind my father and his beliefs and so anyone who questioned him or showed him disrespect I took a dislike to.

Looking back I can understand why my Mum had nothing to do with him, he has been quite destructive in the past and had caused all sorts of problems for Mum and Gary and so she decided to ignore him and tried blanking him out of her life. But at the time it was frustrating for me because I knew Dad was 100% right over his findings and no one wanted to help him or listen and so this would start to make me feel angry. I would slowly start to become intolerant to my Mum's attitude towards him and her extreme lack of interest in the affair and we began to clash and argue.

My Mum was extremely happy when I told her I was just about to start two jobs, she was even more happy when I told her one of those jobs was at Malcolm Harrison's business. Mum had known Malcolm from years ago, she thought it was a good opportunity for me and a good prospect, however she was slightly dubious about my other job; timeshare didn't have the best of reputations.

My first ever whole week at work was the most boring, uneventful, pure drudgery and the worst ever working week I have ever had. It wasn't the people I was working with because they were generally O.K. and were just trying to make ends meet. It was the repetitiveness of the job and the factory conditions that did it for me. I was constantly looking at my watch waiting for the next break or for home time. I was achieving nothing and there was no way I could see myself working there for too long, in fact after the second day I decided that I would only stay until the end of the week and that would give me one weeks wages of £100 which I intended to use for a trip to Potter's in Norfolk that had been arranged by Stuart during that week.

That week felt like the longest working week I have ever had and I truly believe I did the right thing when I walked out after only five days. And every time I see people working in a factory that dreaded memory comes back to me, I also feel sorry for anyone who works in such conditions but I also appreciate the only reason they are doing it is to support their families and I also know if someone came along and gave those people an alternative they would take it.

My Mum was furious at me for walking out of that job, not only had I given up a full time job but in her eyes I had let her down and made her look bad and had also let Malcolm down. I appreciated Malcolm giving me the job and opportunity but if things don't feel right in life you must address them no matter whom it upsets.

I had also started my part time job at TWTI that week; I had worked on the Wednesday and the Thursday. Again the work was fairly repetitive but there was something about the whole set-up and the nature of the people that I liked. And I also found out I was quite good at the job, I created sixteen leads in those two shifts and eights of those leads turned up to the exhibition, it was a good percentage and so Jane was pleased with my initial efforts.

So now I had lost my full time job but had kept my part time job to my Mum's disgust.

I spent the entire £100 I had earned from Space Maker that week on my weekend away at Potter's forgetting to give my Mum any house keeping. The whole weekend was spent getting stupidly drunk and participating in long sessions of cannabis intake. And so in my intoxication and irrational thinking I agreed to a dare that Stuart had presented me. He dared me to have a crew cut and so in the madness of the situation the following morning we all went to the local barbers and I had all my hair cut off.

My mother's reaction to this when I got home was very emotional. She opened the door and burst into tears. She had at that point also been worrying about my recent actions over the past months and was worrying about my future. The fact that my continuous interest in my father's work didn't help the situation either. She thought I was being influenced and brain washed by people and she thought she was quickly losing control of me.

My mother's relationship and mine was quickly deteriorating, we would argue a lot and disagree on most things and the fact I hardly saw her at that point was not helping. I had a job that started at 6pm and finished at 9pm, the job also gave me enough money to continuously go out after work and so I wouldn't get in until eleven or twelve of an evening and as I didn't have to get up for anything I would sleep in until late morning, therefore not having to see my Mum who left the house early to get to work. This pattern to life would continue for weeks and bit by bit my Mum started losing patience with me.

The events that take place in the next couple of months would totally confirm my belief in my father's work, it would also confirm to me the importance of his findings and the seriousness of it but would therefore send my delusional thoughts into overdrive.

My father rang me one day in early May, deciding it was time for my reintroduction to this affair and asked me whether or not I would like to attend a meeting with him, to visit one of the leading forensic handwriting experts in this country to discuss the preparation for a meeting with the Prime Minster, John Major.

Dad had returned from Germany feeling confident about his recent meetings at the Berlin police department.

Within a few weeks of him being back it became clear he wasn't going to hear from them. Dad was never the sort of person to give people second chances and so therefore would never try and get back in contact with people who had ignored him or basically made a judgement against his character, no matter who they were.

He had presented his findings to Berlin and they had backed away. We don't know why but Dad wasn't going to waste his time trying to find out.

The time had come in the affair to involve people from this country, he had been to Switzerland, Austria and Germany but due to lack of funds and people who were basically frightened of the subject, didn't have the success and acknowledgment he had wished for.

And so while in the lounge of 28 Basedale Rd, Dagenham, he started to put together a document called 555c. The naming of this document has nothing to do with the fact that Adolf Hitler's Nazi Party number was the same. It was pointed out to Dad sometime after and so just goes to show one of many coincidences in this whole affair.

The document was put together on an A4 piece of paper. The page that Dad had taken from *Mien Jugendfreund* in the New York Public Library with the August Kubizek signature on it, was placed in the middle of the page, he then surrounded that signature with black tape creating a box around it, which also covered up the date of the signature being 1953.

He then on the outside of the box placed writings from Hitler's Letters and Notes by Werner Maser and also placed three English sections of the writing from his photograph album.

He then photocopied that A4 piece of paper and sent it to some thirty Graphologists and Forensic Document Examiners in this country attaching a letter explaining that part of his family were English and part were German and that the family had a dispute over an antique and he therefore needed statements telling him whether or not the person who had wrote that signature in the black box was the same person who had wrote all the writings on the outside of the box. He sent this document off but without telling them that it had anything to do with Adolf Hitler.

Dad waited patiently for a response and one of the first letters that came through was from a lady called Ruth Myers.

Ruth Myers is based in London and she is one of the leading handwriting Graphologists in this country and specialises in scientific examination of documents and handwriting. She has over seventeen years experience, highly qualified, appeared on TV and radio and had worked for many organisations including banks and the Crown Prosecution Services and has also archived profiles for celebrities, politicians and royalty.

I will quote from the last paragraph of her letter sent to my father.

"It is in the opinion of the examiner based on reasonable scientific certainty that the centred signature outlined in the black box and the outside writings surrounding the same have all been penned by the same author."

Dad then sent her a letter back enclosing what he calls his white album, which contained in depth material and documents relating to all the handwriting on that document 555c and so telling Ruth Myers in the process that the writings were actually penned by Adolf Hitler and the white album also explained that that signature was dated 1953.

So in a way Ruth Myers indirectly had suggested Adolf Hitler had written Dad's photograph album but more importantly had confirmed that the signature in the black box was Adolf Hitler's and so therefore being alive in 1953.

Dad received a number of positive statements from all these experts and so he planned to gather them all together to work on The Album and the other findings.

At this stage he hadn't told any of them (apart from Ruth Myers) that Hitler penned the writings and so he had to be very careful when telling them. And when he finally did, some backed away but others became even more interested.

A man who did back away from this was called Alan Bishop; he lived in Priest Lane, Brentwood Essex. He initially responded to my Dad's requests with a positive statement but when finding out after that the writings were Hitler's, he immediately backed away and accused my father of misleading him and basically accused him of being a con man. But nevertheless he had made an initial positive statement and what makes this man important in Dad's eyes is that he lives in Priest Lane, the same road in fact that I lived in when this whole affair started. And so why this man is important is because anyone who lived in Brentwood, whether it be my Mum, Gary, my friends, my father's friends and people from the Cricket Club, if they were in any doubt, which they all were to the fact that my Dad owned a photograph album belonging to Hitler then they could have quite easily and literally walked to Alan Bishops house and asked his professional view on the matter. He may not of spoken highly of my father but if he was a truthful man then he couldn't have denied his findings. But instead of this happening most people have ridiculed my father, judged his character, called him insane and called him a liar and all sorts of things, which has tarnished his character and has left him without one single friend.

It was also ironic that Alan Bishop had a part time job at TWTI and so I would find myself having to work with this man on numerous occasions.

One of the experts who did contact my father after she had learnt who's writing it was, a lady called Maureen Ward Gandy.

She had sent Dad her initial findings stating the August Kubizek signature was the same handwriting as the writings on the outside of the box and had also sent a number of faxes to Dad's office. A meeting was arranged between both of them in early May 1992 at her house in Crawley to discuss the matter further.

Maureen Ward Gandy is a professional consultant in forensic documents and a handwriting specialist. She studied handwriting for the police and for the Home Office to establish fraud. She also works with the media and the newspapers and has worked with writings from people such as Christopher Columbus and Queen Victoria. She has also done radio shows and has worked for many lawyers, airlines, the Government and trading standard authorities.

So you could say that she is a highly experienced lady whose work and findings are respected by the highest people in the land. She is one of the leading experts in her field in the world.

After the meeting was arranged, my Dad contacted me to see whether I would like to attend.

It was quite an ironic situation really. We were just about to have a meeting with a woman who was going to be responsible for organising a group of forensic scientists from the Home Office with the intentions of presenting the findings from The Album and the other revelations to John Major but there we were not even having enough money between us to pay for a train ticket to get to Crawley. Dad never had a car or much money throughout this whole affair.

I told Dad I would only go if we had a car to take us there, I still laugh today at those requests because Dad had found himself after three years in a great position with great prospects and here I was laying down my demands.

Dad would have walked to Crawley if necessary but here I was insisting that I would only attend if he found us transport.

Dad felt at the time my presence at certain meetings was important and essential. He thought I was the best witness to events possible and because I had started this whole affair by knocking down the shed, he thought in some way I should be involved. He thought there was a real purpose and importance to my life and a destiny.

Ken McCullen was still financing Dad at this point and his secretary's name just by coincidence was Wendy Davey and so Dad would use her credit card sometimes saying that she was his sister.

And on that occasion he used it to hire a white VW van and so I agreed to go and my father picked me up from my house that morning and we headed round the M25 towards Crawley.

We arrived in Crawley thirty minutes early and I remember us parking up outside a pub and Dad sat there thinking about what his intentions were for this lady. He had told me he was going there mainly to discuss the August Kubizek signature and not necessary The Album or the birth certificate. And he told me his intentions were to get Maureen Ward Gandy to get him in front of John Major to discuss the fact that Adolf Hitler was English, alive in 1953 and therefore could still be alive today and a threat to this world but more so a threat to every single Jew left on this planet.

Well this was quite a development for me; I thought the meeting was to do with The Album and an intention to get it auctioned. And so for my father to come out with such dramatic statements and proposals was surprising to say the least. My Dad used to talk a lot to me about what he was going to do and what was just about to happen and a lot of it went straight over my head and so again on that occasion while we were sitting in that hired vehicle outside that pub with no money, the talk about John Major went over my head and I in those situations seemed to be able to turn my hearing off and think about something else.

I at that stage was still only interested in The Album, the fact that Hitler was English and could still be alive meant nothing to me but Dad was now more involved and interested in the cover up and the conspiracy side of things and he felt that it was such an important issue Hitler not dying in the bunker in Berlin that he needed to talk to the Prime Minister about it.

Dad had still not since that journey on the train down to Austria in 1989 ever mentioned anything more to me about the direct connection between a member of our Royal Family and Adolf Hitler, he had kept those thoughts and theories close to himself. But it is because of those theories that certain events over the next few months would take a certain direction in which no one would understand. I would learn of my Dad's theories very soon and how he came about his findings. He would tell me a few months later, on the way home after a meeting with the Richardsons, the feared notorious South London gangsters.

We got to Maureen Ward Gandy's house and I remember her and her husband greeting us at their door as we walked down the pathway. She seemed so pleased to see us and she immediately commented on the friendliness of our faces and said that she felt most at ease in our presence.

We were invited in and I could see they had a made an effort to make us feel welcome. They had also organised lunch for us including strawberries and cream for dessert. The first thing I noticed about Maureen's house was the amount of ornaments to do with Red Indians, she had spent many years studying her trade in America and had dealt with Indians in the past.

We sat in her lounge discussing the affair and Michael, her husband, was in the kitchen preparing lunch. All of a sudden my Dad got up to go to the toilet, which left me in the room alone with Maureen. And so I decided to use that opportunity to have a discussion of my own with her.

She hadn't at that stage seen The Album but she had seen photocopies of most of the pages and so I asked her whether she thought the writing in my Dad's album was actually Hitler's. It had already been confirmed to me by Josephine Day but that was a few years ago and the enormity of the whole thing and my struggle to understand why I was involved made it a perfect opportunity for me to be reassured again. She nodded her head in a positive fashion, which was all I needed. My Dad came back into the room and the meeting commenced.

He sat down and said to Maureen he wanted to raise this whole issue mainly on the August Kubizek signature. (Which was written by Hitler in 1953). He said he wanted to employ her and her forensic skills to 100% authenticate his album, the signature and the birth certificate and once she had completed the work, he wanted Maureen through her contacts to get him in front of John Major. My Dad asked her if this was possible.

Maureen became excitable and was amazed at what my Dad had just said, not because it sounded far-fetched but because, just by coincidence, she had received a hand written letter by John Major just two hours before we had arrived that morning. She was astounded by this coincidence and went hurrying upstairs to bring the letter down to show us. It was basically a letter thanking her for her support through the recent General Election.

If she hadn't already made her mind up to whether she was going to take on this project then I think those set of coincidences made it clear for her.

Dad offered her £555,000 to complete the work but to also raise the matter with John Major.

She agreed and said she would manage a team of experts from the Home Office to work firstly on The Album and then on the other findings. She stressed to Dad that a report coming from the Home Office could not be ignored.

She went on to photograph every part of The Album, (excluding those two postcards of Paris) so she could start her work, she once again stressed to Dad that she would need unlimited access to The Album to complete her work properly.

Dad was very happy on how the meeting had developed and would soon enter into a contract with this lady. He had now employed someone who could complete the forensic side of the work.

One of the last memories I have of that meeting was when Maureen offered to analyse my writing. My Dad encouraged me to have it done but I declined because I didn't want Maureen picking up in my writing the fact I was smoking drugs at the time.

We finally all said goodbye and my father went back there the following day to agree and sign a contract.

Another thing I learnt that day was the theory behind the blind spot. Dad let me drive the van on the way home and I remember creating a near pile up on the M25 due to me not properly looking behind me while I was changing lane.

I drove back into Brentwood and down the King's Rd and pulled the van up outside TWTI, I said goodbye to my Dad and walked inside to start my part time shift at the timeshare company.

That particular journey back to work that day from Maureen Ward Gandy's house was filled with much excitement and anticipation for the future. I had just experienced for the first time the real importance of Dad's work and it was also the first time I had heard the enormity of it from someone other that my Dad. It had also dawned on me the riches Dad had promised me might only be a short time away. He had also told me he was in contact with two other experts, one had a contact at Sotheby's and the other worked for The Mail on Sunday who may be interested in the story.

You can only imagine the excitement running through my mind and once again my shopping list of cars and houses started again.

It had also dawned on me I no longer needed to save for my valeting business and no longer needed to look for another full-time job.

Dad had just entered into a £555,000 contract with a leading forensic expert to work on The Album, signature and birth certificate to present a report for John Major, which I had personally witnessed. And so it was obvious to me there was soon to be a lot more money floating around, whether it was coming from the Government, Sotheby's or from The Mail on Sunday for the rights to the story.

After all that excitement and with my mind racing with all kinds of different thoughts and after witnessing my Dad and this lady talking about their intentions for the most powerful man in this country, I had to walk back into my part time telesales job and try to control myself.

It was so tempting to tell everyone at work that evening about my day but in reality who would have believed it and so why should I of wasted my time and efforts only to be ridiculed. I knew the truth and it was just a matter of me, being patient until everyone else would find out.

That day had also depicted a classic example of the way my whole life has been. What I mean is the balance that has always run through my life and has controlled me throughout this affair. See part of that day was filled with excitement and intrigue but the other half of the day I was brought back down to earth with the monotony of my telesales job. Throughout the whole affair I have had this kind of balance and it has without me sometimes appreciating it kept me fairly level headed. But still nothing could stop my extravagant thoughts constantly running through my mind and they would affect the way I would run my life.

Another thing that was hard to comprehend that day, was I was just a normal seventeen-year-old who was just trying to find his way in life but in the background to it was the bizarre happenings to do with my father and the massive revelations he was involved in which was soon to involve John Major and the American Secret Service.

But I also remember thinking that day to myself; why was I involved in such a thing? Why was it me who knocked the shed down? Why was it me who had started the ball rolling? Why was it my Dad who was discovering all these important revelations? And why was it he kept me constantly updated me with his work?

As I say, there was one half of my life that was ridiculous basically and the other half that was fairly basic and straightforward. But going along that straight forward road knowing there was this complete other side to my life was sometimes very hard and I struggled severely with understanding the meaning to my life.

Greg had been given one of the hardest tasks of all by my father to try and get through and convince my Mum that Dad's album was actually once the property of Adolf Hitler and to try and get her to understand the importance of it.

Dad felt it was time for my Mum's ignorance and plain stupidity to end, he felt it was time to reunite the family to discuss his findings and to discuss the subsequent repercussions. Dad felt he had come to a stage in his work whereby it was essential that my Mum put all her ill feelings to one side and start to support him.

Dad was just about to hopefully hold meetings with John Major to discuss the deception at the end of the Second World War but mainly to discuss the possibility of Hitler still being alive and dangerous and to put a plan together to lure him out of hiding and to maybe bring him back home.

Dad also felt discussing such revelations and ideas with people from the Government could mean the possible involvement of our security services (if they weren't already) and therefore the threat of them made Dad move towards my Mum. He also thought the general support from his family would be a nice thing to help him get through one of the toughest and most frustrating periods of his life.

Greg did try his best to get through to my Mum but to no avail. Dad thought if someone other than us tried talking to her it might just make a difference. Greg would have probably got more reaction if he had tried talking to Max (my dog) because my Mum didn't want to listen to a word he was saying and I was sure even if John Major himself would have turned up that evening to express the importance of it all she still would have sent him packing.

My Mum had a deep resentment towards my Dad, in her eyes it was his fault for the breakdown of their marriage due to his illness, she also thought because of his influence on me that caused the split between herself and Gary but now she could see the direct influence from him to myself that was affecting the way and the direction my life was taking and she hated him for that.

She was able to protect Michael from his spell but not me and it was at this point she was realising I was 100% behind my Dad and she also didn't like the feeling of one of my friends pressurising her into believing something that basically was unbelievable.

She could no longer stand having me around she couldn't risk mine and my Dad's beliefs and way of life rubbing off on my brother. Dad had only just recently tried to kidnap Michael and me from cricket; he took us to a house in Plaistow where I managed to run away to a local police station. Dad was planning to take us both to Europe and I couldn't allow that to happen for my brothers sake and my mothers. So my Mum tried her best to protect him and if that meant having to throw me out in the process then that was what was going to happen. My brother had been shielded from the Hitler affair and so my Mum would do her best to continue that protection, he was just about to do his GCSE's and didn't need any distraction from my Dad or me.

Personally my general attitude towards life at that stage was somewhat odd but in my Mum's eyes must have looked horrendous. In her eyes I was this seventeen-year-old boy who had no future, I was working in a dead end part time telesales job, continuously going out, continuously sleeping in until midday and to top it off was believing in everything that my Dad was feeding me. In my eyes I was just on the verge of greatest and personally responsible for the riches that were heading my way, I had the perfect life in my eyes I had a great job that gave me enough money at the time to do what I wanted and my recent meeting at Maureen Ward Gandy's house did nothing to suppress those thoughts, I knew it was just a matter of time before all my thoughts and fantasies came true.

One of the last things I did before I unknowingly left TWTI was to get my good friend Alister a job, he had just finished his GCSE retakes at St Martin's and needed a job and I thought it would be nice to have someone I knew working alongside me. In a way and not knowing at the time it was the best thing I have done for him because it was there he learnt the basic skills he required to eventually go on to become a director of a stationery company where he still works today but more importantly Al met a girl there who he would eventually go on to marry; Sarah Woodley.

After one more confrontation with my mother she decided it was best I go and live with my Dad once again, she gave me no choice in the matter and basically threw me out. My actions and behaviour in that period might not have been too clever but I know the real reason why I was being thrown out and that was because of my beliefs, involvement and support for my father's work and if that was the case, was I so bad for standing by someone who I knew and could see was right. And was it fair for my mother to have done something like that without even checking out whether what I was involved in was actually true or not, one phone call to Maureen Ward Gandy would have given her that answer. No, instead she believed what her friends thought of Dad's work and so therefore believed my Dad was insane and could not be telling the truth. But the question I have is why would you throw me out of your house and make me go and live with a person who in your eyes was insane?

Dad's reaction when I again turned up at his doorstep was a happy one. There was a lot going on in his life and in the background regarding the Hitler affair. He had tried to reintroduce me into the affair when we visited Maureen Ward Gandy's house, so having me come back to live with him at such a time was in his eyes perfect and meant to be.

He felt I should be more involved and this gave him the perfect opportunity to steer my life in whatever direction he wished.

If I was in any way apprehensive about the future and moving back to Dagenham then Dad straight away took that away. He convinced me everything regarding the Hitler affair was just about to raise up and the riches I had dreamed of were just around the corner, he told me all his different plans for the forthcoming weeks with regards to dealing with all the different handwriting experts. He told me I should stay with him and witness the proceedings take place and once they became public, he said I could hold my head high and have the satisfaction of watching all those non believers and judgers come crawling back for my forgiveness. (Mainly pointing at my family and friends from the Cricket Club)

My first night back in Dagenham was spent watching TV with Dad and Nan. I immediately accepted my fate and with a real sense of anticipation and looking forward to the days and weeks ahead, I quickly adjusted and became totally comfortable with the situation.

My Nan was over the moon to have me back but not for the reasons you may think. Dad's behaviour and way of life had totally become focused around the Hitler affair. He thought after finding that album especially while being in the middle of his church project

165

that he had been given a duty by God and so therefore no-one or nothing was going to stop him in his crusade.

Dad had been working constantly on the affair, day and night and unfortunately my Nan had to witness his near obsession with it, she also had to witness his immense frustration, which on occasions would enter into aggressive and loud outbursts of rage. I guess in my arrival my Nan must of thought I may help with Dad's frustration and anger and may even ease his dedication toward the Hitler affair, she was wrong.

The sleeping arrangements would slightly change from the last time I was there. My Nan this time stayed in her own room, my Dad decided to sleep downstairs in the lounge and so I had his room. The room was a fairly small one with one wardrobe unit in it but with a magnificent view of the railway tracks. And during the weeks ahead I would be rudely awoken by the underground trains going past on the District Line, the fact I could virtually hear everything that was going on by the neighbour next door also didn't help with my sleeping pattern.

I had gone from the luxury of the Hartswood Rd house with its spacious rooms and beautiful surroundings to a mid terrace ex-Council house that was home to my Nan but was now also home to Dad and therefore the home and the centre point to his Adolf Hitler campaign.

The following day, Doug Brown one of my Dad's neighbours drove me back to Brentwood so I could pick the rest of my belongings up. If I was going to move back to Dagenham with my Dad then I wasn't going to leave anything behind. Doug drove a four door Rover a typical kind of Dagenham car, Doug was a fairly big chap who gave the appearance of a gangster with all the tattoos and gold jewellery to go with it. But in reality Doug as I remember was a gentle giant who was struggling to survive and support his family. Dad had got Doug involved into the Hitler affair and I think he was just hoping that something was going to come of it. It was in fact Doug who had introduced Ken McCullen to Dad who became his financier; Ken had invested a large amount of money with the intention of seeing a return from the sale of The Album. Dad had also given Doug a fairly large contract as a finder's fee that would be paid out as soon as The Album was sold. So I think Doug like many others looked at Dad as their saviour.

I walked back into the house in Hartswood Rd with the slight hope that maybe Mum might of changed her mind, I didn't mind staying with my Dad because I knew a lot of positive things were happening but Dagenham wasn't my home, Brentwood was.

As I put the rest of my clothes etc, into bags, Mum and my brother appeared on the landing, Mum said she had reconsidered her decision but after talking to my brother they both agreed it may be best if I go and live with my Dad for a while. The fact my brother may have influenced my Mum's decision sent me into a rage and I told them both exactly what I thought of them and expressed what I thought of their awful attitude they showed towards my Dad and me, I told them how wrong they were about Dad and how they were soon to find out the truth. I walked into my brother's room and emptied all my CD's from his rack. The last thing I said to both of them was, if and when they wanted to apologize to me for their disgraceful treatment of me and realising how wrong there were, I said I would be at my Dads, but I would never again make the first move towards them. My relationship with my brother and Mum at that point was over, I couldn't stand anymore of their judgements towards my Dad's work, and my Mum constantly telling me and thinking Dad was insane became intolerable.

I said goodbye to them both and walked downstairs. Before I walked out the front door Max came up to me, I knelt down and gave him a big cuddle and that's when I finally became emotional and all my anger and fury seemed to melt away but as I was cuddling him all my built up emotion finally came out. I said goodbye to him and walked out the door. It was the last time I ever saw him, he died a few months later suffering from a bad liver, he died just before my Mum was moving into a top floor flat where animals were forbidden, so in my eyes if Max was going to die then he died at just the right time, I was obviously sad to hear he had died but because of my view on it I wasn't terribly upset, it was just something that was meant to be.

Doug could obviously see I was upset and he did his best to cheer me up on the way back to Dagenham. He told me a number of different stories, which in the process did make me laugh. Including a story from when he was a bus driver, a lady had got on his bus and asked him if he went to Tesco's and Doug replied "Yes" so the lady got on but when eventually the bus came to the end of its route with no Tesco's in sight, she asked Doug why he had said the bus went to Tesco's and Doug replied "You said do I go to Tesco's and I said yes, I go every Sunday with my wife." With that the lady angrily got off the bus.

167

My first week back in Dagenham was a real eye opener and the realisation of my situation hit home. If I thought my stay at my Dads was going to be a easy ride then I was truly mistaken, I had walked out of my job at TWTI without telling them, having a part time job while living in Dagenham wasn't practical.

I had also stopped playing cricket for Brentwood. Every one of the members knew of Dad's work. Dad had made a point of writing to every member telling them he owned a photograph album belonging to Hitler and he believed Hitler was alive and he explained in his letter he needed the help of everyone at the Cricket Club to participate in a operation called "Key Man". Key Man was an operation that would entail two hundred plus people flying into Arizona to begin a search for Hitler.

It was an outrageous letter, which made Dad look completely mad in the process. Dad had done it on purpose; he told me he had done it for political reasons. Dad knew that everyone of those members at the Cricket Club would be taking the piss out of him and he would be the focus point of many discussions in the bar after the game. But Dad also knew that in doing it he would have the total support of each and everyone of those members once they got the smallest whisper of it in the media. All Dad had to do was raise The Album through Sotheby's etc, and then he would have everyone round at his house begging for his forgiveness. It was a brilliant plan that took a lot of courage and guts, he was purposely putting himself in a position for persecution, he would use this same approach and plan with a number of different people with the idea that most would ignore his findings, he used to say that once his album became public knowledge it would put him in a powerful position because he would have so many people around him wanting to make up for their ignorance.

See Dad was telling people he thought Adolf Hitler was alive and powerful but everyone thought this was crazy and ridiculous because if you went by Adolf Hitler's birth certificate then it made him in 1992 hundred and three years old and therefore highly unlikely to still be alive. But Dad knew the birth certificate was fake and he believed he knew his actual birth date being 1905 which would have made Adolf Hitler in 1992 eighty seven and therefore a stronger possibility of him still being alive. But in Dad's shrewdness and cleverness he would not let on about that particular knowledge and hoped the media would take this story on and highlight his findings and therefore he would have the support around him from all those people he had contacted in the past. Dad believed Hitler was living somewhere in Arizona probably as a woman and living with the Red Indians, Dad knew Hitler was heavily involved in the occult during the war, he also believed he was still immensely powerful and planning a final attack against the Jews.

This might of made a good plan for Dad but seeing everyone over the Cricket Club looking at me with those side eye glances and having the bar go quiet when I entered made me feel uncomfortable. I felt awkward playing there, I hated the fact that my Dad was right but no one took any notice, instead they took the piss. I had seen two experts by now and they were obviously more qualified than anyone over at that cricket club to determine whether or not The Album was Hitler's. I couldn't bear playing there anymore amongst all those judgers and so I left, hoping though to return within months after they all learnt the truth.

I also received a letter from Alan Lilley, the Essex U19 organiser; inviting me to take part in an Essex U19 trial game against Hutton 1ST XI and it was obviously to determine whether I would make the grade into the U19 arena. I hadn't played any cricket during that summer and I also felt that while living in Dagenham it wasn't practical to be playing for Essex and I guess my priorities had slightly changed, cricket had become unimportant to me and I based more importance on the Hitler affair but I also remember just not turning up to that game, I didn't even ring Alan Lilley to tell him that I wasn't going to be there. My attitude towards Essex and Alan Lilley was that once The Album was sold and I had my millions in the bank I would explain to him the predicament I had been in and hopefully he would accept me back.

Looking back it was a crazy way of thinking and it was at that point I threw my Essex and cricketing career out the window.

Apart from the barking dogs and the trains going past every five minutes, my Nan lived down a fairly quiet road, which was close to the local parade of shops but mainly and more importantly near to the local park; Mayesbrook Park.

The park was situated on the other side of Lodge Ave, which was just a stones throw from my Nan's front door. It was a massive park that had two big fishing lakes; it was also the home to Barking and Dagenham Football Club and Barking Cricket Club. During my stay with Dad I would spend a lot of time walking around that park, it had such nice surroundings and so sometimes while walking I would forget I was even in Dagenham. And on occasions when I wasn't handling the situation or feeling a little down I would go over to the park to get away from it all.

I would also spend a lot of time with my Dad walking round it and it was there I would learn a lot of his thoughts and theories regarding Hitler and this affair and on most occasions the conversation would become rather intense and would always be one sided.

I had to walk beside him while he was constantly talking about Hitler and the affair, he would talk about how he thought Hitler was cast aside and shipped off to Austria when he was young and how he was ignored by his Mother. He would express his beliefs to why Hitler had such a strong dislike towards the Jews and suggested that maybe Hitler was in love with a Jewish girl while in Austria when he was younger. Eva Maria Bruner had picked up in his writing from The Album that he had constructed it for someone he loved. When that album was constructed at the age of sixteen by him, he had no ill feelings whatsoever towards Jews.

On one of the postcards it is written "Synagogue of Worms" and the handwriting experts have not detected the slightest bit of anger towards the Jews when he wrote that word synagogue. So Dad believes he constructed The Album for a Jewish girl that he loved but is it possible he loved her so that much he might have told her the truth of where he actually came from and who his real family were (that being the British Royal Family)?

And so is it possible, after he told her, she would not believe him and laugh and make fun of him and spread his ridiculous beliefs to other Jewish people and in the process have lots of Jewish people laughing at him in his hometown. And how would that have made him feel, people laughing at him and not believing him? I'm quite sure it would have made him feel, very angry especially if he had got beaten up or abused in the process and is it possible that a Jew while beating him up stole his most precious belonging; The Album.

And so was it then while being attacked and laughed at and having his album stolen that he took so much time to construct, was it then maybe in some dark ally somewhere in Vienna that Hitler's hate towards the Jews began? If that is so then his hate began because the Jews laughed at him, but most important of all didn't believe him when he told them he was a member of the British Royal Family.

There would be many more theories that were only theories, but to Dad were important. He had exposed a conspiracy surrounding

Hitler, which proved he was educated in England, could read and write English, constructed the book *Mein Jugendfreund* after the war which most importantly proves he was alive in 1953 and also suggested through his fake birth certificate he was much younger than actually stated.

These findings and the fact Dad owned Hitler's album put him in a strong position to make these theories. History had to be rewritten because what is written in our history books about Hitler's early life is rubbish. Hitler was never in World War One (this will become clear when discussing Hitler's real date of birth) so anything you read about that is rubbish and any photos you see of Hitler being in World War One have been superimposed and obviously the question is who has helped Hitler create such a cover up and why?

During those walks he would also touch on his theories regarding the Royal Family but only enough to make me aware of them. He would mention Queen Mary's name and speak to me on how he thought she could have stopped or even prevented the war through one phone call to her son.

I must admit when the conservation took this route I would begin to stop listening and naturally turn off, I didn't know who Queen Mary was or who George V was and quite frankly didn't care. I didn't even have any interest in the present day Royal Family, they meant absolutely nothing to me and if asked I didn't even know the Queen's first name or the names of any other royals except of course Prince Charles and Princess Diana, but that was mainly because they were on the television every other night due to their much publicized divorce.

When Dad started to talk about his own struggles with the affair he would start to get immensely frustrated, he had been ignored and judged by all his friends and family and he would start to get angrier and angrier, he would say everyone had left him to hang.

But seeing Dad for the first time slip into these rages was somewhat frightening. I remember sitting in the lounge with my Nan one day, (must have been in the first week of being back) and my Dad came in and sat down and started talking to us about the affair and talking to us about how badly he had been treated by everyone and how he was being ignored by all the media. And as he kept talking his voice became louder and louder and he would start to wave his arms around and by now I started to get worried because I had never seen him like this before, he then stood up and started stamping his feet and his arms would aggressively fly up and down, much like when Hitler used to stand and give his passionate speeches in Germany. Dad was furious with me, my Nan, my brother and anyone else in the family and friends for not supporting him throughout this hard time and he would keep saying he had been left to hang by everyone.

I couldn't believe what I was seeing and hearing and wondered how many people in the street could hear what was going on. After he had finished he stormed out of the room and the house. I looked at my Nan for some kind of explanation to what I had just witnessed and all she said to me was that he is terribly frustrated.

It was at that point I wondered if I had done the right thing in supporting him and moving back to live there, I couldn't stand living there if Dad was constantly going to talk about Hitler and having to worry about his rages.

Deep down I wanted to stay, I wanted to see and witness the up and coming events and deep down I felt I should be there, I wanted to try and see it out but if I was going to do that then I needed something to keep me occupied, so therefore limiting my time with my Dad, I decided I needed to get a job.

My good friend Greg had left Victoria Jewellers to work at the Esso Garage in Brook Street, Brentwood as a cashier. Greg always seemed to be looking out for me; he was a very generous and a kind person. If he could see I had no money he would always give me twenty pound here and there, never wanting it back. He would also lend me his jeep if I ever needed to see someone. So he was a good friend but I must admit I did always wonder whether he was only being that like because he knew I was involved in Dad's Hitler affair and so could also see the financial rewards coming my way.

But Greg could see I was struggling even in that first week living in Dagenham and so he managed to get me a job in the Esso but it was working nights. I was always one to go with the flow and so this opening had presented itself to me so I went with it.

Greg gave me a one night training session on the Thursday and he went through all the training and procedures of the job, which didn't take long because it was quite a basic job.

But during that night we were still talking about ways of how we were going to make our millions and whilst watching cars pull up at the garage to get their petrol, we would start talking to the customers who had really nice cars to find out what they did for a living and how they made their money. Some of them wanted to talk others didn't. But one chap pulled up in a brand new red Mercedes SL and when he walked in we both started talking to him and it just so happened he owned Adam Kennedy, which is a large group of estate agents. And after chatting to him for a while and expressing our ambitions he offered us both a job. We both said we would think about it and so he gave us his business card and walked out. Greg decided straight away that selling houses was not for him but he did encourage me to go for it.

After that one night of training I spent one night on my own working there, basically it was purgatory and the job just wasn't for me, there was no challenge in it and also on the Friday night many of my friends who knew I had started work there decided to pay me a visit after the pub, I let them all in and they decided to nick half of the stock out of the shop.

I guess if I had lived fairly near the garage I might have carried on working there but working nights was quite a hard thing anyway, sleeping during the day working at night, it was very unsociable, a pain in the ass basically. But the journey home in the morning after my shift had finished was horrendous. I had to walk from the Esso to Brentwood railway station, get the train to Chadwell Heath and then get another bus back to Dagenham, walk up the hill, then get in fall asleep and then wake up and start the same process all over again, well fuck that, that just wasn't going to happen. I phoned Roger, the manager to tell him I wasn't going to do any more shifts. But what did come of it was the opportunity to work for Adam Kennedy. I phoned him and he set up an immediate interview for me with the Area Manager at their headquarters in Wanstead.

Now for this interview I needed a suit, if I was going to work for an estate agent then I needed to look smart and I needed to make a good impression. I had about two hundred pound left over which was in a saving account my Nan (Vi) had set up for me when I was young. And so I remember going to Romford on that Saturday to Coles in the Liberty Centre. They were having quite a good deal on that day whereby you buy a suit and get a tie for half price plus six free bottles of white wine.

I always remember walking back through Dagenham, I had just bought my first suit and I felt proud of myself, I had my suit in one hand and my six bottles of wine in the other. As I approached the parade of shops where my Nan lived I could see my Dad talking to someone just outside where his office was in Porters Ave. But what I didn't realise was he was trying to convince this man to invest some money into the Hitler affair because Dad had no money and needed more financial investors. It was quite funny really looking back because as Dad was trying to do that and telling this man we had no money, I came up to them said hello and went on to show my Dad in front of this man my brand new suit and tie and the six bottles of wine. Dad had just spent some time telling this man we had no money (which we didn't really) and then I had turned up with all this new gear and so this man just walked off, my Dad wasn't too pleased at the time but we do look back now and laugh.

My Dads office in Dagenham, well it wasn't his office, it was a insurance company along the parade of shops in Porters Ave opposite the Roundhouse pub called John Kimpton which Dad used as his own office, he had a phone there a fax machine and access to the photocopier and he ran his whole campaign from there. But even in those first few days of being back in Dagenham, I would follow my Dad round to that office and witness the huge amount of faxes coming out of the machine from Maureen Ward Gandy, they were faxes regarding The Album and the other finding and basically outlining a further contract between herself, Ken McCullen and my Dad and basically updating Dad on her progress with the report she was preparing. The woman was highly motivated by my Dad's album and highly enthusiastic about the whole subject otherwise why would she continuously have sent him these amounts of faxes.

I felt good the following Monday morning waking up with a purpose; I was just about to start my first day at Adam Kennedy. My interview had gone well but the job had a slight draw back on it because they were only giving me a week's trial and that involved me having to sell one house to keep my job.

My Dad never gave me the best of encouragement when it came to me getting a job, he always thought that was long term thinking on my part, he was always very positive with his work and always thought the beginning of the end was always around the corner and so he thought I wouldn't be in the job for five minutes.

I started my first day at Adam Kennedy's in Romford; I had my own desk and a number of leads to start with. And so my challenge began to sell a house in a week. Well unfortunately I failed my challenge horrendously and at the end of the week they let me go. It is quite a throat cut industry really, I had witnessed in that week somebody getting sacked because she hadn't sold a house in a while but the way it was done and way she came into work and was told was not nice, I did feel sorry for her as she gathered up her belongings, I didn't like the way she was treated.

I tried my hardest in that job I created a number of good leads and showed many people round many houses but maybe I just wasn't a very good salesman, I always thought that I was and was told by people that I would make a good salesman but maybe I wasn't, maybe I wasn't pushy enough, maybe I wasn't professional enough, maybe I just didn't know enough about the houses I was trying to sell or maybe I just wasn't meant to be an estate agent.

And so my career in the estate agent industry ended within one week.

It had become quite clear to me that I was obviously meant to be alongside my Dad to support him and to witness the forth-coming events. I had tried to path out different routes for myself but my fate and the power creating it wanted me beside him. I gave up looking for jobs and decided to get more involved with my Dad, I had always in the past kept my distance from his work, I knew what he had was real and that was all I needed to know but now that I was living there with nothing else to do, I decided I would start to help but more importantly I was there and he had someone to talk to and to discuss his different ideas with.

During those first few weeks of May in 1992 while he was working alongside Maureen Ward Gandy, another handwriting expert was taking an eager interest in Dad's findings.

Margaret White is a handwriting graphologist who used to live in Sutton, she is a founding member of the British Institute of Graphologists and her clients among others include merchant banks, financiers, recruitment/career counselling specialists and commercial companies.

She is again a leading expert in her field of work and once she had seen Dad's documents and the original album she immediately wanted to get involved.

Dad already had Maureen Ward Gandy working on the forensic side of things and so this lady being a graphologist coming along meant both sides of authentication would be complete.

Dad and I were invited to Margaret White's flat to meet her personally and to discuss how she could possibly help in raising this matter.

I remember the meeting quite well, she greeted us in a much similar way as Maureen Ward Gandy did, she made us feel welcome and showed enthusiasm for Dad's work. She had obviously seen all of Dad's documentation by now and could also see the conspiracy surrounding the whole affair.

Most of the handwriting experts who have had anything to do with this affair, if asked will tell you that studying The Album and the documents in *Mein Jugendfreund*, have been the most amazing and sometimes frightening things they have ever seen.

In fact when a lady called Victoria Fabling, a graphologist who was working for The Mail on Sunday, first looked at the August Kubizek signature, she physically came up in red blotches and said to my Dad it was the most amazing thing she had ever seen.

A lot of these experts when realising the writing was Hitler's backed away and cowardly crawled back into their meaningless lives, but some like Margaret White and Maureen Ward Gandy could see something was adrift and wanted to be involved. They were willing to put their reputations on the line because they could see the truth, they could see a cover up had been put in place and so they wanted to be part of a team that was going to be responsible for putting history straight. I'm sure also that the money and publicity created from all this gave them a good incentive.

Another thing I remember about being at her flat was her son Rory, he suffered from Autism but Margaret made no effort to hide him from us and I always remember respecting her for that.

Margaret from then on whenever dealing with anyone who may have known me, would always ask after me, she would always say she respected me deeply for my loyalty towards my Dad, she has also said recently that due to my Dad's delusions over certain things, that I shouldn't be too hard on him.

My Dad offered Margaret a similar contract, as Maureen Ward Gandy's to gather graphologists to raise the issues. Margaret agreed to a £555,000 contract and immediately came up with two suggestions.

Margaret was a Fellow of the Royal Society of Arts in John Adam St and she suggested she book a room for a meeting between all the graphologists that she would invite and for the ones Dad had already contacted. Dad agreed and after a quick conversation with the RSA she booked a room for the 21st May 1992, she also told Dad that she would invite her friend along from the Croydon Post; he was a freelance journalist called David Cullen.

She also made another phone call to Roy Davids and after a forty-five minute conversation with him had arranged a meeting in

June. Roy Davids was the Marketing Director for Sotheby's and had worked there since 1970. He was one of Margaret's friends so if she was telling him she was dealing with someone who owned a photograph album written in English and German, by Adolf Hitler then he was going to listen. Margaret was a highly qualified person and so therefore generated a lot of credibility. That meeting at Sotheby's was to determine whether or not they were going to auction The Album. It was the meeting I was mainly interested in for obvious reasons; I had waited three years for this moment and eagerly waited the outcome of their decision.

The meeting at Margaret's obviously went well and we were both happy with the whole situation. On one side we had Maureen dealing with the forensic side of things and hopefully getting Dad in with John Major and on the other side we had Margaret White managing the graphology side of things and hopefully responsible for the eventual auction of The Album.

One thing that Margaret did suggest to Dad was to try and get a copy of the *Mein Jugendfreund* book with the signature in. Dad was still only working with copies and photocopies of the book.

You could go into any library or bookshop and get this book but it was very rare to have the introduction with the signature in. It was a very strange situation, some books had it in but others didn't and on most occasions they didn't. Dad had the page with the signature on it from the New York Library but Margaret suggested that having the actual book to show people would create a much bigger impact.

Dad had already looked in quite a few places for this book but without success, it appeared that the book just seemed to have disappeared, in fact Dad had returned to the New York Library to take more copies of the book but when he asked for it the librarian told him that someone had stolen it. So it looked like someone was going round collecting these books up; the conspiracy had been exposed by Dad and so now someone was trying to cover up the cover up.

Fortunately they had forgotten to look in the library at Basel University, Dad had asked a friend of his called Ursula Luici from Lucerne, Switzerland to look for the book. Ursula had a friend who studied at the university and it just so happened they had it.

The days leading up to the RSA meeting were quite frustrating for Dad, he needed that book but did not have the money to go down and get it and he didn't want to risk her posting it just in case it got lost. Dad could also see I was beginning to get down with the situation, I knew there was a lot going on in the background but sometimes there would be long periods of time when there was nothing happening and so I would have to listen to my Dad or just sit in the garden watching the trains go by.

And it was one day while in that garden Dad asked me if I wanted to go to Switzerland to pick up the book *Mein Jugendfreund*. He told me I would go by ferry and trains and be gone for two days, back in time for the meeting at RSA. He went on to tell me it was a very important trip, bringing that book back to create the right impact at the meeting.

I agreed to go but there was one slight problem; we had no money for the trip and the days were now passing by and the RSA meeting was nearly upon us.

Richard an employee at John Kimpton's, and had taken an interest in Dad's work, I guess seeing and probably reading all those faxes from Maureen Ward Gandy intrigued him. But Dad offered him a contract if he would put up the money to finance my trip to Switzerland. He wasn't sure at first until he read a fax, which had come through that day from Martin Jocelyn, it was a fake fax organised by my Dad so that Richard would read it. The fax contained details of money to be deposited into an account once a positive response had came from the RSA meeting. After Richard had read the fax he decided he would put up the money for my trip.

I left on the 19th May giving me two days to get there and back, it was cutting it fine and if I incurred any delays I would not make it.

This was my first solo mission in the affair and the importance of it couldn't be higher. The meeting at the Royal Society of Arts was a major event in this affair and was the first time that so many qualified people had been brought together to discuss the situation. The Album was obviously going to be there but if I could get this textbook back in time then it was going to create a massive impact especially as a member of the press was going to be there.

The mission I was just about to undertake was a fairly simple one. All I had to do was get to Lucerne, meet this lady, get the book and get back again. The fact I was carrying a book that proved Hitler was alive in 1953 and proved his birth certificate was a forgery and also the fact so many of these books had gone missing the danger of my mission never entered my mind.

Throughout the whole journey I kept myself to myself and never did anything to bring attention to myself. I rarely spoke to anyone, normally I would make the effort to have conversation with people, especially people on trains who I was going to have to spend so much time with but on this occasion I didn't, I guess the reason for my trip and not really wanting to talk about it made me be quiet. On most occasions I would never talk to strangers about what I was doing or what I was involved in because at the end of the day they weren't going to believe it and so I wasn't going to waste my time to be laughed at or worse belittled.

I arrived in Paris with three hours to spare before I had to board the next train to Lucerne. The last time I had been in Paris I had been with my father and the memory of him pinning me up against the wall in the waiting room flooded back.

This time I was in Paris on my own and I was here of my own accord. I had three hours to spare and so I wanted to make the most of my time in this great city. The two main attractions I knew of in Paris were the Eiffel Tower and Jim Morrison's grave. I had to make a decision quickly to what attraction I wanted to see, I only had time to see one of them.

Well it didn't take me long, I was a big Jim Morrison fan but going to his grave just didn't appeal to me I wasn't interested in the dead and sitting in a graveyard surrounded by gravestones and a load of bones was just not my scene. Jim Morrison's bones may have been in that graveyard but his soul has gone somewhere else and so I wasn't going to spend my three hours in Paris there.

I got the Metro round to the Trocadero and walked out of the station eagerly awaiting my first view of the Eiffel Tower.

It was a beautiful sunny day with lots of tourists around and as I walked out of the station the enormity and splendour of the tower hit me, I just stood there for a moment to take it in. I had obviously seen the Eiffel Tower on the TV before but seeing it for the first time in real life was somewhat incredible.

I didn't have much money, once again my train fares had taken up much of my funds but I did have just enough money for a ticket to enter the tower. I bought my ticket and decided to walk up the stairs to the top, I could have got the lift but it felt more of challenge to walk the stairs. When I eventually got to the top the view was awesome and breathtaking, you could see for miles around and see everything in Paris, it was amazing.

I got back on the train and my journey to Lucerne begun, I sat there feeling quite lonely daring not to talk to anyone, I was never very good at lying and so if anyone asked me what I was doing in Europe I would have felt it hard to have lied.

If there was a presence in my life then they were doing their job well that journey because my whole trip to Lucerne and back was trouble free and not one person approached me and even on the trains I had the whole carriage to myself, so therefore feeling comfortable and secure in my journey.

If this mission had been an introduction to further missions then it had succeeded. It was a mission that gave me the experience of travelling alone but also gave me an insight into performing a mission with an importance. The fact that I was picking something up from this lady in Switzerland that proved Hitler was alive in 1953 and so therefore could still be alive seemed at the time not to be important but in reality was the worst nightmare for many people including every Jew in the world. That book was going to be showed to many experts and a member of the press but hopefully to John Major to show him the importance of it and there I was with the responsibility of bringing it home. If there was a threat out there then I never witnessed it and so if that book was meant to be back in London for the attention of the Government then due to fate and whatever power in the world, that's where it ended up.

I arrived at Lucerne station and a worrying thought started to enter my mind, maybe this lady may not turn up to meet me and so my whole journey would have been a waste of time.

I was wrong, in fact she made the effort to meet me on the platform and it was her that came up to me to introduce herself. I don't know how she knew me but I didn't care at the time, I was just pleased she was there, I followed her to her car and she whisked me away to the outskirts of town where she lived.

I entered her flat and there was another lady in there, once again she kept herself in the background and had no input into the conversation. Ursula made me some dinner and while I ate it she asked me a number of questions regarding this book that she had got for Dad. She obviously knew the importance of it and knew of my Dad's album and I guess having me there made it a perfect opportunity for her to pick my brains; the fact this other lady was in the background listening in made me feel slightly uncomfortable. She seemed to want to get as much information out of me as possible in the short period of time I was there, I had nothing to hide and had no instruction otherwise so I told her what she wanted to know.

After a good hour of being there Ursula drove me back to the Lucerne railway station, it was during that journey that she passed me the book that I had come all this way for. I took it and said thank you, I instinctively opened it to the introduction page and was pleased to see the signature of one August Kubizek dated 1953. I placed it in my bag and tried to forget about it. We arrived at the station and Ursula escorted me to the right platform, she wished me luck and said goodbye.

I remember getting on the train and sitting down and preparing myself for the long journey back. As the train pulled out of the station I took the textbook out of my bag that had just been given me. *Mein Jugendfreund* by August Kubizek, I started to look through it and couldn't understand a word of it because it was written in German, but I did recognise the signature, birth certificate and the postcards written by Hitler to August Kubizek, I remember looking up at the other passengers on board and just wondered what they might think if they knew what I did. The fact I had come half way across Europe for this book and also if it hadn't have been for this particular book The Album would have definitely been sold by now, really I should have hated that book, I should have thrown it out of the train window but deep down I knew it was important and deep down I knew I had been born to be part of what was happening, I could feel some kind of presence around me and I felt that my life had a real purpose to it, so I put the book back in my bag and enjoyed the rest of my journey.

If MI5 were involved by this stage, then I still wonder to this day why they didn't stop me getting that book back to my Dad. It was a perfect opportunity for them. I was alone in Europe with the second most damaging book (after The Album) in the world, that if ever became public knowledge would create amazing unease amongst most people on this planet. The fact Hitler didn't actually commit suicide in 1945 and was possibly still alive was a thought most people could not comprehend. So many of these books had gone missing in recent times and if MI5 were involved, is it possible they actually wanted that particular book back in England? Because the whole of my journey was trouble free and in fact when I got to Calais and it was looking like I was going to be late back for the RSA meeting, I was suddenly transferred onto a Hover Craft and back into Dover within minutes. If they were involved and wanted this meeting to go ahead the question I have is why? And for whose purpose was it really for?

I arrived back at Victoria Station, London with two hours to spare before the meeting at the Royal Society of Arts begun. It had been a short trip but one I will never forget, I enjoyed my time in Paris and enjoyed the adventure to Lucerne.

If I was in any doubt as to whether my trip to Switzerland was right or not then what happened next 100% confirmed to me it was. As I got off the train at Victoria and looked up, I spotted my Dad in the distance walking across the entrance to the underground, now for that to happen amongst thousands and thousands of people using that station, was in my opinion a confirmation of my efforts. Fair enough I had arranged to meet my Dad but he was walking off in a different direction but for me to see him in that split second just confirmed to me my trip to Lucerne was 100% right and worthy.

As I saw my father I quickly ran towards him, I greeted him and he asked me whether I had the book. I said yes. He told me to follow him and we made our way to the Savoy Gardens where we had tea and a sandwich. As we sat there I passed him the book he had so long been searching for; mission accomplished.

If that mission was meant to whet my appetite for further adventure then it surely did, I loved the sense of travel and adventure and the suspense of not really knowing what to expect at the end of the trip also made it exciting. But being part of the Hitler affair and having a purpose behind each trip gave my journeys a real reason and if that initial trip had been a trial of some kind then I had passed with flying colours.

We stayed in the gardens until 4.40pm then we made our way to John Adam St, where Margaret White was waiting for us outside the Royal Society of Arts.

The meeting was held in a room called the Coffee room and present were: Thomas Davey, John Davey, Margaret White, Victoria Fabling (British Academy of Graphology and worked for The Mail on Sunday), Bridget Hickey (Graphologist and friend of Ruth Myers), Elizabeth Hoben (Graphologist), Roger Moncad (Leading Graphologist), John Wilcox (Graphologist) Renna Nezos (Principal at the British Academy of Graphology), David Cullen (from the Croydon Post) and one or two other experts.

My father sat at one end of the table and Margaret sat at the other, Margaret had been put in charge by my father and seemed to be relishing the responsibility.

My father began talking and explaining to all the people present how this whole thing had started and he joked by saying that the whole affair that had taken over his life and virtually destroyed it was actually started by me when I knocked the shed down.

He placed the photograph album in the middle of the table and the book, *Mein Jugendfreund*. Each expert in turn studied all of the writings, being the writing in The Album, the August Kubizek signature and the birth certificate.

And everyone agreed that all were penned by Adolf Hitler.

David Cullen, the journalist who was witnessing the event turned round and said, "This whole affair resembles the Watergate scandal of the early seventies coming out of Washington."

With that Elizabeth Hoben responded "John, if you don't mind me saying so this affair makes the Watergate scandal look like the back page of The Beano."

The Watergate scandal was responsible for the American President Richard Nixon resigning, so when Elizabeth Hoben made that comment the importance of what I was involved in started to kick in a little more.

Renna Nezos got up from the table and without saying a word walked out. We don't know why but Dad had two possible reasons why she might of left that meeting;

Renna Nezos was the highest qualified and most experienced person in that room and along with Victoria Fabling had suggested that Margaret White wasn't qualified enough to manager such a task and team and Dad believes that might be the reason she left.

Renna Nezos had also picked up in Hitler's writings the Anglo-Saxon and Latin and Dad believes that after actually seeing The Album and listening to the others talk about how scandalous and damaging the whole thing was, that she became frightened and decided she didn't want any more to do with it.

The leaving of this woman meant nothing to me, the fact she had turned up in the first place obviously meant she knew whose the handwriting belonged to because otherwise after studying Dads documents initially she would never have turned up.

As I sat there at the table in the RSA, I was witnessing all these handwriting experts become quite intrigued and excited by the whole thing and to watch that was also exciting for me. I obviously knew The Album, signature and birth certificate was Hitler's but to have so many experts in one room all agreeing was a great feeling and gave me a real belief in Dad's work. Sometimes when I find it hard to come to terms with my life and start to doubt what I have been involved in, I just take myself back to that day and remember what all those experts had said.

That meeting had been set up by Margaret White mainly to gather the experts and discuss the best way of raising these issues. Victoria Fabling said she would talk to someone at The Mail on Sunday to see whether they were interested in taking the story on and to investigate it further, she told my Dad she would write to him soon.

The other journalist there David Cullen took numerous amounts of notes and Dad told him he would send some tapes and more documents to him so he could investigate further. This man had just been at a meeting that would make unbelievable reading for any newspaper and so he found himself purely by accident in a once in a lifetime opportunity. This story at that time was immense and any one who had the courage to take it on would find themselves extremely wealthy at the end of it but as Elizabeth Hoben had suggested this affair was highly political and dangerous and so it was going to have to take someone with guts and courage to take on.

It turned out that the main point to the meeting was to prepare everyone for the meeting at Sotheby's the following month. All the experts had come to the conclusion the best way to raise this affair publicly was by putting The Album up for auction; it was the best way to bring attention to the other issues.

Everyone said goodbye to each other and the four of us, myself, my Dad, Margaret and David Cullen left the building together and headed for the Embankment Tube Station.

As we were heading for the station my Dad turned round to Margaret and David and told them he had to make a phone call and so he would say goodbye. We all said our goodbyes and went our separate ways. When they were out of sight I turned to my Dad and asked him who he needed to ring, he said no one but we couldn't have gone into the tube station with them because we didn't have enough money for the train tickets and so pushing our way through the barriers would have looked stupid and most embarrassing.

It was quite an ironic scene really, we had just come out of a really dramatic meeting with great potential and Dad was also carrying an album by Hitler, which was obviously worth a lot of money, but we were standing there without even enough money to get a train ticket.

We waited around for a while and then we walked down to the Embankment and managed to slip through the barriers and get on the underground back to Dagenham.

It had been a long few days for me but they were worth it, I got back to the house in Dagenham where my Nan greeted me and I sat down that evening and enjoyed one of her special dinners. Sitting in that house that night with no job and money meant nothing because I was filled with excitement and hope for the future and couldn't wait for the meeting in June to take place at Sotheby's.

In the few weeks leading up to that meeting a number of things happened which may have caused the breakdown of that meeting. A falling out between my Dad, Margaret White and Maureen Ward Gandy occurred.

My Dad and Margaret fell out because of David Cullen the journalist from the Croydon Post. Dad had sent him two tape recordings of this affair and a number of documents relating to it and when after a period of time not hearing a word from him, Dad wrote him a letter telling him exactly what he thought of him and faxed it through to his office for everyone to read. See, my Dad never liked complacency and anyone who had had his documents and not responded in quick time would receive a fairly stiff letter. In Dad's mind everyone who had received his highly important documents and not responded quickly were not worthy of them and so he would take the opportunity away from them.

But the letter Dad sent to David was not the kind of letter you send through a fax machine and had upset him and in the process he contacted Margaret. Margaret phoned my Dad and asked him what on earth he was doing, see Dad never had enough patience with anyone in all this and due to his principles had sometimes ruined perfect opportunities to finish this affair. My Dad and Margaret's communication slightly broke down from then, she still had her contract and still agreed to come to Sotheby's but she was upset with Dad for sending that letter to her friend.

Maureen Ward Gandy and my Dad's financier Ken McCullen had put a contract together behind my Dad's back that entailed Maureen having The Album in her bank so she could work on it at her pleasure, the contract also entailed Dad wouldn't receive any monies until Maureen and Ken were paid out. This contract had been constructed without any involvement from my Dad. Ken had already put £7500 into this project and when he found out Maureen was involved and was going to be responsible for raising the issue, he decided he wanted to go over and see her just to be reassured about Dad's work but in the process they both tried to come up with this contract. When Ken turned up to present Dad with it, he went completely mad and sacked both of them. He couldn't believe they had done such a thing and Maureen wanting The Album permanently just wasn't going to happen. Maureen might have been able to get Dad in front of John Major but my Dad had his principles and no man or nothing was going to get in the way of them.

Dad truly believed Hitler was still alive and was conducting his business the way he thought Hitler would have approved. This sounds far out and having to live with someone who thought like this was very hard. Dad had also mentioned to me in the past very briefly and at the time I thought he was joking, that he intended to give The Album back to Hitler.

When Maureen received the news about being sacked, she was devastated and continued to send Dad a number of faxes to try and make sense of what was happening. Maureen had already completed most of her work and was just about to involve her friends from the Home Office; she had already completed her own report, which entailed a fifty-three page in-depth scientific analysis on The Album, which she still has to this day.

After a short time my Dad did calm down and Maureen was back on the team but I'm not sure she totally trusted him after that. The work with her friends from the Home Office had been put on hold by Dad and all efforts were now focused around Sotheby's. Dad explained to Maureen what was happening and invited her to the meeting. Dad thought that a fifty three page leather bound report from a leading forensic expert would go some way in convincing Sotheby's that The Album was Hitler's. Obviously if they agreed initially to auction The Album they were going to do their own checks on it but having that report and all the other experts present would go a long way in breaking the ice. See that album was written in English and Hitler was known not to understand English, so having this album written in English and Dad stating it was Hitler's was sometime very hard for people to believe.

One of the experts that does stick out in my mind is Victoria Fabling, she had a unique kind of energy about the affair that no other expert had. She seemed to be involved, not because of the financial gains but because she could see what Dad had was right and could also see the conspiracy that had taken place and so I think she wanted to be part of the team to put things straight and I think she felt it was her destiny to be involved.

And as promised she wrote to my father explaining to him that she had approached the editors at The Mail on Sunday regarding his findings and the story behind them but the paper had printed similar stories in the past and had got their "fingers badly burnt" over it.

So why was The Mail on Sunday told off for printing such stories? Well because the Government and the Security Services don't want the general public to know the truth and that's why the Mail on Sunday told Victoria that they couldn't do anything with Dad's story. This similar attitude was shown to me when I have been dealing recently with Martin Townsend, the editor from the Sunday Express. The story behind how I became in involved with him and his newspaper is amazing and truly borders on a super natural experience that powerfully brought us together which in the process would suggest to anyone that The Sunday Express were meant to have the story and meant to do something about it.

But what Victoria Fabling did strongly suggest was that Dad should contact John Major directly, she said the revelations he had discovered were massive and should be discussed with no other person than John Major. Now for Victoria, who was a highly qualified expert who worked for The Mail on Sunday and had a good reputation, to suggest such a thing in writing surely would suggest to anyone the enormity of what I was involved in but reading such a letter while living in Dagenham with my Nan was somewhat surreal.

She went on to say she would be present at the Sotheby's meeting in two weeks time.

And that day quickly approached in June 1992 and it was a day I had waited for, for many years and all my dreams had gone through my head depended on the outcome of this meeting.

We all made our way up to London by tube, that being myself, my Dad, Dougie Brown and Ken McCullen and on the way we met up with Martin Jocelyn who had taken a few hours out of work to attend the meeting and one of my Dad's other friends Pete Ness.

Dad had arranged to meet Margaret White at Brown's Hotel in Mayfair. The meeting was due to begin at 12o/c and so we were due to meet her at 11.30am but for some reason she failed to turn up at the time arranged and so we made our way to Sotheby's on our own. I could see in Dad's face that he was fuming because Margaret had not been at the hotel waiting for us but I guess he was hoping she was delayed for some reason and would arrive later.

We got to Sotheby's and Roy Davids introduced himself and he took us over the road from the main building and into another building that was also owned by Sotheby's and into a large meeting room surrounded by antique paintings and a large table in the middle.

We sat down and waited for the experts to arrive. Roy Davids brought some refreshments in and left us in the room. As promised Victoria Fabling arrived with the other experts who were present at the RSA meeting.

One of those experts was still missing, Margaret White, she had organised this meeting in the first place and was financially going to gain from the outcome. Another lady who didn't turn but sent her husband instead was Maureen Ward Gandy.

The two main people in Dad's eyes who had been put in charge of their respective teams and had been given large contracts and who were going to present to Sotheby's in their professional way, their results and findings of The Album were not there. And now I could see Dad was starting to rage inside, "how dare they let me down", he must have been thinking. There were other experts there but Margaret carried creditability because she knew Roy Davids and Maureen Ward Gandy was important because she was a forensic scientist and she was going to bring that 53 page report along that no one could argue against, so I guess you could understand why my Dad was angry.

The real reasons why they didn't turn up are unknown but Dad believes the breakdown in communication with them previously may have had something to do with it another reason is that Margaret White and Maureen Ward Gandy were great rivals in their work and one being a graphologist and the other being a forensic scientist respectively meant sometimes their work clashed and so Dad believes that maybe they just didn't what to face each other.

So the start of the meeting hadn't gone quite as planned but there were still enough experts there to answer any questions Roy Davids might have and I guess the fact that Maureen's husband was there must have carried some weight.

Roy Davids came back into the room with a much younger looking man who looked like he had just stepped out of university and basically looked like a pompous idiot who should never have been there in the first place to make his tactless comments.

The photograph album was placed in the middle of the table and the experts present explained to them in their scientific way, how and why The Album was written by Hitler.

I was sitting next to my Dad and I could sense his unease with the situation. The Album being on display for so many people at one time was something he wasn't use to. Roy Davids begun to move closer and closer to The Album and leant down over it and studied the writing for himself. He made his way back to his chair and asked Dad a question, "As you may probably know it is documented Adolf Hitler never wrote in English, in your opinion why is he in your photograph album?"

It was a question no expert could answer. They could tell you why the writings were Hitler's but none of them could answer why he was writing in English.

I guess the answer was obvious really but to tell someone Hitler was actually English and them to believe it was impossible no matter how much evidence you had.

All of the experts knew that the English in The Album was written by Hitler at the age of sixteen but none of these particular experts knew of the traits of Anglo Saxon and Latin in his writing, it seemed it was only the European experts who could detect it.

And there was only one person in that room other than my Dad who knew his theories regarding Hitler being a member of the Royal Family. So the question that Roy Davids had asked was extremely hard to answer without making Dad look ridiculous.

If Sotheby's were going to auction that album they had to first know where it had come from but more importantly why it was partly written in English. Sotheby's had to know all the facts before making a decision to whether they were going to auction it.

The fact The Album was found in a garden shed in Dagenham was somewhat hard to explain and probably not believed by Sotheby's. Unfortunately Dad only had theories to how it ended up there. As Dad was talking Roy Davids colleague made his way round the table towards The Album. I could see my Dad was beginning to get angry at all the questions he was having to answer but I learnt after that he was still fuming at the fact that Margaret White and Maureen Ward Gandy hadn't turned up. Dad went on to explain to Roy Davids that a number of experts have suggested that Hitler was actually educated in England which was why he could write English, that's all Dad said about it and Roy Davids didn't continue questioning him.

If Sotheby's were going to auction The Album then it meant putting their whole reputation on the line. Auctioning something that belonged to Hitler was controversial in the first place especially as Jews owned the company but auctioning something belonging to Hitler that proved he was English would have brought mass and somewhat unwanted attention to Sotheby's. If they were going to do it and had the guts to go through with it, it would be the most amazing auction ever and the question is; which organisation or person in the world would pay almost anything to have that photograph album back in their possession?

At this stage of the proceedings it didn't look like the meeting was going too well because even if Roy Davids believed The Album was Hitler's the fact it contained massive revelations meant it was going to be somewhat hard to auction, if The Album had been totally in German it would have been a different matter.

Maureen Ward Gandy's husband, Michael who was attending the meeting on behalf of his wife, was carrying in his bag, as we learnt after, the fifty three-page report that categorically stated that The Album, which was on that table, was once the property of Adolf Hitler. Michael as we understand had brought the report along to show Roy Davids and we believe it was at this stage that he was just about to produce it and therefore would have taken away any doubt Roy Davids may have had but due to what happened next it never happened.

At that moment Roy Davids colleague had made his way round the table and was now studying The Album for himself, he then turned round to my father and said to him The Album reminded him of a musical box. I guess it was a fairly innocent comment but he made those comments at a time when my father was finding it hard to control his emotions and I guess him saying that sent my Dad over the top.

My Dad as I say was angry that Margaret and Maureen hadn't turned up and I guess if you could imagine the way he was thinking and his emotions at the time of the meeting, he had been through a lot building up to it. He also knew that Hitler was English and a member of the Royal Family and possibly still alive which no other person in that room knew about and so the questions Roy Davids was asking were somewhat hard for him to answer honestly. See even at that point Dad had made a comment to me, that he never intended to actually sell The Album but would go through the proceeding and put it up for auction to lure Hitler out of hiding, it was crazy thinking and I didn't believe his plans at the time. My plan was to sell that album and live happily ever after but Dad had other plans. Dad knew The Album was never going to be sold but he was going to use the publicity of the auction to raise publicly the other issues. Once again it was a good plan but for me made no sense whatsoever.

But with that sly comment just made by Roy Davids colleague, my Dad entered into one of his rages in the middle of Sotheby's, in the middle of this meeting, with all the experts around and he just started letting off steam at everyone. But it wasn't a pretty site and it wasn't the sort of thing you do when you are holding a meeting with one of the directors of Sotheby's and it ended with my Dad storming out of the meeting room leaving The Album on the table. Martin Jocelyn got up and followed him out of the room, I just sat there not believing what he had just done, this was the day I had so long been waiting for and Dad seemed to be doing his best to fuck it all up.

Martin managed to calm my Dad down with a few glasses of water and a good chat and eventually they came back into the room and Dad made his final comments to Roy Davids. If Roy Davids had any doubt to whether he was going to auction that album or not then my Dad's outburst of anger did not help the situation.

Everyone shook hands and Roy Davids said he would notify us in writing of Sotheby's decision on whether they were going to auction my Dad's album or not.

My father was still quite angry and Roy Davids decision to notify us in writing in two weeks time was not the kind of decision my father had been hoping for or expected.

He picked up his album and carefully wrapped it in cloth and placed it back into a small safety box and back into his briefcase and he walked out of Sotheby's with myself, leaving everyone else behind, we made our way back up Bond Street towards Oxford Street.

After a hundred yards or so I could hear someone calling us "John, John, please wait." And it is a scene that truly sticks out in my mind.

Victoria Fabling had come hurrying out of Sotheby's chasing us up the road to catch up. And as the three of us stood there she turned round to Dad and said to him, that whatever the outcome from

Sotheby's it is unimportant, what you have and what you have discovered is far more important than them and she said that the revelations were so serious she urged my father once again to contact John Major.

I don't think Victoria was involved in this affair for the money, I think she felt she belonged to the project, that she was meant to be involved for some reason. She could see that Dad was upset over Sotheby's and the pressure that he was generally under. I will always remember and appreciate her for her efforts and advice.

Her words had also made me a little more aware of the importance of Dad's affair and it began very slowly to sink in that what I was involved in was not all about money.

That was the last time I ever saw Victoria Fabling but the short time I did know her and reading her letters will always be with me. I tried tracking her down recently so I could get her views on these events but I found out she has moved to Canada and no longer studies graphology. I will say now, she is not the only graphologist in all this who after being involved in the Hitler affair decided to seek another form of work.

But I still remember on the way home that day, the feeling of eagerly waiting for Sotheby's response, Dad may have flipped out during the meeting but that didn't change the fact his album was Hitler's. It would be a long two weeks and it wasn't just me who was eagerly waiting for the response, obviously everyone who attended that meeting some way or another had a reason for wanting to know the outcome.

Another bizarre meeting I attended in and around that period while waiting for a response from Sotheby's was with the Richardsons.

Martin Jocelyn who seems to have been involved in this affair right from the start had driven over to Dagenham one night to tell my Dad that the Richardsons wanted to talk to him about his album.

The Richardsons were in the middle of constructing their own book and it included material regarding Eva Braun apparently living somewhere in the South of England but most importantly their book was trying to prove that Hitler's mother was actually Queen Mary.

The Richardsons had found a publisher to print their book, in fact I believe it was the same publishers in Australia who had printed Spycatcher, the only thing that the Richardsons needed before printing went ahead was actual prove that Queen Mary was indeed Hitler's mother.

Now just by coincidence Martin Jocelyn's brother, Mark, owned a restaurant south of the river and it was frequented by the Richardsons, and just by chance Mark overhead a conversation by them about their book and the content of it and suggested to them to talk to my father. Well that's what I've been lead to believe, sounds like bullshit to me nevertheless a meeting was set up and I for some reason I was invited.

Martin nor his brother wanted to attend the meeting, even though Mark had passed my Dads details onto the Richardsons I think he wanted as less involvement in all this as possible. I guess having meetings with the Richardsons to talk about Hitler and the British Royal Family was too much for some people to handle.

The meeting was shrouded in secrecy and Dad was lead to believe that all the Richardsons wanted to talk about was his album, Dad at this stage knew nothing about them knowing anything about the Royal link.

We had to get the underground all the way to Brixton where a car was waiting for us to take us to a hotel in the middle of the countryside somewhere in Surrey.

A Jewish man called Mark who seemed to be a generally nice chap met us at the station, he drove a four door Vauxhall Astra and he opened the doors for us to get in. And he drove us to this hotel that was run and owned by the Richardsons, we didn't know what to expect and our driver who did his best to make us feel at ease gave no clues away.

The whole experience for me was quite a nervous one, it wasn't quite like any of the other meetings I had attended before and this whole cloak and dagger stuff was quite a strange experience for me.

We eventually got to the hotel and it was a beautiful picturesque place, a typical country hotel that had a warm and cosy feel to it, even though I was surrounded by all these gangsters. We were greeted at the door by two heavies and we were shown straight through to one of the conference rooms.

Charlie Richardson wasn't actually present but he was obviously aware of the meeting and had suggested to his colleagues that maybe it wasn't a wise idea getting involved with such research.

Again even the Richardsons were doing their best to welcome us and to make us feel comfortable. Drinks were supplied and lunch was put on including prawn cocktails to start with.

As we entered the room there seemed to be quite a few people there, the head Richardson came straight up and introduced himself and in the process introduced everyone else. There were three or four of the Richardsons present and there was also a couple of historians from Cambridge University and a few people from The Sun newspaper. If the Richardsons' book was going to go ahead then they had to get the right information and the historians were there to help in that department, the journalists from The Sun were there because the Richardsons wanted as much publicity for their book as possible and so I think they were just there to witness the proceedings.

During lunch it was a period of general chitchat, getting to know the people we were surrounded by and I guess Dad was easing himself into the subject. Throughout lunch and the whole meeting a tape recorder was placed in the middle of the table obviously to record all what was being said.

I was sitting next to one of the Richardsons and he was this fairly large kind of bloke who looked like he was ready for a boxing match not a discussion that could bring down the House of Windsor. During lunch I thought I would try and make conversation with him and I turned round to him and said, "What do you do for a living?" he looked down at me and said, "I kill people." I looked away and thought how pleasant, if only my Mum could see me now.

I finished my lunch and Dad had started his talk about the affair, I had heard it many times before and so I decided I would leave and go to the toilet. I got up and left the room leaving my Dad to it. Before I re-entered the meeting I went up to the bar and ordered myself a drink. There was this girl sitting at the bar and she turned round to the barman and told him not to charge me, I said "thank you" to her and we began to chat. I didn't realise at the time but I was chatting up the daughter of one of the main men. And as we sat there in deep conservation, one of the heavies came up to us and started talking to me for some reason, rudely interrupting my conservation. And for some reason he started to make a point. He said, that if a load of police cars turned up he would go behind the bar get his guns and start shooting at them.

It was a bizarre thing to tell me and it definitely put an end to the conversation I was having with this girl. But if he was trying to scare me for some reason then still to this day I don't know why.

I had enough of talking to him and made my way back to the meeting. Dad was in full flow and I sat back down and started to listen. One thing that was slightly strange was that one of the historian's mobile phone would constantly keep ringing, Jerald was a so called historian but I believe there was more to him than meets the eye. I knew that this chap's phone ringing would be pissing my father off and I knew it was only a matter of time before he said something and so that was making me feel slightly uneasy.

Now what happened next was a complete shock for the both of us, but a shock for different reasons. A shock for me because of the amount of money they were offering Dad and also because of the information they wanted. For Dad it was a shock because he was unaware that the Richardsons knew of such information but he also became aware that the meeting being held that day was purely for this information, he thought the meeting was for the Richardsons to help him raise the Hitler issues but instead it was actually so that Dad could help them raise their issues.

The main Richardson turned round to Dad and said, "We need your help to prove that Adolf Hitler is the son of Queen Mary, if you can produce such evidence then we will pay you seven million pounds."

Suddenly I became instantly interested in the conversation, seven million pounds was like winning the lottery and all Dad had to do was provide the simple proof they required. Now for someone else to mention a link between Hitler and the Royal Family had sparked an interest in me, hearing my Dad talk briefly to me before didn't really mean much but now as I sat in this hotel surrounded by historians and journalists, it started to intrigue me.

Dad had never told me which member of the Royal Family he thought grew up to be Hitler but as I sat there I desperately wanted to know more. Everyone at that table was not interested in The Album or the other revelations, it was just the link between Hitler and the Royal Family that was the main interest, Dad's album could have been worth millions but they weren't interested, they just needed that vital piece of proof and their book was complete and ready for publication.

Dad couldn't quite believe what he had just heard from that man. It had startled him and he didn't know quite what to say. It was the first time someone else other than himself had mentioned this.

"If I'm going to talk about the Royal Family then you are going to have to turn that tape recorder off."

One of them nodded and as it was nearest to me, I attempted to switch it off but for some reason I couldn't and in my Dad's frustration he leant over me and pounded his fist upon it, which in the process did switch it off. I started to feel even more uneasy.

The conversation that took place from then on will always stay in that room and for me to reproduce it would be wrong but I will say the Richardsons were not happy with the outcome of the meeting. Dad refused to help them with their book, I'm not sure whether it was because he didn't have 100% proof himself at the time or whether he felt it wasn't his place to divulge such information to people who were only interested in making money out of it.

The fact Dad had in a way turned down seven million pounds that day, didn't really sink in until a few weeks after. At the time I was more intrigued and concerned over my Dad's theories over the Royal Family. It was now becoming clear I was involved in something far more important than money and if it involved our precious Royal Family then I wanted to know everything.

If an organisation such as the Richardsons who had historians and members of the Press present and who were willing to pay my Dad seven million pound for this information then subsequently I wanted to know more about this Royal involvement. I also wanted to know why my Dad had not passed that information on to them.

I didn't know too much about our Royal Family at that stage but I obviously knew they were the most powerful organisation in the world and now it seemed in a strange way that I was part of that. Dad had damaging information about the Royal Family but he was not willing to disclose it. It appeared he had a kind of respect for them and thought it wasn't his place to talk about it. A chat with someone like John Major would have been more appropriate, the Richardsons wanted to sell millions of books but John Major would of wanted to protect this country.

If it was my destiny to have knocked my Nan's shed down so that my Dad could expose the fact Adolf Hitler was in fact a member of the House of Windsor and therefore was it actually my destiny to bring that organisation down, but a question I do have if that's not the case; why have I been burdened with this knowledge throughout my life, struggling to come to terms with not knowing what's happening in the background? But if this is all true why out of all the millions of people in this country is it me who knows this powerful knowledge and another question, if it is all true why is it that I have been allowed to continue my path and not suffered a similar fate as Princess Diana did in Paris in 1997?

At the end of the meeting that day, Jerald passed his phone number onto my father and asked him to ring him. Mark then drove us back to Brixton where once again we got on the underground back to Dagenham.

Jerald after that meeting would continually turn up at our house in Dagenham and Dad would subsequently disappear for many hours with him, I'm not sure why this was happening, maybe it was because Jerald was a historian and was fascinated with Dad's work or maybe it was because he actually worked for MI5 and was finding out exactly what Dad knew or maybe they were both working for MI5 trying to establish what exactly the Richardsons knew.

The one thing I have learnt, many years after was that every person who was present at that meeting, except my father and me, received a phone call telling each and every person to leave this subject alone, so subsequently the Richardsons' book never got published. I don't know who made those phone calls but if someone or some organisation is threatening the security of the Royal Family then the most powerful and frightening organisation in this country who are given carte blanche when it comes to protecting them, that being MI5 probably in my opinion made those phone calls.

During the tube journey I was itching inside to talk to Dad about his theories on the Royal Family. We got off the train at Upney and while walking through Mayesbrook Park he began to tell me.

I was seventeen at the time when all these events took place and for me to remember everything that went on is impossible, it is also very difficult to get over the different emotions I was going through but I know it was sometimes very hard to come to terms with my life.

During that walk round the park that day, even though I was fascinated to hear Dad talk I still remember my mind switching off to his voice and I had to concentrate very hard to understand what he was saying. I had to listen to my Dad on numerous occasions continuously talk about this affair and so I had automatically learnt to switch off. So on this occasion when I actually wanted to listen I still found myself not listening and thinking of other subjects.

But obviously over time I would learn more of his theories and as time went past it would all sink in and even if his theories aren't true I did 100% believe them. And they obviously affected the way I ran my life and my paranoia over the Security Services I guess started at that point, knowing that Hitler was a member of our Royal Family I thought this was a secret that the Establishment would want to keep to themselves and having some seventeen-year-old boy knowing such information I thought would be a liability.

It's been quite difficult to know when in my story to write about this particular issue. It is also the one revelation, which has affected me the most, it is also the one revelation that I find the hardest to come to terms with and believe. My Dad has had brief reports done on the handwriting of these two people and has had a computerised ear matching with Hitler and this particular person from our Royal Family and those results would suggest that they are the same person. I know for a fact that Dad's album was once written by Hitler, I also know that The Album proves he was educated in England, I also believe that Hitler, through the 1953 August Kubizek signature, was alive after 1945 and I know his birth certificate is a forgery.

I also know that finding a photograph album in a garden shed in Dagenham is somewhat unreal but I still struggle to believe when my father tells me that in fact Prince John did not actually die when he was thirteen but grew up to be the leader of the Third Reich.

Dad believed right from the start, when he realised his album was written by Hitler, that he was a member of our Royal Family. When Professor Dr. Wulf Listenow in Zurich suggested to him that Hitler must have been educated in England because of the traits of Anglo Saxon and Latin in his writing, he then came to the conclusion through common sense I guess, that if Hitler was associated with England it must have be through our Royal Family.

He didn't know at that stage which member it was but when Elisabeth Klein had picked up in Hitler's writing in the Third Reich, that he suffered from epilepsy then it became quite clear to Dad while studying the Royal Family Tree which member he thought grew up to be Hitler.

Dad was looking for a member of the Royal Family born in the late 1890's or the early 1900's, not forgetting Hitler's birth certificate is a forgery and written by himself. And a member which fell into that category was Prince John, born 12th July 1905, and wasn't it a massive coincidence that he actually suffered from epilepsy, so when Dad found that piece of knowledge, he became convinced Prince John eventually become Adolf Hitler.

A question that springs to mind at this point is; if that is all true, do you think our Royal Family would have left Hitler to die in Berlin? Or do you think they would have rescued him and flown him the hell out of there? And if that is true where did he go and what has he been doing since?

Prince John is a relatively unknown member of our Royal Family, which until recently his existence has been hidden away and kept quiet from the public. There is very little in our history books about him and only a few photographs.

My Dad was convinced Prince John grew up to be Hitler even by reading the small amount of knowledge that was available but when The Independent newspaper, on the 11th February 1998, printed which it thought was the first ever picture of Prince John, Dad knew by just looking at the picture and the similarity between them that it was in fact Prince John who grew up to be Hitler and so it wasn't a great surprise when he went on to have the right ears of Prince John and Hitler matched by computer and the results came out positive.

On September 11th 2001 ("just by coincidence") Bonham's auctioned some photos of George V and Queen Mary and their children, including postcards written by Prince John. Prince John writings have also been studied and compared with Hitler's by handwriting experts, I have read some of their replies and they are very positive but still further work needs to be done for me to say that they 100% match but what with the matching of the ears there is a lot of positive evidence to suggest Prince John is Hitler and that evidence along with the other revelations needs to be investigated and looked into, if not for me then how about for all those millions of people who died in the Second World War. The truth always comes out in the end and in this case it's just a matter of when.

For those of you who don't know and there are many who don't, Prince John is the Queen's uncle and was the prince who was hidden away by George V and Queen Mary because he suffered from epilepsy and they couldn't risk him having a seizure or a fit in public. He was therefore moved to a separate establishment away from the Royal Family and was looked after by Lalla Bill at Wood Farm, Wolferton near Sandringham, Norfolk and it was there he received his education, a private education that would have been of the highest level.

It is stated in our history books and in a recently made drama by the BBC, that Prince John died at the age of thirteen due to a massive epileptic fit and he is buried at Sandringham Church, which was described as a very private ceremony.

The fact that our Royal Family have tried to keep Prince John a secret for so many years is very strange in itself, so why now after so much time have they decided to let us know about him. First there was the picture and article in The Independent and more recently there has been the much publicized drama called The Lost Prince which was first shown in 2003 and created much attention from the media regarding the fact that the Royal Family actually tried to hide one of their members from the public.

The story is controversial but could you imagine the reaction if the media and the people of England found out Prince John didn't actually die at the age of thirteen but was instead shipped out of the country to live with close friends (maybe relatives) in Austria and eventually took over Germany and went to war with Britain; his own country?

During that period while we were waiting for Sotheby's to reply my Dad went to Basel, Switzerland to try and talk to the university about the book *Mein Jugendfreund*. The book he had was from their library and Dad thought the university might actually be interested in the revelations that were contained in one of their books.

But once again due to him having no money he got arrested in Basel and put in jail and while the police went through his belongings they noticed an overdue book from Basel University and they sent it back, therefore Dad lost his only copy of *Mein Jugendfreund* with the signature in it.

While Dad was away I decided to phone Sotheby's and try and get their decision over the phone but they said to me they had made their decision but they would put it in writing.

When my Dad found out that I had phoned Sotheby's he went completely mad. Dad when dealing with organisations and individuals would always do everything by letter, it was so he had proof of dealing with people and had proof of their decisions over the affair. Everything was documented and copied and he had letters from everyone who was involved in this which he believed would be part of his own book when this whole affair ended. So me ringing Sotheby's and getting an answer over the phone may have jeopardized them sending Dad a letter.

Everyday I woke up and waited for the postman to arrive to bring that good news from Sotheby's I was so looking forward to. The letter did come eventually and I remember waking up one morning in June 1992 and walking downstairs and my father had said he had received the letter from Sotheby's and he asked me to come into the lounge so I could read it.

No matter what kind of letter my Dad received throughout this whole campaign he could always see a positive side to a negative letter.

But this particular letter I was reading I could only see negativity and as I read on a huge feeling of disappointment came over me.

The letter from Sotheby's basically said they were unable to auction Dad's photograph album because they felt it was far too political for them to deal with.

It was a hard letter for me to read, I had waited anxiously for their response over the days but I had over the years dreamt of the auction and so Sotheby's turning my father down instantly had an effect on me.

I sat there and thought it was the end. I couldn't see where my Dad could go from here, not only had Sotheby's turned The Album down but Dad had also just recently turned down £7,000,000 from the Richardsons. So I sat there and started to wonder what I was really involved in and where it was going.

My father's outburst of rage during that meeting at Sotheby's I don't think helped in their final decision also his behaviour towards Margaret White's journalist friend, David Cullen I think was unnecessary but it happened and therefore broke Margaret and my Dad's working relationship down, I also believe that my Dad's attitude towards Maureen Ward Gandy was not right, he had sacked her over some small disagreement which most people would have ignored knowing the fact she was trying to get him to see John Major.

So I sat there wondering if maybe it was the end of the road for me and maybe it was time for me to get on with other things. For my father it was just another organisation that had gone down the drain and would be kicking themselves once his relations became public but I could never look at things like that.

He seemed to have these opportunities come his way but he would only follow them so far and then destroy them and that just wasn't the way I lived my life, I always went through with certain situations as far as they would go and this letter coming through from Sotheby's I think maybe was a sign for me to move back to my Mum's and try to establish some kind of reality on my life.

It also seemed that anyone involved with my father around that period stepped away from the affair. Dad's financier Ken McCullen, had enough from that point on, Dougie Brown moved to the Gascoigne Estate in Barking and so his last hope was resting on that result from Sotheby's, you can only imagine his disappointment when he had to move out of his home and into a tower block in Barking. All the experts disappeared and we didn't hear from them again. I don't think it was 100% down to the Sotheby's decision but due to Dad's attitude towards The Album and the way he conducted himself through this and because of his bizarre beliefs regarding Hitler.

As I've said before Dad believed that Hitler was alive and believed in his mind he was very close to him and therefore would act using his strong principles thinking that Hitler may be judging his every move.

I stayed at my father's home for another month, I don't think it was through choice, it was because I had no other option, convincing my Mum that I wasn't going to have anything more to do with my Dad and try and go out and find a career was quite hard.

My father wasn't affected at all with the Sotheby's decision and went about his business as normal finding the next person or organisation to send all his documents to.

Maybe I'm being a bit hard on my Dad but it did appear that he would get himself into a great position where maybe he could have ended this whole wretched thing but instead he would back away. It was like he was hiding something from people. When he sacked Maureen Ward Gandy she was just about to involve her friends from the Home Office to work on The Album and therefore would have had the evidence necessary to approach John Major but due to my Dad's strong principles he backed down and believe me I have asked myself why so many times, I even actually wondered if The Album was indeed Hitler's and was there something Dad was hiding. Deep down I knew it was but I could no longer live with my Dad knowing he was going about his business in this way.

I had played no cricket that summer, hardly seen any of my friends and was living off the dole and living with both my Nan and Dad that was at times very hard. My Dad was not the easiest person to live with and him talking about the affair constantly didn't help either, I was being suffocated by it and there was something inside me telling me to get out. The fact that Dad strongly believed Hitler was still alive and living somewhere in Arizona affected the way he went about this affair. If I had of been in charge I would have sold The Album ages ago and hopefully would have been living a normal life by now but because Dad had gone onto find out all these different revelations the affair has seemed to go on forever, he had become more interested in the conspiracy and believed it was his duty as a Christian to expose it, he also thought that Hitler was still alive and dangerous and having his album Dad thought was a bargaining tool when the shit hit the fan.

Obviously for me to stay with my Dad knowing his beliefs and knowing he was always just waiting for something to happen and I had just seen all his efforts with all the different handwriting experts basically go up in smoke, I thought while I was still fairly young I would try and sort my life out. It was becoming unbearable living in the shadow of Hitler.

Due to my Dad's beliefs and proof that Hitler did not commit suicide in Berlin in 1945 and it was a possibility he was still alive, Dad thought that it was his duty to start telling Jewish people about it, he also came to the conclusion after debating with myself over Victoria Fabling's comments regarding John Major that he would put together a number of documents and send them to The Israeli Embassy and Downing Street.

I was not with my Dad when he took a number of documents, (including handwriting reports of The Album and the other findings and numerous telephone numbers of experts around the world who had studied The Album), to Downing Street. Dad personally went up to London to hand delivered them to Downing Street. In the process giving John Major a massive document that proved Hitler was English and could possibly still be alive but without a doubt alive in 1953, surely no Prime Minster could ignore such evidence?

The same set of documents was also hand delivered to the Israeli Embassy in Kensington and on that occasion I was present. It was the last thing I did before I left to go back to my Mum's.

My Dad was in no way whatsoever anti-Semitic, he only ever wanted to help the Jews, he truly thought they were once again in danger and wanted to warn them. He wished dearly that a Jewish organisation would help him in his quest and sometimes I wonder when he has got in a good position and backed down it was because the people helping him were not Jewish.

Again Dad truly believed and still does that Hitler is alive and planning a massive attack on the Jewish race, he believes Hitler is going to blackmail the whole world and demand the killing of every Jew.

Dad thought if a Jew or a Jewish organisation would help him to find Hitler, it would go a long way especially when giving him his album back to maybe turning him around. Sounds completely crazy I know but if you can imagine that Hitler is alive and dangerous and all of a sudden my Dad did find him and gave him back his precious beloved album that was constructed by him possibly for a Jewish woman. Wouldn't it be amazing if Dad could turn round and say to him that it was because of a Jew he made it so far and was able to return his album? I'm sure that would go along way spiritually in changing Hitler's views on the Jews. Because if that ever happened then any man would surely appreciate it would have taken a numerous amount of miracles to have got to that point and surely no man could ignore God.

Entering the Israeli Embassy is a huge task in itself and entering such a place to talk about Adolf Hitler was somewhat nerve racking. But if anyone reading this actually believes this story then you would think the Jews would have been interested in such revelations. Because don't forget they did lose six million of their own people to Hitler, so surely them receiving evidence that he may still be alive would be something that would interest them.

Just as we approached the embassy Dad told me to be careful what I said inside, he said they knew what we were coming for and so it was most likely the whole building was being bugged. And on this particular occasion I believed him, I had seen and witnessed too much and so if Mossad or MI5 were monitoring us at that point it wouldn't have surprised me.

Even before we were allowed through the security gates we were asked lots of questions. I guess just to confirm why we were there and who we were. A man came out of the building and the gates opened and he showed us in. I can't remember being searched but again this man asked us more questions regarding our visit and then he eventually took us upstairs and showed us into a small room with just a table and a few chairs.

We were now, in legal terms, on Israeli ground and they could have done what they pleased with us and looking back on that day it showed my Dad had absolutely nothing to hide but truly wanted to get through to the Jewish people.

A man entered the room and sat down and Dad briefly went through his work and the findings and gave this man a set of documents, the same set in fact that John Major had just recently received. The man took them and we all said goodbye.

The fact we were invited to the Embassy in the first place, I believe is significant. That invite would never have come unless they were interested in my Dad's work; they are not the sort of people who like to waste time.

Dad never received any acknowledgement from the Jews, not one phone call nor one letter asking him to discuss this matter further. In fact all the Jews that he has ever dealt with throughout this campaign and believe me there have been hundreds, they have all ignored him. I know the subject is hard for them but you would have thought that Hitler getting out of Berlin in 1945 would have been something they were interested in. The fact it seems he is English and could still be alive because don't forget Prince John was born in 1905 and therefore at the time would have made him 87 is again information you would have thought the Jews would of wanted. But instead they all ignored my Dad and either they were all too scared of the subject or most importantly just didn't believe it and refused to check my Dad out by making just a few simple phone calls to one of the handwriting experts. Let us all pray that their ignorance towards my father's work is not regrettable but some might already say due to certain events happening in the world today that time has unfortunately run out for them. My Dad's classic saying is "It only ever took a phone call," and it is pointed mainly at all the Jewish people who have received my Dads documents, it means basically make a phone call to see whether my Dad is telling the truth before you judge him as being mad, it could just save your life.

A letter from John Major though was sent to my Dad and when I read it, it was fairly encouraging but also fairly disappointing at the same time. There was no invite for my Dad but instead John Major had said he had found my Dad's work very interesting but because it wasn't in his "remit" he could not deal with it but he said he had passed it on to a different section of the Government.

After reading that letter I used to wonder to myself why the Prime Minister of England wasn't interested in proof that Hitler was English, a member of our Royal Family, alive in 1953 and therefore could be alive and possibly dangerous, surely that proof and evidence is the job for any Prime Minster to investigate further?

That whole period was very difficult for me to live through because I had witnessed so many of the handwriting experts work and could see for myself that my Dad's work was 100% right. But when it came to dealing with organisations Dad seemed to get knock back after knock back which sometimes was very frustrating.

Looking back I can see why things didn't work out because basically it was meant to be, other things were meant to happen later on, anyway if things had of worked out then I would never have written this book.

Sometimes I wonder what has been going on in the background while all this has been going on. I believe there is a part of this story that has been hidden from me, I don't know why, maybe I was being allowed to see so much but only as much as I could handle at the time. Which for a seventeen-year-old seemed to be quite a lot. Sometimes I wonder if I went through all those different events with the handwriting experts etc, so that my belief in Dad's work would become solid and when later on in my life when I lost faith I could always look back and remember those events e.g. the meeting at the Royal Society of Arts.

Looking back now, even though it appeared all those organisations had ignored Dad, I do stop and wonder that maybe one didn't because in the October of that year 1992 Dad was holding meetings with the FBI and you just don't walk into that organisation. So I do wonder sometimes which Government agency over here organised those meetings in Washington and what was the true purpose of them?

Dad was in Washington for eight days during mid October, staying at the Harrington Hotel, which is virtually opposite the FBI Headquarters. He held meetings with two agents from the FBI there, Agent Brewer and Agent Harris, and a lady called Debbie Campbell who I believe was a forensic scientist working alongside John Hicks, who was the Assistant Director of the FBI at the time.

Dad, as I have been led to believe was there to discuss the August Kubizek signature with them. It was possibly the one revelation that the US may have had some interest in because obviously if Hitler was alive and living on their ground then they would have wanted to know about it.

The FBI agreed with Dad that the signature of August Kubizek was actually written by Hitler and they had asked him to get hold of the original signature for them. Dad said he had tried to contact Leopold Stocker, (the publishers of *Mein Jugendfreund*) but to no avail. Dad told them it would be a lot easier if they approached them rather than himself.

After those meetings Dad flew home from Washington with the knowledge the FBI were going to contact Leopold Stocker to get hold of the original signature. They had already agreed the signature in the textbook was the handwriting of Hitler's but getting the original just confirmed it for them.

Dad had not talked to the FBI about any of the other revelations; it was just that one that may have sparked their interest. I guess having Adolf Hitler living in your country for the past 40 odd years would have been embarrassing for them.

Dad received a few letters from the FBI during the first few weeks of him being back and again they were urging him to get hold of the signature. And once again Dad told them to contact Leopold Stocker themselves.

Dad as I believe never again heard from the FBI, but that doesn't mean they didn't continue with further investigation. See these revelations (apart from The Album) are not copyrighted to my father they are for anyone to investigate and study. That book *Mein Jugendfreund* can be bought anyway or borrowed at any library, so go and buy it or borrow it and take it to your local handwriting experts and ask them if the birth certificate, postcards and if you're lucky enough to have a copy with the signature in, are written by Hitler and at what age?

By this time I had moved back to my Mum's. She was now living in a three bedroom flat in The Limes, Ingatestone, Essex.

Living with my Nan and Dad had become intolerable; the feeling of repeatedly having my hopes raised and then dashed was doing me in. It had been quite an exciting time for me and I had witnessed stuff that no normal seventeen-year-old does but unfortunately nothing major had come of all those events and I just couldn't see an immediate end to it. I left my Nan's midway through August, I didn't leave on bad terms and my Dad knew I was leaving because I didn't know how long the affair was going to last and he knew I wanted to go back home where all my friends were. I hadn't seen many of my friends through the summer apart from Alister who came over to see me once in a while to see if I was O.K.. So I left Dagenham to try and build my life back again.

But no matter what I went on to do in my life the fact I was carrying the Hitler revelations around in my head became a massive burden because no matter what I was doing it was always on the edge of my thinking and hovering over me like a bad nightmare and my thinking started to develop a little like my Dad's, because it was always being drummed into me whereby I was always preparing my mind for the day that all this would hit the media and therefore put my Dad and me in the spotlight.

207

This way of life and thinking was not healthy and the power that was controlling my destiny must have realised that. I was sent down a fairly normal road for a while but only for a while and then crazy things started happening again but how long could I continue this way of life? And what effect was it all having on my mentality?

One of the conditions, if I was to stay with my Mum, was that I either had to get a job or go back to college.

The next few months leading up to Christmas were a little strange because looking back they were very similar to the year before.

I decided to go back to college. I enrolled for a one year BTEC Business course along with my friend Al who had just finished his GCSE retakes at St Martin's.

For me to enrol in that course was a way for me to bide my time. I had spent quite a dramatic summer with my father and even though nothing had come of his efforts, I still had a deep faith in him and a faith that something was going to come of it all and so I thought enrolling in a one year business course, a course that I had mainly covered at Thurrock college, would firstly be an easy time for me but would mainly keep my Mum happy until that day eventually came along.

Once again at that point of my life, I was only living it day by day waiting for something big time to break in the news, I was never interested in my future or what I was going to be doing as a career, I was only ever interested in the Hitler affair.

It was great being back in the Brentwood area, I had missed going out with my friends and I had missed my cricket and so I began playing again.

I think for me to bore you with stories about me going out and my cricket achievements, probably stories that have no meaning when compared to the Hitler affair would be pointless and boring, so I will just summarise the main points so you can understand how and why I have lead up to certain events which happen in the future.

It was August 1992 and I had a few weeks left of the summer before college began and I think it was being shown to me that I should make an effort and go back and start playing cricket for the remainder of the season. I was living in a flat in Ingatestone and while standing in the lounge at weekends I could see Ingatestone playing cricket, the flat had a perfect view of their field, and at that point England were also playing in the Test match and so the cricket was on the television as well. I remember standing there realising to myself I was actually missing not playing.

I decided to play the rest of the season for Hutton, which was one of Brentwood's rivals. I couldn't go back to Brentwood I felt uncomfortable there, so I joined Hutton and had a fairly successful few games but I could still sense a stigma even there, my Dad had friends throughout the whole of Brentwood and so rumours about people seem to travel fast and spread easy and so I sensed peoples disbelieve and judgements even at that club. But I still played the rest of the season out but it just didn't feel like home, it didn't feel where I should have been playing, Brentwood Cricket Club was my home and I missed playing there and missed my friends.

I also tried to get a job. I went back to TWTI in Brentwood where Jane was still manager but she refused to give me my job back. She thought the way I had left a few months previously, whereby I had just walked out without saying anything to anyone, was wrong. Al did his best to convince her to give me my job back explaining I had gone through a lot recently but she was having none of it. But what happened next was a stoke a luck for me, (If you believe in luck that is and as my good friend Phil used to say "There is no such thing as luck") Jane was promoted to Marketing Manager of the whole company and was moved to the head office in Grays and subsequently the Brentwood office received a new manager. And this development gave me the opportunity to go back into the Brentwood office seeking my old job back and to present myself to the new manager, obviously not letting on to her that I had worked there before and basically that's how I got my job back. When Jane did eventually find out I was working back in the office she thought because of the way I had done it and the cheek of it, that she would let me continue to work there.

Life for me was beginning to rebuild itself, I had started playing cricket again and had managed to get my part time job back and I was just about to start college, which for my Mum was a good thing, I knew I was just going there to bide my time waiting for whatever my Dad thought was going to happen. I was secretly still involved with my Dad, I had just kept my dealings away from my Mum but obviously I was still intrigued to know what he was doing and so we did keep in contact but the contact was always only between me and him and on a small scale.

Another thing that happened in that period and it was in a period when the Government had just received all of Dad's documents and

Dad was also dealing with the FBI in Washington that Robert Dickman appeared on the scene. Robert is my cousin and until that point in my life I had no knowledge of him, the family had lost contact with him when Neville, Rob's Dad, my uncle, died. But when I realised he was working for the Government as a Civil Servant, I immediately became wary of him. Not necessarily straight away but when I was in hospital I started to become paranoid over everyone in my life and every situation. Paranoid about who people were and why they were associated with me and I used to study how I had come into contact with them. Rob saying he was a Civil Servant, because at that time I had read in many spy books that some undercover spies would say they were Civil Servants. So in my paranoia I did think he was an MI5 agent and subconsciously I was aware of him, which probably did affect our relationship. Later on in the story when my Dad was dealing with Al Fayed I found out at the same time that Rob knew him and I guess it was the mystery around the whole thing and the coincidence that made me wonder. There's probably nothing in it but because of what I was involved in and the organisation he worked for I guess I was just being cautious and surely anyone who may believe this story would understand why I thought that of him.

Part of the course at college running up to Christmas involved me having to do one weeks work experience which I did at Next in Brentwood. I met Emma there who was the Manager of the store but it was an important meeting for me because of what she had and was selling. I got to know her quite well and learnt she was selling her first ever car, a gold Renault Five. She wanted five hundred pound for it and so for me to raise that kind of money I was going to have to save. So I started working hard at TWTI and was putting most of my earnings into my saving account. The Renault was a far cry from the 911 Porsche I had expected by then but it was a nice little car and it was something I was saving for and so was going to appreciate.

Another person who worked in the Next shop in Brentwood was a chap called Matt Flain. We became quite good friends over the next year or so and we would spend much time going out to clubs and parties together. But initially when I first met him at the shop he told me a story that was very coincidental and it was like fate had brought us together. In fact this whole story seems to be packed with coincidences, that some would say were only coincidences but others may say that it was the work of God.

He told me that he was waiting for a sum of money to be paid to him from an investment he had made a few years ago and he said once he had received the money he was going to be fairly well off and so this story he was telling me began to intrigue me. And it turned out it was Matt's Dad Bob, who had invested some three hundred pound into my Dad when he first went to Zurich back in 1989 so that money hadn't come from Bob. Bob had actually asked his son for it thinking it was a sound investment. And while I listened to his story a strange feeling came over me when I realised that Matt's money was actually used by my Dad for the Hitler affair and I wondered what his reaction was going to be when I told him I was also mixed up in that affair and it was in fact my Dad who had spent his money but had failed to return it, let alone the extra cash that was promised.

Fortunately Matt like myself appreciated the coincidences of it all and we both felt it was quite strange and I went on to tell him that in fact what my Dad had was real but it seemed to be taking longer than expected. And I had also invested some money into the affair and was also waiting for my return. Matt and my friendship grew from there.

It was my eighteenth birthday that year in December and my Mum knew I was making an effort to re-build my life, she knew I was working hard and saving hard and I was doing quite well at college, purely because I was just repeating the work I did at Thurrock and so my course work marks were quite good. And as my Mum could see I was putting in an effort to put my life back on the right track, she had gone into Next, without me knowing and met Emma and paid her the rest of the money outstanding for the car. (I had paid Emma two hundred pound deposit).

And on my eighteenth birthday my Mum surprised me with that car, I remember waking up and she told me to look out the window and sitting in the car park below with all balloons around it was that Renault Five. It was obviously a shock to me that my Mum had done such an amazing thing for me especially after what I had recently put her through but it is something I will never forget. The car wasn't the most expensive car in the world but that wasn't the point, the fact she had even bought it in the first place meant a lot to me, I had caused my Mum a lot of worry over the years and we hadn't always seen eye to eye and my constant support for my father had deeply affected our relationship.

Even though that car was quite old and probably had been round the clock a few times, it was a car that had got me through some potentially bad times, it had also provided me a life-line to my friends and job when once again I ended up living in Dagenham with Dad and if it hadn't of been for that car I would have probably of gone under a long time before I actually did. The car gave me my freedom and provided me with many good memories but without it I would definitely have been ill a lot earlier in my life.

That freedom quickly brought back some old habits and I started to spend a lot of time of an evening sitting in some dark country lane smoking pot again with Matt and a few other friends and the same kind of pattern as before was developing.

Early in 1993 I had to do another period of work experience for my college course and this time I asked Jane at TWTI if I could do my work experience for her in Grays, the Brentwood office by now had shut down and the whole operation was being run out of the Grays office at the Queensgate Centre.

Considering that me and Jane didn't quite see eye to eye while working together in the Brentwood office and especially after the way I had previously left, I was quite surprised when she agreed to my two weeks work experience and it was the perfect time for me to begin work there because the company was moving from Grays to bigger offices in Harold Hill, Romford. I spent the two weeks preparing and helping them with the move and then eventually helping them set up the new offices, which included a lot of computer work, preparing new scripts and other general paper work needed for the telemarketing operation. It also included me helping out with the recruitment campaign for the office which included taking phone calls from possible new employees and I even helped out with the interviews, which at the time was quite strange because of how young I was.

I think Jane during those two weeks could see how enthusiastic and well organised I was and could also see the amount of energy I was putting into my work. Everyday I started at 9.00am and finished at 5.30pm and then I would hang around for half hour and then start my shift in the evening until 9.00pm, so I think they could all see my enthusiasm for the company and I believe Jane got together with the chap who owned the business; Barry Hurley and after those two weeks were up they offered me a promotion as Jane's assistant which obviously I accepted.

There was something about that company I loved, it wasn't your normal everyday business, it was quite a laid back place and I was surrounded by normal everyday people who were just trying to get on in life, even the boss, Barry Hurley was a fairly down to earth character who had been brought up in the East End and had made good for himself, he was a very successful man but a man who seemed to never forget where he had came from. I had enormous respect for him and in a way he reminded me a little of my Dad before all the Hitler affair started. Barry had a number of very loyal members of staff who would basically do anything for him and had spent many hours working for him making his business successful, it's just a shame that Barry in the end didn't really appreciate that.

After my two weeks of work experience I again, to my Mum's horror, left college and went to work for TWTI as the Marketing Manager's assistant. My hours for this job again were not conventional hours; I started at 2.00pm and finished at 9.00pm.

It was the last time that I ever went to college; I had tried it twice and due to me wanting to get on with my life left.

Now once again due to my hours at work and extra money that was coming my way, I was able to start going out more with my friends and so exactly like before I began getting in late at night and not getting up until the afternoon, which my Mum totally disagreed with, she was also not happy with me leaving college so I could go and work for a timeshare company.

During this period my Dad had asked me to secretly meet him outside one of the pubs in Shenfield. When I arrived he was with a man called Martin Hogdson. Martin was someone who Dad had played a lot of tennis with during the eighties and he had just recently become involved in the Hitler affair. Martin, before he got involved had a girlfriend who I believe he was going to marry, a good job as carpenter earning £500 a week, he had a car and a van and was just about to move into his own house. Now because of this affair and his true belief in my Dad's work, Martin over time lost everything including his job and girlfriend and totally dedicated his life to exposing the Hitler revelations but in the end due to him getting too deeply involved ended up in Warley Mental Hospital and due to him wanting to totally escape from my Dad and the affair he had to move away without letting anyone know where he was going.

My Dad told me that Martin was financing a trip so they could go to Jersey. Dad was going there to construct a video of this whole affair but before he left he wanted to let me know where he was going and why.

The video that was made in Jersey was a two-hour video of my Dad talking in his hotel room about The Album and the other findings, and in fact I have got a lot of my information and finer detail from it while writing this story. The video explains everything about the revelations and gives details about every expert who has ever seen or dealt with my father, it is a powerful video that I found hard to watch realising what I was involved in.

The video at the end suggests Hitler may be alive and my Dad is directing the end comments towards John Major and after explaining everything and providing telephone numbers of all the experts suggests to John Major it may be time for a meeting, Dad says he needs to ask him a particular question.

Before he left to make that video my Dad gave me a hundred pound in cash, he said if anything happened in the news etc., I should make my way to an address in Ramsgate and wait for him there. Dad was always thinking something was just about to break in the news, he was always so positive about everything but he also knew the danger we would all be in when the shit hit the fan.

I remember saying goodbye to them and driving round the corner to the local ATS and with that hundred pound I bought a new exhaust for my car. Even though I believed all my Dad's work there was something telling me inside it was never going to break in the news.

The video that my father made was sent to a number of different organisations including; John Major, MI5, MI6, all the newspapers, many university's, CIA, FBI, Israeli Embassy, many organisations in Israel and many many individuals that just happened to cross my Dad's path.

It was at this point I later found out that MI5 were actually involved in this affair and I found out at a time when I was doubting the whole importance of it all and so when I was told I realised then that if MI5 were interviewing people over this affair then it was obviously important. MI5 were involved and therefore must have investigated the revelations and any individual who may have been involved.

My Mum had been asked to visit Brentwood police station one day because Gary, who was now living in the house in Hartswood Rd, had received a video from my Dad and was unhappy with its content and felt it was an intrusion on his privacy and so he contacted the police over it. The police must have watched it and because of its content and what it is suggesting contacted MI5. And my Mum sat in a room at Brentwood police station being interviewed by them. Now for some reason the MI5 agent who was interviewing her had made a point of telling my Mum whom he was working for, he said, "I don't have to tell you this but I work for MI5 and you may or may not know that we are responsible for the internal security of this country."

When my Mum told me this I questioned her more about the interview, it was intriguing to think that she had been interviewed by MI5, an organisation that had intrigued me so much but also had worried me over the years sometimes to the point of madness. She never told me the whole detail of the interview she says, conveniently enough, she can't remember the rest, but as I say she told me that information when I thought the affair had no substance and in a way it gave me some added faith I needed at the time.

Now once again it was at this point in the story that my Mum suggested I went to live with my Dad again.

At the time I used to say she threw me out but while writing this story and trying to see it from her side I can kind of understand why she did it. She was unhappy with the way I was running my life, she didn't agree when I decided to leave college and certainly didn't agree with my job and what with all those late nights and her probably knowing I was out doing drugs and by now she had cottoned on to the fact that I was still involved with my Dad. Dad would ask me to do something like make a phone call for him or write a letter and so eventually my Mum found out and I think when she was dragged down the police station and interviewed by MI5, I think that was the last straw for her.

Again I was upset that my Mum had asked me to leave and the thought of living in Dagenham again filled me with dread.

I gathered my belongings again and drove my car towards Dagenham, on the way I decided I would stop off at St Peter's Church in South Weald. I was low and confused with my situation and wondered what my life was all about. I didn't really want to go back to Dagenham and I so desperately wanted this Hitler affair to end, it was like a dark cloud constantly hovering over me.

I walked up to the church doors remembering all of Dad's work regarding the locking of them and I wondered to myself whether these doors were going to be locked. They were not, so I walked in and sat down, I felt quite connected to this church in some way I guess probably because it was the same church that my Mum and Dad got married in.

At that point in my life I don't think you could call me a typical churchgoer and in fact that was the first time I had gone into any church to pray. I may not have been conducting my life quite how God may have liked but then it was he who had put me in certain situations and had burdened my life with the Hitler affair. Even as an eighteen-year-old I could sense some kind of power controlling my destiny but at times I found it hard to acknowledge and sometimes I would even curse that power for putting such a pressure on my life. But as I sat there in that church I prayed for some kind of release and an end to it all.

My stay at my fathers was made slightly easier because of a number of reasons but mainly because I had my own car and was able to get to work but most importantly I could still travel to Brentwood where my friends were. It was also made easier due to my job at TWTI and so I wasn't constantly with my father like the last time but the main thing that made my stay a lot easier was the fact that my Dad's friend Martin Hodgson had also just been thrown out of his house by his mother because of his constant involvement with my Dad, and so he was now living at my Nan's house in Dagenham and so my father had him to direct all his thoughts and frustration at.

Martin was a hundred percent dedicated towards the Hitler affair and he truly thought it was his destiny and a privilege to be involved in such a thing.

And so instead of my Dad trying to get me involved in everything and suffocate me with continuous talk about Hitler and the affair it was Martin who my Dad started to direct all his efforts at.

Martin at that point had just helped Dad with the making of that video and had financed the whole trip to Jersey. He was also involved in preparing documentation that was attached to those videos and the sending off of them.

My interests in the affair at that point had slightly faded and I was more concerned over my job and enjoying myself with my friends. I think my Dad's antics and the general lack of response and development from the year before had dampened my spirits towards the affair, I stepped back from it thinking maybe my Dad had had his one chance, the year before at Sotheby's.

It was still quite an enjoyable period for me and not all of my stay was unhappy. We did have our laughs, I got on well with Martin, he was quite an outrageous character really and out of all the people I have met throughout this, he was the one that, apart from myself, put himself totally out for the affair and sacrificed everything for it and for someone to do that because he truly believed in what he was doing, is in my opinion honourable. He had a nice personality and a good sense of humour and he made me laugh a lot throughout my stay there but if there was some kind of godly reason why I was there that time in 1993 then I'm not too sure what it was. As I say I spent most of my time working or going out and hardly had anything to do with what my Dad was doing. I guess you could say I was there to witness what they were doing. My Dad was also constructing and writing his own book, which I found very hard to see him do because he used to write with such emotion and would sometimes get very angry at whatever he was writing about.

But during my stay I was mainly out, if not at work then out with my friends in Brentwood and so I wouldn't return until late at night sometimes hoping everyone was asleep and I used to get up about midday and go off to work. And on most occasions I would wake to hear my Dad ranting and raving to Martin about the affair and all the people who had let him down. My poor Nan, who I haven't really written enough about in this book, was mainly confined to her room wanting to stay out of my Dad's way. She would stay in her room reading books and her newspaper. It must have been hard for Nan because it was her house and she not only had my Dad living there but Martin and me. She did go out to her club a lot but I did feel sorry for her really because her home had been taken over by the Hitler affair. My father I think didn't get on as well as he should have with my Nan because of her constant denial and rejection over the whole Hitler affair and her lack of support for him and so he thought she was wrong.

At TWTI, I was totally in charge of the recruitment, I was only eighteen but I seemed to have a great feeling about people and it was only people I communicated well with during the interview that got the job, I was never interested in people's qualifications or CV's and so if I seemed to get on well with them I would offer them a job. This was not the most conventional way of employing people but then this was no ordinary firm. However unconventional my methods may have seemed, TWTI after only a short time had a remarkable telesales operation and on most occasions we filled all the exhibitions with eager couples wanting to pick up their travel documents.

I was sitting at my desk one day and my good friend Scott confidently walked through the door and asked me for a job. He had found out I was helping to run the show and he needed a job to get him through the summer while he waited for his A-Level results. I don't think we had a formal interview but I may have gone through the motions just for a laugh.

And so once again fate had brought us together and our friendship began again.

Scott was a confident character and was always liked by most people; he would always put himself out for people and would spend time listening when sometimes talking is not always appropriate.

We began to spend a lot of time together mainly going out after work and we seemed to get on and communicate well. I would stay round his parent's house on numerous occasions and even once stayed there for a whole week while his parents were on holiday. The whole of that week was spent partying and smoking copious amounts of cannabis.

That friendship during that summer was a great help getting me through hard times back in Dagenham and in a way Scott and our continuous partying helped me forget about it all.

Another person who I have a lot to thank for is Hazel. Hazel lives in Aveley and she was the general secretary for the marketing operation during the day and I over time would spend many hours with her and if I was ever upset or down she in her own way would make me feel a lot better. She had a great gift as to know when I wasn't feeling right and also an amazing outlook on life that she would try and pass on to me. And at the time I listened to her and tried to look at life in a different way, she used to say things like, " Don't look at what you haven't got, look at what you have got," and "Don't worry about the future, just go with the flow," and at the time these kind of comments made so much sense to me and helped me get through my hard times while living with my Dad.

Dad by now had basically put The Album to one side and was just concentrating on the revelations and by now he was just mainly dealing with Jewish organisations, he thought it was his duty to try and let Jews know of his findings and warn them of the danger they may all be in.

But also at this point, my Dad along with Martin would go off on all kinds of adventures and they both believed they were following signs from God. They would go to places such as Osborne House and Sandringham; Dad thought that because the musical box in the children's nursery played Tannhauser by Richard Wagner (Hitler favourite piece of music) it was another confirmation that Prince John was in fact Hitler. They also went to Sandringham because that is where Prince John spent most of his time and especially at a place called Wolferton where he was hidden away at Wood Farm by the Royal Family. Dad always felt very close to Prince John and felt deeply sorry for him because of the way he was treated earlier on in his life mainly by his mother, Queen Mary. Dad believes that Prince John loved his mother dearly and if in fact he did go on to become Hitler then Dad believes his outbursts of rage and anger during the war was mainly caused by his mother, a mother who rejected him and sent him packing when he was young because he was an embarrassment.

Dad strongly believes that Prince John's body should be exhumed, as like it has been suggested also for Princess Diana. And through DNA would prove one way or another whether (unless of course he had a twin that no one knew about) Prince John did actually die at the age of thirteen.

I don't believe personally that Princess Diana's body should be exhumed, I think it is quite obvious she was murdered and therefore there is someone somewhere who knows all the answers and I think exhuming her body would be wrong and an unnecessary pain for many to have to witness especially her two children. There are questions that need to be answered regarding the end of her life and I think the quicker it happens the better, I think the media etc, are totally hanging this whole process out so they can produce as much money from it as possible. But I do believe the truth should be known and made public, as she used to say, she was the people's princess and so I feel we have a right to know why and who killed her. But once that knowledge has become public and once the right people are punished for their involvement, I then think it is time to truly let her go and let her rest in peace, if not for her sake then for the sake of Prince William and Prince Harry.

I feel, not that I know them that they are a caring and sensitive pair but if over time they are pushed too far by our media could turn the other way. And I think Prince William, a man who will have so much responsibility and power when he's older should have his emotions towards his Mother left alone because I don't think it will take too much more before he may lose control of his patience and let's just hope it doesn't result in the same carnage as another member of his family produced when he also become infuriated over his mother.

With regards to Prince John's body being exhumed I think it maybe a good idea, if after reading my story the people of this country do have any doubts, then unless the Queen or MI5 come forward and explain, then I feel it may be the only way to find out if indeed Prince John is buried at Sandringham.

Dad had decided if The Album was not going to be examined or used for anything, then it was best kept in a safety deposit box. Dad one day during the summer of 1993 asked me whether I wanted to go to Phoenix. There were a number of reasons why but the main one was to take The Album and place it in a bank in Scottsdale. The other reason was to place all of Dad's paperwork into storage and to try and find someone who may take this whole affair on. Dad was expecting me to find a person to finance him so he could also join me in America and raise all the revelations through the American Press.

Martin sold his van for a thousand pound and gave me all the money so I could buy my plane ticket and have some money left over for my stay.

We travelled up to Kensington and purchased my tickets through STA Travel. I was flying with Virgin from Heathrow to Los Angeles and then onto Phoenix from there.

I was fairly nervous leading up to my departure, the thought of having to carry Hitler's photograph album all the way to America was quite daunting, what would happen if I lost it? Or someone stole it from me? How could I possibly return to England and tell my Dad that.

And why did I have to travel all the way to Phoenix? Well my Dad had spent a lot of time there previously when dealing with the Indians and had made many friends there, he had also been there in recent years and had already opened a safety deposit box in a bank in Scottsdale, he had also hired a storage facility for all the paperwork that went with this affair. But why Phoenix? Dad believes Hitler is alive and living somewhere in Arizona and due to some very spiritual happening that happened to him in previous visits he decided that Scottsdale would be his base and so he thought it was an appropriate place for The Album to be, he also believed

Hitler when found, would read his story and go through all his paperwork with him, so that's why it was all kept and stored there

At the time I just went along with it, I guess two weeks in America was an offer not to refuse. I didn't take too much notice then of the way my Dad was thinking but as I write his story and looking back at what I was doing it does now all sound a bit far out.

Putting The Album in a bank in America was a negative move in my opinion, having it so many miles away from everyone back in London was a bad move but for Dad it was a positive move and suggested to him he was a step nearer to his destiny.

When I told Scott where I was going he became instantly intrigued and as I had become good friends with him and trusted him, I told him the whole story. And I remember telling him while driving along the A12 towards Brentwood from work one day in my Renault and by the end of it we both agreed I would be driving a 911 very soon.

But Scott throughout my whole life has supported me through my troubled times and has had a great belief in what I've been doing, he has never mocked the affair and as I've said before he even introduced me to his Jewish university mate Dominic Woolfe, who had showed an interest in my Dad's work, his uncle was the Chief Editor of the Jewish Chronicle and Dominic invited me to his home in Mill Hill for the night to discuss this affair and the findings.

Even today Scott had given me great support while writing this book and where others have suggested that I shouldn't be wasting my time doing it, he has given me encouragement that is totally appreciated and just helps when sometimes I even started to wonder if I was doing the right thing. In fact he has read every stage of this book while I've been writing it and has made some very helpful comments and suggestions.... cheers mate!

Once again my journey to America was a little like the one to Switzerland the year before whereby I kept myself to myself and kept my head low and never attracted attention.

I was carrying Hitler's photograph album and I knew how valuable it was and by that point I think I started to believe that it was an item that carried great power and had to be protected and looked after.

The Album was kept close to me the whole time and I made sure it went on the plane in my hand luggage. I would have looked a right idiot if I had lost it because my suitcase went missing.

The flight to America seemed to fly by, I think it was mainly to do with the entertainment offered on board, I was quite surprised when I sat down at the beginning of the flight to notice a small T.V in the back of the seat but even more surprised when I realised I could spend the whole journey playing PlayStation games.

The first thing I noticed when I arrived in L.A. was how beautiful the women were but again because of what I was carrying and the mission I was on I made no effort to exchange conversation with them.

The flight from L.A. to Phoenix only took an hour and while on that plane I was also surprised to see a telephone in the back of the chair and so while sitting there in mid air I decided to phone my hotel in Phoenix, to make sure they were expecting me and if it was possible for them to pick me up from the airport. They were expecting me but they suggested I got a taxi to the hotel.

As I sat there the man sitting next to me had heard my English accent and started to talk to me and while I sat there listening to him, he reminded me a little of one of the characters from Knots Landing. He was a friendly chap with typical American confidence; he gave me his phone number and said if I needed anything while I was staying in Phoenix to let him know. As the conversation went on, he asked me why I was in Phoenix and so I told him, it slightly put an end to the conversation and it was quite funny to see him quickly walk off when we landed.

The suitcases I was having to carry were extremely heavy, due to all of Dad's paperwork and so I was pleased when an airport porter came up to me and helped me to the taxi but I did wonder why when we got there he was still hovering around me and then I realised I hadn't tipped him.

My first night in Phoenix was stayed in at The Day's Inn in Scottsdale, but after one night due to them being fully booked I moved to The Sunburst, which was a beautiful hotel within walking distance from the bank. And in fact that was the first thing I did, I knew I wasn't going to be able to relax until The Album was safely put away.

I walked into the bank, and a woman who seemed to be the friendliest person, greeted me. She told me that she had been expecting me after speaking to my father earlier on that day. She showed me to my Dad's safety deposit box and left me alone, I then walked into a private room and opened it. As I remember there was some paperwork it in and a tape cassette.

I placed The Album in it, shut the box and placed it back in the wall.

I have no idea what was on that tape but knowing my Dad it was probably a message for the FBI or the CIA, just in case one day they wanted the contents of that box. Dad by now had kept two of the postcards separate from The Album; they were the postcards Dad had not let Michel Ziegler see in Berlin. He used to say to me that they had important writing on them that no one had seen and keeping them separate from The Album was a bargaining tool if or when the Security Services ever picked us up. That was his insurance, if anything happened to him or the family, then those cards would have been released to the press and that's something the Establishment would not have wanted.

I said goodbye to the young lady and left. Not realising I would be back the following year to retrieve it for a trip to Vienna.

The next thing I did was to get rid of Dads' paperwork; I got a taxi from the hotel and made my way to the storage facility. Dad had given me some extra cash to pay his storage right up to date, which I did.

When the man showed me to Dad's unit I was extremely surprised when I saw the amount of bags already in it, I checked what was in them and again they were all filled with correspondence regarding this affair, letters to and from all sorts of people.

The last thing I had to do before I could totally relax was to get Dad's video transferred onto US format so that if I did meet anyone who showed any interest in the affair, I could just give them the video.

I asked the man at the storage unit where the nearest shop was that may do that for me and he told me the way and I always remember the surprise on his face when I told him I would walk there. Due to the heat in Arizona, it seemed no one walked anywhere but drove instead.

I think the main reason I decided to walk was that I was trying to save my money and the man had told me it wasn't that far and so getting a taxi would have been an unnecessary expense.

Before I left for the United States, Dad had given me a number of people to contact who he had met previously and one of those people was a Jewish man called Jeff Lowe, he had moved to America from Vienna to escape the Nazis during the Second World War.

Dad had met him when he last visited Scottsdale and they had shared some very personal stuff together and my father thought this

223

man was important for some reason because Jeff told Dad a story about a time he went out into the desert and saw two hands appear in the sky and how they turned into a white dove and flew away. (Dove is a sign of peace) So Dad suggested that I contacted him and that he would show me around and make me feel welcome.

As I walked along the pavement towards the video shop, the heat was becoming unbearable and I felt the sun burning my neck, I became immensely thirsty and my stomach was shouting out for food but as I struggled on walking through this very quiet neighbourhood. I started thinking about Jeff Lowe and I thought to myself whether I should ring him or not, and as I thought this I looked down towards the pavement and to my utter astonishment I saw the word Jeff chiselled out in the concrete. I stopped walking and to make sure I wasn't seeing things, I knelt down and felt the actual indentations. I got back up and as I was always the sort of person who followed signs, I thought to myself after seeing that while thinking about him, I should without any doubt ring him.

Many strange things throughout this whole affair have happened to me for example when I knocked the shed down and found a photograph album belonging to Hitler but seeing Jeff's name in the concrete like that while I was thinking whether I should ring him or not, was a powerful moment for me. But still to this day I don't know the meaning of it because that night I did ring him and he wasn't in and I left a message on his answer phone but he never contacted me and so I wonder if Jeff Lowe is an important person maybe for the future.

I managed to reach a Pizza restaurant before I collapsed, the heat was ridiculous and if I hadn't of found that restaurant I would have definitely collapsed on the street somewhere.

I finally arrived at the video shop and they informed me they didn't do format transfers but I didn't care, in fact I was relieved, it meant I didn't have to worry about handing them out.

I got back to the hotel and now I could start to relax and enjoy the rest of my stay, having The Album and Dad's paperwork on me was a massive pressure and so I was relieved to have off loaded it.

I walked into the hotel's restaurant and began to order my dinner. As I sat there drinking my beer an immense feeling of deja vu came over me, I had the strongest feeling my Dad and Martin were just about to walk in, the feeling was so strong I even put my cigarette out and placed the ashtray on another table. (My Dad would have been furious at me if he knew I had been smoking) I even started to look towards the entrance of the hotel to see whether they were going to walk through it.

That feeling that night was very strange and a little worrying, I got up from my table cancelled my order and went back to my room.

It had been a very strange day, the pressure of carrying The Album was immense but the relief when I put it in the bank was great. The shock of seeing all those bags in that storage facility was slightly worrying as well, I hadn't realised the amount of work Dad had actually put into this affair but storing every bit of paperwork that was relevant to it, I guess in some people's eyes is a bit strange. Then there was the heat that got to me, then seeing Jeff's name in the concrete was an amazing experience for me and it was an incident that gave me a massive faith in what I was involved in. The feeling at the dinner table was a bit odd as well and again slightly worrying but what happened next really did freak me out and I began to wonder whether I was in the right place.

I phoned my Dad to give him an update and to tell him that I had transferred hotels and to tell him that The Album and paperwork was safe. As I gave him the telephone number of the hotel the feeling that came over me when I read out the last three digits was quite overwhelming, the last three digits of The Sunburst Hotel in Scottsdale are 666.

I don't know whether it was due to the pressure I was under or the sense of not really knowing what was happening to me or maybe I had suffered from a little bit of sunstroke but that night I was constantly sick and felt very dizzy and had to spend the rest of the evening in bed.

This whole story, no matter what you believe in, is a powerful affair and if you are going to compare any human to the devil then it has to be someone like Hitler. Hitler did delve into the occult and used it to help him make decisions during the war, he also truly believed he was being guided by some power and I believe he thought it was his duty to eliminate the Jews.

Phoenix is a very spiritual place and someone turning up with an album belonging to Hitler may have caused some tremors and so I believe I was coming under some pressure from some unseen power. But where there is evil there is also good and throughout this whole affair I have tried to do the right thing, I'm not a horrible person and I have a strong faith but being so associated to something so powerful and to someone who was responsible for killing millions of people means I have had to go through some very strange and tough times. If this affair is meant to have a worthwhile and peaceful ending then if that means God is helping me get to that point, then you can bet your life on it that the Devil is going to try and stop me.

I explained to Dad what had happened to me earlier on in the day, and he told me to stay cool and try and relax, he told me not to worry about talking to anyone about the affair but to enjoy myself instead. He said he would get in contact with a friend of his called Jeannie who lived in Scottsdale who had a daughter of my age.

I spent the next week totally relaxing and enjoying myself. I would drink and eat at a typically American bar called Jets, which at times was quite hard to get in because of my age, in America you have to be twenty-one to drink in the bars. During the day I spent most of my time around the pool and pool bar, in fact it was at that bar I received a phone call from my Dad, he was kind of hoping maybe I had made contact with someone who may have had an interest in the affair. I don't think he was too impressed when the receptionist at the hotel told him I was at the pool bar and no doubt Martin found it even less impressive because at the end of the day it was his money I was using to fund the whole trip.

Jeannie's daughter had turned up one night and took me to a house party, it was like no other party I had been to before. Everyone there seemed to be immensely rich and the cars these kids were turning up in were amazing but unfortunately as I remember the majority of the people there were very unfriendly and just seemed to worry about what they looked like. We left fairly early and she took me back to the hotel.

The following day she took me to Phoenix Zoo, which by our standards is the most amazing zoo you will ever go to. I always remember on the way there though, we were behind this pick up truck and we pulled up at the traffic lights and this chap got out and reached into the back for something but the girls who I was with were convinced he was going to pull out a gun and they all started panicking and putting their heads down, I just sat there in amazement at it all and just watched him get back into his truck, but apparently there was a lot of shooting in that part of town and so they were just being cautious.

I spent a few more days in Phoenix and then decided to fly back to LA to spend some time there. The one major thing I didn't do while I was in Arizona was to visit The Grand Canyon, there were two reasons, one I didn't really have enough money to go there but the main one I think was I didn't have anyone to share the experience with. Hopefully one day I will return with my family, not only to go to the Grand Canyon but I would love to retrace my steps to that video shop that day and find that pavement slab with the name Jeff on it, in fact I would love to find it before this book gets published and take a photo of it and have it printed in this book. It would go a long way to prove I was telling the truth, not that I'm trying to convince anyone that this story is true because in my opinion it doesn't matter if you believe it or not because at the end of the day I know it's true.

I had been warned by a number of people in Phoenix to be on my guard while being in LA, they told me it wasn't quite as friendly and as nice as it was in Phoenix. This obviously made me slightly nervous about the place and it wasn't long until I found out for myself just how bad it was. LA in my opinion is an awful place and you wouldn't get me going back there in a hurry.

I remember getting on the coach from the airport to my hotel and the minute I got off it, a homeless man came hurrying up to me begging me for money and nearly mugged me.

That was my first real memory of being in LA on my own and so obviously it unsettled me and I became very aware of my surroundings.

I was staying in Santa Monica and had heard a lot about how nice the place was and in particular the beaches. Before I left the hotel I made sure I was wearing the most inexpensive clothes I had, I didn't wish to attract any more homeless people.

As I walked along the coast and up and down the famous Santa Monica Pier, all I could see was vast amounts of homeless people hanging around and it started to infuriate me, a place that is surrounded by so much money I thought would have no such problem, the fact it did, meant to me that something was wrong somewhere. How can you have a place with so much wealth but then so much poverty and homelessness? I know it is the same in most cities but as I stood there that day I decided to myself that if I ever became rich and influential, then I was going to sort out the homeless problem in LA. That sounds a bit bizarre but my Dad had made me believe I was going to be this powerful figure one day because of the Hitler affair and so after I witnessed for myself the scale of the problem, I then started to believe that maybe my Dad was right, maybe I was meant to have seen those problems for myself because I truly believed I was going to be back there one day to sort it all out.

I didn't feel comfortable in LA, maybe it was because I was all alone in a big and dangerous city but something definitely felt wrong and so I spent most of my time there in my hotel room, longing to go home. Scottsdale was great, a beautiful place and most of the people there were very friendly but L.A. was a totally different ball game, it was a different experience from the last time I was there with Mum and Gary, and I guess if I had been there with a few friends and wasn't limited to my spending I might have had a better time.

I went into the local STA travel agents who were conveniently around the corner from the hotel and got my flight brought forward. My stay in LA seemed to be pointless, I had done what I needed to do in Phoenix and so now I wanted to go home.

I had enjoyed my trip to America it was an experience that I will always remember, I felt quite privileged to have had the opportunity to go there in the first place but the strange feelings and experiences I had come across in Phoenix made me truly aware of some kind of power in this world and from that period I tried to open my mind up to it and started to follow my instincts. And I wonder sometimes whether me putting The Album in a bank thousands of miles away was in fact for that reason, maybe my trip had nothing really to do with The Album maybe it was so I could experience that power.

Anyway one of the best feelings of that whole trip was when I looked out of the plane window, on the way home and could see London, I was home again and it was a great feeling. No matter where I've been in the world, I have always looked forward to coming home. England is my home and I'm proud of that.

13/4/04

I have been writing this book now for just over five months and even though I have enjoyed it, I have continued to wonder whether I'm doing the right thing or more importantly whether my efforts are just a waste of time.

For me to complete my story would again take me another five months but at this stage, without the backing of any organisation I'm not willing to sacrifice any more of my time towards this subject.

The up and coming part of this story was very hard to live through and so retracing it again for this book, I would need to see a true purpose for it. I will attempt to get this story so far published and if I can see an interest in the book then I will attempt to complete the rest.

I have written this book in my spare time but when you have a family that spare time is important, I also have my own business, which has suffered a little due to me wanting to finish it so badly.

And so today I decided to stop, I've lost so much already to this affair. I have rebuilt my life, which now includes my wife and two children and so I cannot allow myself to lose them due to this subject.

Part two of this story, if it ever gets written is mainly about my struggle to escape from the whole subject.

If this book does get printed then I hope everyone appreciates I never wanted all this pressure and no matter what comes from this, I truly hope it is for the better and the good.

Part two includes my life until the present day, I could even write a book about writing this book, so much has happened. I have a great story, which surrounds the Daily Express, a story that is so coincidental and was put together not by me but by the man running the show.

Even while writing this story I have had to spend a few days in The Priory and a week in Warley Mental Hospital not coping with a number of different pressures that seemed to hit me all at the same time. I even managed to write a couple of chapters to this book in there and I guess some will say the whole book was probably written in there.

Also the death of two of my friends has in one way had an effect on the way I have written this story. One of those friends was called Simon (Dappa to his friends) he committed suicide in January 2004, it affected everyone around me but affected me more personally because I knew just how he felt before he died. Yes, I once tried to take my own life. Why? because of the Hitler affair and it is something I will cover more deeply in the next part. Also my close friend Phil Apicella died on Mother's Day 2004 of a heart attack, Phil was the one friend who I was really looking forward to reading this, he had witnessed me struggle through my hard times and also had a great belief in this story.

The next few years of the story would include my travels around Europe, which includes me working in France and Switzerland and also my travels back to Phoenix and on to Vienna, where I sat with Paul Eisenburg the Chief Rabbi of Austria discussing the Hitler revelations and what they possibly meant for Jewish people. I also met Alois Shaffer (The graphologist who had studied the birth certificate) and witnessed his utter shock while studying the signature of August Kubizek, he also spent the day with us when we held a meeting at Christies. I also sat with Eva Maria Brunner, a leading handwriting expert in Vienna who spent four hours with me in my hotel room explaining why The Album was written by Hitler, she also explained why there was no other place than England where Hitler could have been educated.

That moment in Vienna along with the time I spoke to August Kubizek's son, was the moment I truly became aware of how serious this affair was. And it was at that point when I was twenty-one that I started to become unwell.

The story surrounding my illness is immense and worth writing just so other mentally ill people can read it because if I can overcome my illness after the things I have been through then I hope this story would encourage others.

My illness believe it or not is the one thing out of all this that I really looked forward to writing about. It will be hard but worth it and if it helps just one person get through that hell, then it's worth doing.

A large part of the next stage is to do with that and with the rebuilding of my life after Hitler and how I have managed to get married, have two children, my experiences while working for Royal Mail and the influential contacts I have made while working for them and myself and how I went on to own my own business.

But there are also stories surrounding my involvement with Royal Protection and also a story about a conversation I had with a lady from MI5 regarding this book. And two amazing stories that while in London my path crosses with Princess Anne, (outside Bonham's,) and the Queen. There is also the very spiritual and personal story regarding Princess Diana regarding the evening she died and how that tragedy affected my mentality and my opinion at the time, on the Royal Family. There is also my story that surrounds the story of Prince John and how I was lead to believe he grew up to be Adolf Hitler, the main publicity surrounding Prince John was exposed in 1998 and 2003 and I will write about how that knowledge of believing that, affected me and my life and how it again made me ill.

I truly hope this book hasn't offended anyone, it wasn't supposed to, I have only written the truth and what I have experienced while living with my Dad. My Dad's ideas and theories may not all be true but I know some of them are and I think they should be recorded. I know this story may be difficult for some races to read and comprehend. A Jewish man recently read this story, he was in fact the first Jewish person to read it and just by coincidence he is also a good friend of Prince Charles. He phoned me and told me that my story would in no way offend the Jewish people. He also said in his opinion Prince Charles and his family would not be offended or concerned by anything written in this book (mainly because he thought this story was unfounded, untrue and a figment of my father's imagination). However when this person told me this, it took a lot of pressure off me because obviously I have wondered deeply what the Jewish people and the Royal Family may have thought of this story.

It was suggested to me by a publishing company to get permission from everyone who is mentioned in this book but I haven't done that. I think anyone mentioned should feel privileged to be in it, I think this book could be part of changing history and so if an individual had been fortunate enough to be part of it, then why should I change their name. No matter what part you have played it is important and may have unbeknown to us all played a crucial part.

And so as I write my last words I look to the future with great anticipation and look forward to seeing my book in its completion.

I have enjoyed doing this and it truly shows you can do anything if you put your mind to it, I've been quite surprised at the amount I have written and the detail I have remembered.

I have not mentioned too much about my wife in this story and that's mainly because she features more in the second part but I do wish to thank her for her patience while I've been writing this and wish to thank her for supporting me through my troubled times.

I hope you have all enjoyed reading this and I hope soon to be completing the next part.

Thank you.

Printed in the United Kingdom
by Lightning Source UK Ltd.
103912UKS00002B/25